SOCIAL WORK I

Social Work in East Asia

Edited by

CHRISTIAN ASPALTER
*Bejing-Normal University—Hong Kong Baptist University United
International College, Zhuhai, China*

ASHGATE

Published by
Ashgate Publishing Limited
Wey Court East
Union Road
Farnham
Surrey, GU9 7PT
England

Ashgate Publishing Company
110 Cherry Street
Suite 3-1
Burlington
VT 05401-3818
USA

www.ashgate.com

British Library Cataloguing in Publication Data
A catalogue record for this book is available from the British Library

Library of Congress Cataloging-in-Publication Data
Aspalter, Christian.
   Social work in East Asia / by Christian Aspalter.
      pages cm
   Includes bibliographical references and index.
   ISBN 978-1-4724-1309-3 (hardback : alk. paper)—ISBN 978-1-4724-1310-9 (pbk.)—
ISBN 978-1-4724-1311-6 (ebook)—ISBN 978-1-4724-1312-3 (epub)
   1. Social service—East Asia. 2. Social problems—East Asia. 3. Public welfare—East Asia. 4. East Asia—Social policy. 5. East Asia—Social conditions. I. Title.
   HV410.5.A87 2014
   361.3095—dc23

                                                                         2013050279
ISBN: 9781472413093 (hbk)
ISBN: 9781472413109 (pbk)
ISBN: 9781472413116 (ebk – PDF)
ISBN: 9781472413123 (ebk – ePUB)

MIX
Paper from
responsible sources
FSC
www.fsc.org   FSC® C013985

Printed in the United Kingdom by Henry Ling Limited, at the Dorset Press, Dorchester, DT1 1HD

Contents

List of Figures and Tables

Figures

Tables

Notes on Contributors

Christian Aspalter is Professor and Founding Head of the Social Work and Social Administration Programme at the Beijing Normal University–Hong Kong Baptist University United International College in Zhuhai, China. His journal publications include 'Developing Ideal-Typical Welfare Regime Theory' (*International Social Work*), 'The Welfare States in Poland, Czech Republic, Hungary and Slovenia: An Ideal-Typical Perspective' (*Social Policy and Administration*, with J. Kim and S. Park), 'The Welfare State in Cross-Cultural Perspectives' (*International Social Work*), 'The European and American Social Dream: The Competition of Welfare Regimes' (*Journal of Comparative Social Welfare*, with J. Weidenholzer), 'Strategies of Welfare State Reform in Aging Societies' (*Hallym International Journal of Aging*), 'The East Asian Welfare Model' (*International Journal of Social Welfare*), 'Freedom, Dehumanization and Welfare: An Asian Perspective' (*Journal of Comparative Social Welfare*), 'Social Security in China and Chile' (*Korean Journal of Policy Studies*), 'Development Constraints and Social Policy in India: A Political Explanation' (*Journal of Comparative Social Welfare*), 'Democratization and Welfare State Extension in Taiwan' (*Welt Trends*), 'Population Policy in India' (*International Journal of Sociology and Social Policy*), and 'Politics and Its Impact on Social Policy in Taiwan, Hong Kong and Mainland China' (*Social Policy Review*). His book publications include *Active Ageing in East Asia* (with A. Walker, 2014, forthcoming), *Health Care Systems in Europe and Asia* (with Y. Uchida and R. Gauld, 2012), *Debating Social Development* (with S. Singh, 2008), *The State of Social Welfare in Asia* (with A. Dashkina et al., 2008), *Securing the Future for Old Age in Europe* (with A. Walker, 2008), *Understanding European Social Policy* (with P. Abrahamson, 2008), *Welfare Capitalism Around the World* (2003), *The Welfare State in Emerging-Market Economies: With Case Studies from Latin America, Eastern Central Europe and Asia* (2003), *Neoliberalism and the Australian Welfare State* (2003), *Discovering the Welfare State in East Asia* (2002), *Democratization and Welfare State Development in Taiwan* (2002), *Conservative Welfare State Systems in East Asia* (2001), *Understanding Modern Taiwan* (2001), and *Importance of Christian and Social Democratic Movements in Welfare Politics* (2001).

Ernest W.T. Chiu is Associate Professor at the Department of Social Work and Social Administration at The University of Hong Kong. His publications include, 'Healthy Longevity and Health Care Service Needs: A Pilot Study of the Nonagenarians and Centenarians in Hong Kong' (*Asian Journal Gerontology and Geriatrics*, with S.L. Cheung et al.), 'Long-Term Care Policy in Hong Kong: Challenges and Future Directions' (*Home Health Care Services Quarterly*), 'China's Policy on Rural-Urban Migrants and Urban Social Harmony' (*Asian Social Science*, with Y. Li), 'New Wine or Old? From Colony to SAR—Elderly

Welfare in Hong Kong' (*Chinese Journal of Social Work*, with L. Ko), 'After the Handover in 1997: Development and Challenges for Social Welfare and Social Work Profession in Hong Kong' (*Asia Pacific Journal of Social Work and Development*, with S. Tsang and J. Mok), and 'Governmental Policy and Social Exclusion of Rural-Urban Migrants in Urban China' (*Asian and Pacific Migration Journal*, with Y. Li), as well as 'Professional Services and Training: Meeting the Diverse Needs of Older People' in S. Chen and J.L. Powell (eds.) *Aging in Perspective and the Case of China: Issues and Approaches* (2010), 'Assessment in Social Work Education—An Emerging Issue' in L.C. Leung and K.F. Chan (eds.) *Social Work Education in Hong Kong—Theory & Practice* (2008), and 'The State of Welfare in Hong Kong' in C. Aspalter et al. (eds.) *The State of Social Welfare in Asia* (2008).

Zulkarnain A. Hatta is Associate Professor of the Department of Social Work of the Universiti Sains Malaysia in Penang, Malaysia. His publications include 'The Impact of Spiritual Intelligence on the Health of the Elderly in Malaysia' (*Asian Social Work and Policy Review*), 'Exploring Traditional Approaches for the Helping Profession: The Sufi Model' (*Tawarikh: International Journal for Historical Studies*), 'Towards Establishing School Social Work in Malaysia' (*Asian Social Work and Policy Review*), 'Spirituality and Governance in the Development of Human Capital' (*Social Welfare Journal*), as well as 'Spiritual (Sufi Path) Approach to Stress Management' in A. Husain (ed.) *Twenty-First Century Psychology: Spiritual-Religious Perspectives* (2009) and 'The Role and Importance of the Helping Services' in S.C. Mey (ed.) *The Adaptation of Mentoring in Organization* (2008).

Huang Pei Jie is currently a Ph.D. candidate at Department of Social Policy and Social Work, National Chi Nan University in Puli, Taiwan. Her dissertation was 'A Study of Social Work Professionalization in Taiwan: Historical Analysis of the Power Structure.' Her Publications include, for example, '*Multiservice and Integration Difficulties: An Analysis of the Welfare Service for Marriage Immigrants in Taiwan*' (2009, with X.D. Fang et al.), and her current research topics focus on power, social structure, and social work; social policy analysis; expressive arts therapy; philosophy of social science; self-narrative study; and non-profit organizations and social enterprises.

Hubert Liu is Assistant Professor at Department of Gerontological Care and Management, Chang Gung University of Science and Technology, Puzi, Taiwan. He wrote his PhD dissertation 'Winding Route to Consensus-building: Democratisation and Taiwan's National Pension Scheme' at the Graduate School of International Cooperation Studies, Kobe University, Japan. His research interests include geriatric social work, elderly welfare policy, welfare state theories, as well as social policy and social work in Japan and Taiwan. His forthcoming publications include 'Taiwan' in C. Aspalter (ed.) *The East Asian Welfare Model: Towards Ideal-Typical Welfare Regime Theory* (forthcoming), 'Financing the Welfare

State System in Taiwan' in C. Aspalter (ed.) *Financing Welfare State Systems in Asia* (forthcoming), as well as 'The Welfare State System in Japan: With Special Reference to Financing Health Care, Long-Term Care and Pensions in a Super-Aged Society' in C. Aspalter (ed.) *The Ashgate Research Companion to Welfare State Systems* (forthcoming).

Oyut-Erdene Namdaldagva is a senior faculty of the Social Work Department, The Mongolian State University of Education in Ulaanbaatar. Her research areas are gerontology, social work education, management of social welfare programs and projects, community based services, and service utilization. Her publications include, for example, 'Professional Social Work Education in Mongolia: Achievements, Lessons Learned and Future Directions' (*Social Work Education*), as well as *Health Education for TVET Students and Teachers* (2011, with C. Baigalmaa et al., in Mongolian), *Human Rights Manual for Social Workers* (2010, with C. Baigalmaa, in Mongolian), *Social Work Fieldwork: Theory and Practice Importance* (2008, et al., in Mongolian), *Review of Social Work Development in Mongolia* (2008, with S. Enkhtuya et al., in Mongolian), as well as *Assuring Income Security in Old Age: Views of The Mongolian Elderly* (2010, with G. Mujahid et al.).

Kitipat Nontapattamadul is Associate Professor at the Faculty of Social Sciences, Thammasat University, in Bangkok. He has published a great number of key books in social work and social policy in Thailand, for example, *Foundations of Social Work Theory* (1995, in Thai), *Social Welfare and Social Work: General Perspective* (1994/2010, in Thai), *Social Policy and Social Welfare* (1995/2011, in Thai), *Qualitative Research in Social Welfare: Concepts and Methods* (2004/2011, in Thai), *Critical Theory in Social Policy and Planning* (2006, in Thai), *Contemporary Social Work Theories* (2010, in Thai), *Comparative Social Policy* (2012, in Thai), and *Development of Social Work in ASEAN* (2013, in Thai). His journal publications, for example, include 'Working With Women Who Experienced Family Violence: An Assessment of Thai Social Welfare System' (*Thammasat Review*), and 'Integration into a Mosaic Society: The Laotian Refugees in Calgary' (*Thammasat Review*).

Rosaleen Ow is Senior Lecturer and Head of the Department of Social Work, National University of Singapore. Her publications include 'Elderly Health' (*Asia Pacific Journal of Social Work and Development*), 'Poor Hemodialysis Outcome: Identifying Social Risk Factors in Elderly and Non-Elderly Patients in Singapore' (*Asia Pacific Journal of Social Work and Development*), 'Do Caregiver Beliefs Matter? An Exploratory Study of Palliative Caregiving Decisions in Singapore' (*Asia Pacific Journal of Social Work and Development*), 'Development of a Research Proposal to Explore Needs and Service Utilization Among the Conjugally Bereaved in Singapore' (*Asia Pacific Journal of Social Work and Development*), 'Negotiating Challenges: Social Development in Asia' (*Asia Pacific Journal of Social Work and Development*), 'Hope Among Terminally Ill Patients in Singapore:

An Exploratory Study' (*Social Work in Health Care*, with I.M.H. Woo), 'Meeting Healthcare Costs: The Case of Childhood Cancer in Singapore' (*International Journal of Social Welfare*, with K.H. Ng), as well as 'Needs and Issues of Persons with Disabilities' in K.K. Mehta and A. Wee (eds.) *Social Work in the Singapore Context* (2011), 'On the Move, Social Work Education: The Singapore Journey' in S. Stanley (ed.) *Social Work Education in Countries of the East: Issues and Challenges, Social Justice, Equality and Empowerment* (2011), and 'Singapore: Practice and Challenges' in E. Blyth and R. Landau (eds.) *Third Party Assisted Conception Across Cultures: Social, Legal and Ethical Perspectives* (2004).

Jem Price is Senior Lecturer at the School of Applied Social Sciences, The University of Brighton, UK. His particular areas of interest include social work and ageing, better practice with lesbian and gay service users and global social work perspectives. His publications include, for example, 'Professional "Imperialism" and Resistance: Social Work in the Philippines' (*Trabajo Social Global*), as well as *Queer in the Head: An Examination of the Response of Social Work Mental Health Services to the Needs and Experiences of Lesbians and Gay Men* (1997).

Zarina Mat Saad is Senior Lecturer at the Department of Psychology and Social Work, School of Social Development at the Universiti Utara Malaysia, in Kedah, Malaysia. Her publications include 'The Impact of Spiritual Intelligence on the Health of the Elderly in Malaysia' (*Asian Social Work and Policy Review*), as well as 'Parents Involvement of the Orang Asli Community in Their Children Education' in F. Shaffie and R. Yusoff (eds.) *The Development of Marginalized Community in Malaysia: Towards Self-Empowerment* (2008, in Malay); 'Social Work Practice With the Elderly' in A.H. Hillaluddin et al. (eds.) *Social Work Policy, Legislation and Practice* (2005, in Malay); and 'Dealing With Death and Grieving' in A.H. Hillaluddin et al. *Social Work Issues and Education* (2005, in Malay).

Ku Yeun Wen is Professor at Department of Social Work, National Taiwan University and President and Founder of the Taiwanese Association of Social Policy. His journal publications include 'Is There a Way Out? Global Competition and Social Reform in Taiwan' (*Social Policy and Society*), 'East Asian Welfare Regimes: Testing the Hypothesis of the Developmental Welfare State' (*Social Policy and Administration*), 'Developments in East Asian Welfare Studies' (*Social Policy and Administration*), 'East Asian Welfare Regimes: Testing the Hypothesis of the Developmental Welfare State' (*Social Policy and Administration*, with Y.J. Lee), 'Social Change and Social Policy in Taiwan: New Poverty, M-Shaped Society and Policy Implications' (*International Journal of Japanese Sociology*, with James C.T. Hsueh), 'Effectiveness of Social Welfare Programs in East Asia: A Case Study of Taiwan' (*Social Policy and Administration*, with C.C. Huang), 'Resource Allocation in Families With Children in Taiwan: Do Poverty and Family Structure Make Differences?' (*Journal of Poverty*, with C.C. Huang), 'After Massification: The Quest for Entrepreneurial Universities and Technological Advancement in

Taiwan' (*Journal of Higher Education Policy and Management*, with K.H. Mok and K.M. Yua). His other publications include *Welfare Capitalism in Taiwan: State, Economy and Social Policy* (1997), 'Social Development in Taiwan: Upheavals in the 1990s' in K.L. Tang (ed.) *Social Development in Asia* (2000), 'Towards a Taiwanese Welfare State? Demographic Change, Politics and Social Policy' in C. Aspalter (ed.) *Discovering the Welfare State in East Asia* (2002), 'Welfare Reform in Taiwan: The Asian Financial Turbulence and Its Political Implication' in C. Aspalter (ed.) *The Welfare State in Emerging-Market Economies* (2003), 'Social Security' in I. Holliday and P. Wilding (eds.) *Welfare Capitalism in East Asia: Social Policy in Tiger Economies* (2003), 'Social Welfare Development in Taiwan: Class Interests and the Politics of Social Policy' in S. Singh and C. Aspalter (eds.) *Debating Social Development* (2008, with C. Aspalter), and 'Perspectives on Ageing in East Asia: The Embeddedness of Institutions' in T.H. Fu and R. Hughes (eds.) *Ageing in East Asia: Challenges and Policies for the 21st Century* (2009, with S.J. Shi).

Foreword

In his poem, 'The Ballad of East and West', Rudyard Kipling (1895) famously lamented the fact that, as was commonly believed, 'East is East and West is West and never the twain shall meet' (line 1). Globalization, of course, is nothing new. But today, thanks to new information technologies, we are globally interconnected in ways that were never before imagined. With a wealth of knowledge at our fingertips, political causes are advanced, and so are professional ideologies. The communications revolution, in short, has facilitated the diffusion of values, knowledge, and ideas. It has also enhanced the ability of representatives of professional groups and to organize across national borders.

Social work has not been unaffected by these developments. Historically, social work has been an essentially local activity, bound by its own rules, regulations, and belief systems. In the United States, for example, the profession has been strikingly insular with a focus largely on individual therapy as opposed to a focus on structural change. And until recently, European theoretical advances – for example, harm reduction modalities, restorative justice initiatives, anti-oppressive formulations – were largely ignored by US schools of social work education. At the same time, regarding Asian influences, the transfer of professional knowledge has been largely from West to East. This insularity, however, may be a thing of the past.

Several factors account for the expansion of social work knowledge into new territory. First, are the social and economic forces of globalization mentioned above. Second, the mass migration of populations fleeing from war and natural disasters alerts the profession to the need for greater cultural sensitivity. Third, the growth of NGOs attracts media attention to human rights and child welfare issues related to mass trauma. Our shared awareness of the urgency for coordinated global action to ensure the environmental sustainability of the planet is a theme that unites us all.

Social work today, in North America and elsewhere, is truly becoming an international profession. Many social workers who practice in their homelands draw on knowledge that is international in scope – knowledge of advocacy, counselling, and community organization. Many others are practicing across borders, such as in nongovernmental organizations, in nations wrestling with the aftermath of war, refugee crises, and child welfare issues. One promising development is the increasing acceptance by universities and professional associations of academic credentials earned in different parts of the world.

The internationalization of social work is seen as well in the expanding membership of schools of social work and professional associations in the International Association of Schools of Social Work (IASSW) and the International Federation of Social Workers (IFSW). Today, 90 social work organizations, including those in most of the countries covered in this book – Hong Kong and mainland China, Japan, Malaysia, Singapore, Mongolia, and the Philippines – are members or provisional members of IFSW. Asian universities are represented in IASSW as well.

Within this climate of global interconnectedness and shared concerns about social and economic sustainability and human rights, the publication of *Social Work in East Asia* is a timely and much-needed addition to the social work literature. Social work has looked West since the earliest days of the profession; it is now time to turn toward the East. Big things are happening in this part of the world consistent with burgeoning economies. The editor, Christian Aspalter, brings to the shaping of this book an expertise informed by extensive academic and consultative work in Hong Kong, Japan, Malaysia, the Philippines, Singapore, South Korea, Taiwan, and Thailand. Aspalter has selected as chapter authors individuals that are key experts on the country whose social welfare system is being described; they are all highly knowledgeable concerning the unique challenges facing practitioners in their particular country or region. Each chapter, accordingly, is highly informative and should be of major interest to practitioners and policymakers in the East as well as in the West.

Readers of this book will learn of vast differences in the form that social work takes and in the innovations that are developed across the Asian continent. In some of the countries, you will see, social work is an established and honored profession; in others it is a relatively new discipline. Whereas the strong social change thrust of social work has been viewed as threatening to some of the governments under consideration—both communist and capitalis – elsewhere, legislative policy has fully embraced support for this professional field. And yet, there is much common ground. In all the countries represented in this collection, an allegiance to the mission of social work shines forth. At its core, this is a dedication to helping people, especially the most vulnerable of populations—the young and the old and persons with disabilities – to get their needs met. There is a dedication also to social change efforts to improve social welfare offerings and the preservation of personal and natural resources. Aspalter's advice, which is offered in the concluding chapter of this book, is well taken:

> For social services we have to get more and more out of the counselling room, into the community and, very important, into the natural environment … One can do so much more out there in the open, among the trees with the birds singing, while one is enjoying the wonderful scenery that nature provides us with. (169)

Katherine van Wormer
Professor of Social Work, University of Northern Iowa

Chapter 1
Introduction

Christian Aspalter

As yet there is no theory on the possibility of different social work regimes around the world, or in any particular region of the world. Also, although the overall welfare state systems have been successfully categorized into families of nations from an 'ideal-typical' perspective (cf. Aspalter, 2006, 2011, 2012; Esping-Andersen, 1987, 1990, 1992, 1999; Hicks and Esping-Andersen, 2006; Aspalter et al., 2009) – that is, families of welfare state systems, or welfare regimes, or types of welfare capitalism (cf. Appendices 1.1–1.2) – there is no systematic ideal-typical classification of social work service systems. The comparison of social work service systems is located on the meso level of welfare system comparisons.

There are three major levels of welfare system and/or welfare policy comparisons:

a. macro systems: classifying whole countries, or in some instances semi-independent or independent regions;
b. meso systems: gender policies or family policies, employment policies, health care policies, education policies, and so on; and
c. micro systems: policy level solutions, be they particular policies or technical solutions within those policies and/or programs.

For example, gender policy comparisons (Lewis, 1992, 1998; Sainsbury, 1993, 1999; Hobson, 1994) are among the most developed studies at the meso level. Findings of meso-level analyses do not correspond, not by a long way, to the findings of macro-level analyses *because they study different objects*. Welfare state systems are intrinsically different from their sub-level policy fields. Their relationship is not one that resembles the relationship between mother and daughter. Instead, national welfare state systems have their own logic, strategy, constitutional constraints, system environments ('outside' conditions, for example, population characteristics, prevalence and severity of social problems, national policy and political contexts, and so on; for a thorough introduction to social system theory, see Luhmann, 1984, 1995, 1997), and so forth.

That is why sub-level policy systems develop their own solutions, that is, emphasis of different policy objectives, policy strategies, and institutional structures. These correspond to their own '*system environments*' (that is, the *outside world*), which are very different from the system environments of the overall national welfare state system.

For this reason, sub-level policy systems are more sensitive to different conditions: for example, more sensitive to particular pieces of legislation, or even a smaller number of experts and their level of organization or political/societal influence, their educational background and preferences.

The empirical evidence as shown in the in-depth case studies below has laid the groundwork for a better understanding of social work systems or social work service systems, from an international, comparative perspective. The analytical determinants in each case vary quite a bit, the way we would expect following the implications of and theoretical foundation outlined by Luhmann's social system theory (Luhmann, 1984, 1995, 1997).

This book was designed to give authors – who are/were on the ground, who are country specialists with the best understanding of what is going on in the, in most cases, rapidly developing field of social work – more freedom, that is, more room to focus on determinants that have been and/or are most important in their country or region. The particular historical, political, institutional, and social determinants of social work developments are, by and large, varied across case studies in all of East Asia, be they developing or already developed countries or regions.

Mongolia is a former socialist country now with multiparty democratic rule. Singapore and Malaysia are single-party dominant countries, and so was Japan until recently. Taiwan, Thailand, and the Philippines, like Mongolia, have developed a highly competitive democracy with vibrant party competition in free, democratic elections. Hong Kong is a society that has been determined by the flow of migrants and, formerly, refuges from mainland China. Hong Kong exhibits a large presence of overseas NGOs and a strong influence of government bureaucracy, as set up under colonial rule by the British, with the absence of universal suffrage.

In communist countries governments' attitudes towards social work have been more conservative in the past, arguing that they did not need social work because everything was taken care of by the party or work unit. They believed that communist societies do not have social problems and, hence, do not need social work services. Mainland China, for example, has completely reversed its stand on social work in recent decades, now fully supporting social work, as extended economic development, urbanization, the fast aging of society, and the loss of factories and jobs due to economic globalization have spurred the growth of old and new social problems.

On the contrary, some major capitalist countries, like Japan, did not like social work since most practitioners tend to be members and activists of left-wing political parties, or left-leaning in their political inclination. Democratic party competition, wherever it grew strong, pushed a great deal for general support of social work legislation, social work licensing, and social work employment by the government, as well as social work educational programs, especially at university level. Social work institutions became particularly strong alongside government support of social workers in general when left-of-centre or less conservative political parties rose to power, gathering strong support from the social work community, such as in Taiwan or South Korea.

In Hong Kong, another capitalist hub, the conservative government was and still is wary about social workers, who are often community leaders and organizers, sometimes supporting the government and sometimes not. Conservative governments in Far East Asia want full support and full control of key experts and/or experts in key positions in society.

In Hong Kong, therefore, social workers in the past have been identified as troublemakers, or social or political mobilizers – if they demanded a welfare state or a particular benefit or policy, that was too much for some governments to take. Even if the government itself supported the policy and the construction of a welfare state system in the end, it had to be the government, who proposed those policies and programs, and not grassroots, community organizers or social movement leaders.

In Taiwan, on the contrary, social work development was determined by both the government and the social workers themselves. In Thailand, the government is more of a driving force behind social work development than the social work professionals themselves.

In Mongolia, the relationship between the government and the social work sector may be described as being more symbiotic, given the severity and prevalence of ostensible social problems such as child labor, homeless children, child prostitution, unemployment, and so on.

In Thailand, a peculiar mix of an ideology of nationalism and the king's support for welfare to counteract the effects of 'selfish capitalism', saw social welfare in general and social work in particular in a more positive light. However, the beginnings of social work development in Japan did not materialize into a strong development of the social work profession. It is only with recent changes in the Japanese policy arena, that is, pushes for greater social welfare due to heightened electoral competition, that social work development has seen a period of revival and relative extension.

In Singapore, the government works hand in hand with social workers to prevent social problems rather than to cure them, under the umbrella of the government's philosophy of achieving and maintaining 'social harmony' and full-fledged support from most of its citizens in democratic elections.

Full legislative and policy support by the government was easy to obtain in some countries like Mongolia, hard to get and then overtly strong (hence causing its own problems) in others as in Taiwan, and never really took off in still others as in Japan.

Sometimes the meaning of social work itself, in the local language and cultural context, causes a developmental constraint for a social work system. In Thailand, for example, the terms 'social work' and 'social assistance' are confusingly used (cf. Chapter 6).

Moreover, in most countries/regions covered – such as, the Philippines, Japan, Mongolia, Malaysia, and Hong Kong – social work is not strictly defined but is broadly conceptualized, and includes volunteer services and, at times, contributions made by rich donors. This circumstance has led to an overall weakness due to vague professional boundaries.

4   *Social Work in East Asia*

Another key determinant is the educational background of social workers; for example, in Malaysia and Thailand, we have the problem of non-trained social workers or non–social work majors taking up social work practice, or teaching core social work subjects. There is a generation of social workers with an educational background in history, arts, sociology, or psychology, and so on. Even though they receive in-house training or continuous educational courses, this will have an impact on the overall development of the social work profession.

As the contrasting experiences of the case studies in this book volume show, the time of inception of social work education and professionalism does not correspond to the speed of social work development, or general level of social work development achieved. Other determinants and circumstances far outweigh the impact of time, which is also important to some extent.

Social work first developed in Japan and Russia in the 1920s, India in the 1930s, Thailand in the early 1940s, the Philippines in the late 1940s, Singapore and Hong Kong in the early 1950s, Malaysia in the early 1970s, Taiwan in the 1990s, and Mongolia in the late 1990s (see the case study analyses in this book).

The following case studies set out to describe the current state, as well as the past development, of social work systems in East Asia, with particular reference to the development of social work as a profession and special emphasis on the history of social work development, social work education, the organization of professional social workers, the licensing and legislation within the social work system, as well as special topics, such as, for example, social work indigenization.

In Chapter 2, Hubert Liu sets out to explain the fundamental causes of the relative uniqueness of the Japanese social work system and its development. Even though Japanese social work was instigated by developments in the West, and started to develop in the early 1920s, the Japanese path of social work development parted with that of most Western, as well as neighboring Far East Asian countries and regions. During the time of Imperial Japanese expansion and subsequently World War II, social work development in Japan was frozen, as it was seen to be left-leaning, and hence friendly with communist forces abroad. Hubert Liu shows that American occupation, at its onset, led to a great deal of influence from American social work, which could in return have built on strong development since the 1930s. Even though American social workers were supervising Japanese social workers in the beginning, this did not change the evolution of the Japanese social work system, as they mainly focused on providing direct social work services, and not on building a social work system. The Japanese authorities, thereafter, deinstitutionalized social work, by designing a lower educational level for social work, and by putting voluntary social work organizations directly under the control of the government, which still saw social work as a left-leaning profession. This negative governmental attitude was prevalent until the 1980s but 1987 onward a new period of accreditation started, with the implementation of the national licenced social work system. It was a top-down decision, and employment in social work services was not connected to obtaining a social work licence. The government, according to Liu, saw the increasing need for social work services provided outside the government, as its own role was on the decline due to fiscal cuts. The new Certified Social Worker and Certified Care Worker Law of 1987 added to the confusion about the uniqueness of the social work profession by not clearly distinguishing between the roles of the former and the latter. It is for this reason that the fate of social work in Japan has been and is lying in the hands of bureaucrats, and the government in general, who are rather wary about the role of social workers, due to the dominant conservative ideology.

The next chapter by Oyut-Erdene Namdaldagva (Chapter 3) highlights the particularly interesting case of Mongolia, a former socialist country that suffers from a great number of social problems, being generally poor, but having developed a great deal of democratic party competition through universal suffrage. The end of the socialist, one-party state in Mongolia meant that new room was created for the development of a general social welfare system in the early to mid-1990s. Contrary to other countries in Far East Asia, full government support for both the social security system and the social work system contributed positively to welfare state and social work development in Mongolia. The 1995 Law on Social Welfare pushed for the development of a national professional social work system, giving a clear definition of social work and its professional ethics. Nonetheless, the people at large still have difficulty narrowing down the roles of social workers. The golden time for professionalization of social work in Mongolia came roughly between 2001 and 2002, when three major social work associations were formed. Oyut-Erdene Namdaldagva shows clearly how, in the special case of Mongolia, the social work system was integrated into the wider social security system, by way of policy papers, legislation, and institution building. Especially in the case of Mongolia, a multitude of forces, including economic, political, cultural, and social factors, contributed to the birth and relatively quick development of the social work profession and services. In 1997, a special emphasis on developmental social work was created. This, however, still lacks full-fledged implementation at program level – in training and service programs. Namdaldagva calls for an evidence-based focus in designing and running social work services.

Huang Pei Jie and Ku Yeun Wen analyze the case study on Taiwan (Chapter 4) and argue that the social work profession was defined by the strategy of gaining legitimacy through the intervention of state power rather than through professionals' practical qualities. The authors show that even though the beginnings of social work existed in Taiwan during the Ming and Ching Dynasties, the main impetus came from the post-upheaval period under Japanese colonial rule (1895–1945), especially the 1920s and 1930s, as the Japanese government sought to build Taiwan as a southern base of its empire, and to gain new legitimacy through social welfare and social work services. It was, however, only after the lifting of martial law that social work was able to develop in the 1990s. Similar to the experience of Japan, Taiwan saw a discontinuation of social work development in most of the post-war period, under martial law and Kuomintang rule, due to the Kuomintang's dislike of welfare policies of all kinds (Aspalter, 2002a). The peak of social work development in the 1990s was the 1997 promulgation of the Social Worker Law.

While this piece of legislation was a major victory for social work, it also meant to a great degree a loss of professional autonomy, in which most social workers had to obey and act upon the wishes of the government and forego their professional imperatives to act in the interests of their clients, and not the interests of the state. Later on, professional organizations resumed control and gained more autonomy, by way of negotiation meetings and public hearings.

Chapter 5 by Ernest W.T. Chui looks at the peculiar development of social work in Hong Kong. The end of the Chinese Civil War in 1949 brought millions of refugees (along with foreign NGOs) from the mainland and abroad. The 1966–1967 social riots brought a change in colonial social politics in Hong Kong. Subsequently, the government built the foundations of a new welfare state system between 1971 and 1974 (Aspalter, 2001a; Chan, 1996). Just like in Mongolia and Thailand later on, social work in Hong Kong arose from the general (felt) need (by the government) to establish a welfare state system of some kind (Aspalter, 2001a, 2006, 2011). Ernest Chui explains that in the 1970s, the reliance on international funding for welfare NGOs diminished and the government had to step in to fill the void, as a new welfare paradigm evolved. The government tried to prevent social unrest by increasing social assistance, public housing, and education services, as well as heavily subsidized public health care with very low levels of out-of-pocket payments, which are quasi-universal in nature (Aspalter, 2007).

Social work was, as a result, lifted to new heights. The development of social work in Hong Kong had foreign roots, until the political context of the Great Cultural Revolution on the mainland and local riots in Hong Kong in the late 1960s made it paramount for the government to step in and build a welfare state system; one that chiefly focused on (a) social assistance, (b) public housing, (c) heavy subsidies in health care and education, and (d) social services (with around 80 per cent of manpower stemming from NGOs, and 95 per cent for those being financed by the government (Aspalter, 2002b).

Even though professional social workers organized themselves as early as 1949 into a professional organization, it took decades and the help of a complete paradigm change in social welfare politics for the new partnership with the government to form. The government is benefiting from the innovative drive and efficiency of private NGOs, while it has kept control by way of being almost the sole funding source.

Ernest Chui concludes (as do government agencies as, for example, in the neighboring Guangdong Province on the mainland) that the Hong Kong social work profession – after having witnessed the indigenization of a largely Western social work profession – is very well prepared to help the Chinese mainland with a myriad of social problems, with its high standard of education for social workers and provision of social work services (which fit perfectly under the umbrella of the the communist government's current focus on policies that create and boost 'social harmony').

In Chapter 6, Kitipat Nontapattamadul first explains why the Thai government was implementing its first social security law as late as 1990. The government was, up to then, arch-conservative and did not see any need to establish any kind of welfare state system, with religious charities and traditional family and kinship relations filling the void. It is intriguing that in Thailand in 1954, a social insurance act was approved by the then government, but not implemented (which resembles the case of South Korea quite a bit, where the pension and health care systems, even though long approved, have only been implemented recently [Aspalter, 2013]).

Kitipat Nontapattamadul depicts the rise of Thaksin Shinawatra as prime minister and his elevation in the common people's esteem, especially in the poor countryside where his policies of universal health care and micro-credits have found widespread popularity. Succeeding prime ministers Abhisit Vejjajiva and Yingluck Shinawatra have in essence continued the extension of the realm of the welfare state, with a particular focus on the universalistic idea of 'social welfare for all' (Aspalter, 2009).

While the roots of professional social work reach back to the early 1940s, and the first social workers association was established in 1958, the recent boost for the development of social work services came as a result of the overall drive to establish some kind of new welfare state system. Kitipat Nontapattamadul demonstrates that new laws that boosted the social work profession were enacted between 1999 and 2008 and the social work licence law followed in 2010. Hence, both the Thaksin Shinawatra and the Abhisit Vejjajiva administrations contributed significantly to social work development.

Social work development in Malaysia is analyzed by Zulkarnain A. Hatta and Zarina M. Saad (Chapter 7). After giving a thorough introduction to social welfare development in Malaysia from its early beginnings, Hatta and Saad reveal that the institutional framework at the ministerial level kept on changing (with a lot of ministerial reshufflings) while the development of social welfare legislation and particular legislation supporting the development of professional social work services in general, as well as in each particular field of social work, continued steadily throughout the post-war period. In 1973, the first social workers association in Malaysia was founded, much later than in Japan, Thailand, the Philippines, Singapore, and Hong Kong – but much earlier than in Taiwan or Mongolia. The passing of a social workers' law followed only very recently, in 2010.

The second part of the chapter concentrates on the particular development path of social work education in Malaysia, which influenced the unique patterns of employment opportunities, and thereby the overall development of social work as a profession. While early on there was strong input from other disciplines, due to the requirements of international social work associations, the names of programs changed and they are now called social work programs. In this way it was possible to develop a stronger sense of identity.

Hatta and Saad emphasize the great need to establish professional and educational standards in Malaysia, paying special tribute to social work educational policies and the accreditation process. Paramount to any further improvements with regard to the overall development of professional social work, will be the distribution of social work jobs to social workers, not to any graduates, based primarily on their grade point average.

The chapter by Rosaleen Ow (Chapter 8) also puts forward the pivotal idea that the type of social welfare policies and programs will determine the political will and actual room for development of professional social work services. Singapore has developed a welfare state in a class by itself (seen from a real-typical perspective) (Aspalter, 2001a,c, 2002c, 2012) being influenced (just like Hong Kong) by British social workers from the very beginning. The first formal training of social workers took shape in 1952 but the formation of a Singaporean social workers association was delayed until 1971. This reflects the incremental welfare ideology of social policy in general, as exhibited by the Lee Kwan Yew Administration for most of the post-war period (Aspalter, 2001a).

In the field of social welfare services, the government's key approach is characterized by the principle of '*Many Helping Hands*'. Rosaleen Ow underlines the active role of the Singaporean government in planning, regulating, and facilitating the development of new social work services by shouldering the development costs as well as recurrent costs, as appropriate. In the main part of this case study, Ow sheds a great deal of light onto the development of different social work services, sector by sector.

Ow comes to the conclusion that the nature and practice of a social work system, as in the case of Singapore, is to a large extent the outcome of particular social, political, economic, and cultural forces, rather than the 'intent of social work' as such. In addition, she states that even though social workers have been contributing to social development and social policies of all sorts, they also heavily rely on political will and the existence of international collaboration, as well as being the beneficiaries of overall social development and specific social policies.

Last but not least, Rosaleen Ow states the importance of preventative social work services that contribute to nation-building by participating in the development of human potential and community building.

The last case study, on the Philippines, has been contributed by Jem Price (Chapter 9) and provides a strong international point of view, putting social work development in the Philippines into the wider international context. Catholic social teachings have made inroads into the social politics of almost all Catholic countries in the world (Huber et al., 1993; Kersbergen, 1994, 1995; Aspalter, 2001b, 2011). Nonetheless, in the first two decades after World War II, it was the American-trained social work pioneers who set up the first schools of social work and constituted the Philippine social workers association as early as 1947. And in 1965, the first law was passed to regulate social work, and particularly the operation of social work service centres.

In the main part of his chapter, Jem Price investigates the influence of local political institutions, particularly the personal power and influence of elected representatives, and a pluralist structure of local government units. He also analyzes the impact of the colonial history and American political influence during the post-war period, and the important contributions of the United Nations and international welfare NGOs. After discussing the issues of indigenization of social work practice in the Philippines, and the importance of social work education,

Price sums up the overall conclusions of this very insightful chapter, noting at the end that much-welcomed economic and social development also bear risks of developing effects detrimental to overall development.

In Chapter 10, I go on to elaborate the developmental social policy approach, as first developed by James Midgley (1995, 1996; 1999, 2001, 2003, 2008), while breaking down overall policy paradigm to the level of social work services (Midgley and Aspalter, forthcoming). In the earlier part of the chapter, I introduce the meaningful paradigm of societal human capabilities in social policy and social work, which focuses on the development and defense of *individual human capabilities* (including physical and mental health, education, and so on), *social capabilities* (mutual support networks, mutual aid, solidarity, and so on), and so far much-neglected *cultural capabilities* (habits, customs, traditions, people's cultural participation, as well as cultural preferences and traits).

Thereafter, the chapter focuses on real case studies of social work services that have helped shape the new societal human capabilities paradigm, and then the adoption of the developmental social policy model and objectives on the practical level of social work services – with cases of innovative, special social work services in point that have been collected from a wide range of countries and regions (South Africa, Sri Lanka, Russia, Malaysia, Hong Kong, and mainland China). The main part of this normative study applies in great length the major imperatives given by the developmental social policy theory that James Midgley of the University of California at Berkeley set up and made popular around the world. The normative theory of developmental social policy can, as a matter of fact, easily be understood and applied by all sides.

The policy proposals given are theoretically and empirically founded and seek a new way forward, out of the woods of ideological battles of the Right versus the Left, into the light of empirically founded, evidence-based social policy that helps to create better – more efficient and more effective – welfare state systems all over the world, with practical guidelines given for the development and reform of (a) welfare state systems in general, (b) specialized fields of social policy, and, last and here most importantly, (c) social work service systems, while taking care of local variations and contexts; as well as universal truths in policymaking and service provision.

Appendix 1.1: Advantages and Disadvantages of the Ideal-Typical and the Real-Typical Methodology in Welfare State Comparison

	Real-Typical Method	**Ideal-Typical Method**
Purpose	Focusing on the reality of welfare state institutions, their similarities and differences across nations; researchers focus on details, on institutional differences rather than their similarities, for better clarity on 'micro cross-national' level.	Focusing on average features of each regime cluster, used as a 'yardstick' to facilitate broad cross-national comparisons; as a consequence, minor and some major differences are omitted for the sake of better clarity on the 'macro cross-national' level.
Theoretical Basis	Researchers' own method of distinguishing system features	The theory of Max Weber on 'ideal types'
Major Advantages & Disadvantages	*Advantages:* Delivers the detailed picture, focuses on particular administrative and regulative set up, as well as legal and administrative technicalities; i.e., this methodology is more sensitive to program-level and short-term developments, enables further analysis of welfare state institutions, also when building on knowledge derived from ideal-typical theories and models, enables greater clarity on national and policy level in welfare state comparison. *Disadvantages:* The grand picture at international level may be unclear or contradictory, some important similarities on international level, especially with regard to policy outcomes and strategies may be omitted (cf., e.g., the importance of the principle of *functional equivalence*), the models set up change quickly over time, and often lack substance, i.e., a strong theoretical fundament.	*Advantages:* Delivers the greater picture, focuses on *functional equivalences* (different systems or system structure deliver the same outcome, for example: housing ownership is *functionally equivalent* to some extent to pension income), provides a perfect starting point for further real-typical welfare state regime analysis, enables greater clarity on international and global level of welfare state, comparison; i.e., it is very helpful when comparing a larger number of welfare state systems. *Disadvantages:* Details at national level may not appear, especially with regard to the institutional set-up of systems as well as administrative technicalities and legal provisions, some important policy levels and areas may not appear, the one or another country may not fit, or may not easily fit in an ideal-typical model (not every welfare state system has to be part of an ideal-typical welfare regime, some are atypical or simply drifting in between different welfare regimes, or changing from one to another).

Source: Aspalter (2012).

Note: cf. also Aspalter (2005, 2006, 2011, 2012).

Appendix 1.2: Summary of Key Elements of Five Ideal-Typical 'Welfare State Regimes' in Macro Cross-National Comparison

	The Social Democratic WR in Scandinavia	The Christian Democratic WR in Continental Europe	The Liberal WR in Anglo-Saxon Countries	The Pro-Welfare Conservative WR in East Asia	The Anti-Welfare Conservative WR in Latin America
Main Welfare Ideology	*Social Democratic*	*Christian Democratic*	*Liberal/ Neoliberal*	*Pro-Welfare Conservative*	*Anti-Welfare Conservative*
Social Rights	*Universal* Social Rights	*Performative* Social Rights	*Clientelistic* Social Rights	*Productive* Social Rights	*Regulative* Social Rights
Welfare Mix	Universal social security and welfare services	Bismarckian social insurance, NGO-based welfare services	Asset- and means-testing, limited social insurance, company-based welfare services	Universal social investment in education, health care, housing; Bismarckian social insurance and/ or provident funds	Bismarckian social insurance and/ or provident funds; universal and means-tested social assistance, health care services
Emphasis on: State Market Family Individual	Strong Weak Weak Strong	Strong Weak Strong Weak	Weak Strong Weak Strong	Increasing Decreasing Strong Weak	Decreasing Increasing Strong Weak
Degree of Decommodification	High	Medium	Low	Medium-low	Medium-low
Degree of Stratification	Low	Medium	High	Medium	Extremely High
Degree of Individualization	High	Low	High	Medium	Medium
Countries/Regions	Sweden, Norway, Finland, Denmark, Iceland	Germany, Austria, Netherlands, Belgium, France, Switzerland, Portugal, Spain, Italy, Poland, Czech Republic, Hungary, Slovenia, among others	United States, Australia, New Zealand, Canada, United Kingdom	ML China, Hong Kong, S.Korea, Japan, Taiwan, Thailand, Malay- sia, Singapore, Indonesia, among others	Chile, Argentina, Brazil, Uruguay, among others

Notes: WR = welfare state regime; findings on the first four ideal-typical welfare regime are based on Esping-Andersen (1987, 1990, 1992, 1998), Aspalter (2006, 2011, 2012), and Aspalter, Kim and Park (2009).

References

Aspalter, C. (2001a), *Conservative Welfare State Systems in East Asia*, Westport, CT: Praeger.

Aspalter, C. (2001b), *Importance of Christian and Social Democratic Movements in Welfare Politics: With Special Reference to Germany, Austria and Sweden*, New York: Nova Science.

Aspalter, C. (2001c), Different Worlds of Welfare Capitalism, *Discussion Paper Series No. 80*, GPPP, Australian National University, Canberra.

Aspalter, C. (2002a), *Democratization and Welfare State Development in Taiwan*, Aldershot: Ashgate.

Aspalter, C. (2002b), The Hong Kong Way of Social Welfare: An NGO-Based Welfare System, in *Discovering the Welfare State in East Asia*, edited by C. Aspalter. Westport, CT: Praeger.

Aspalter, C. (2002c), Singapore: A Welfare State in a Class by Itself, in *Discovering the Welfare State in East Asia*, edited by C. Aspalter. Westport, CT: Praeger.

Aspalter, C. (2005), East Asian Welfare Regime, in *The Challenge of Social Care in Asia*, edited by N.T. Tan and S. Vasoo. Eastern University Press: Singapore.

Aspalter, C. (2006), The East Asian Welfare Model, *International Journal of Social Welfare*, Vol. 15, pp. 290–301.

Aspalter, C. (2007), The Asian Cure for Health Care, *Far Eastern Economic Review*, Vol. 170, No. 9, pp. 56–59.

Aspalter, C. (2009), Securing the Future for Old Age in the Asia and Pacific Region: Short-Term and Historical Challenges, *keynote speech* presented at the ISSA International Social Security Association Conference '*Regional Social Security Forum for Asia and the Pacific*', hosted by the Government of Philippines, Manila, October 21–23.

Aspalter, C. (2011), Developing Ideal-Typical Welfare Regime Theory, *International Social Work*, Vol. 54, No. 2, pp. 735–50.

Aspalter, C. (2012), Real-Typical and Ideal-Typical Methods in Comparative Social Policy, in *Routledge Handbook of the Welfare State*, edited by B. Greve. London: Routledge.

Aspalter, C. (2013), Social Policy in Korea: Theory and Practice, paper presented at *Social Development and Social Policy: International Experiences and China's Reform*, organized by the Institute of Public Policy, South China University of Technology, Guangzhou, China.

Aspalter, C.; Kim, J., and Park, S. (2009), The Welfare States in Poland, Czech Republic, Hungary and Slovenia: An Ideal-Typical Perspective, *Social Policy and Administration*, Vol. 43, No. 2, pp. 170–85.

Chan, R.K.H. (1996), *Welfare in Newly-Industrialised Society*, Avebury: Aldershot.

Esping-Andersen, G. (1987), The Comparison of Policy Regimes, in *Stagnation and Renewal in Social Policy*, edited by M. Rein and G. Esping-Andersen. New York: M.E. Sharpe.

Esping-Andersen, G. (1990), *The Three Worlds of Welfare Capitalism*, Cambridge: Polity.

Esping-Andersen, G. (1992), The Three Political Economies of the Welfare State, in *The Study of Welfare State Regimes*, edited by J.E. Kolberg. Armonk: M.E. NY: Sharpe.

Esping-Andersen, G. (1999), *Social Foundations of Postindustrial Economies*. Oxford: Oxford University Press.

Hicks, A. and Esping-Andersen, G. (2005), Comparative and Historical Studies of Public Policy and the Welfare State, in *The Handbook of Political Sociology*, edited by T. Janoski et al. Cambridge: Cambridge University Press.

Hobson, B. (1994), Solo Mothers, Social Policy Regimes, and the Logics of Gender, in *Gendering the Welfare State*, edited by D. Sainsbury. London: Sage.

Huber, E.; Ragin, C., and Stephens, J.D. (1993), Social Democracy, Christian Democracy, Constitutional Structure, and the Welfare State, *American Journal of Sociology*, Vol. 99, No. 3, pp. 711–49.

Kersbergen, K.v. (1994), The Distinctiveness of Christian Democracy, *Christian Democracy in Europe*, edited by in D. Hanley. London: Pinter.

Kersbergen, K.V. (1995), *Social Capitalism: A Study of Christian Democracy and the Welfare State*. London: Routledge.

Lewis, J. (1992), Gender and the Development of Welfare State Regimes, *Journal of European Social Policy*, Vol. 3, pp. 159–73.

Lewis, J. (ed.) (1998), *Gender, Social Care and Welfare State Restructuring in Europe*. Aldershot: Ashgate.

Luhmann, N. (1984). *Soziale Systeme* [Social systems]. Frankfurt a.M.: Suhrkamp.

Luhmann, N. (1995), *Social Systems*. Stanford, CA: Stanford University Press.

Luhmann, N. (1998), *Die Gesellschaft der Gesellschaft* [The Society of Society]. Frankfurt a.M.: Suhrkamp.

Midgley, J. (1995), *Social Development: The Developmental Perspective in Social Welfare*. London: Sage.

Midgley, J. (1996), Toward a Developmental Model of Social Policy: Relevance of the Third World Experience, *Journal of Sociology and Social Welfare*, Vol. 23, No. 1, pp. 59–74.

Midgley, J. (1999), Growth, Redistribution and Welfare: Towards Social Investment, *Social Service Review*, Vol. 77, No. 1, pp. 3–21.

Midgley, J. (2001), Growth, Redistribution, and Welfare: Toward Social Investment, in *The Global Third Way Debate*, edited by A. Giddens. Cambridge: Polity.

Midgley, J. (2003), Poverty and the Social Development Approach, *Poverty Monitoring and Alleviation in East Asia*, edited by in K.L. Tang and C.K. Wong. New York: Nova Science.

Midgley, J. (2008), Developmental Social Policy: Theory and Practice, *Debating Social Development*, edited by in S. Singh and C. Aspalter. Hong Kong: Casa Verde.

Midgley, J. and Aspalter, C. (forthcoming), Theory of Developmental Social Policy, in *Development and Social Policy*, edited by C. Aspalter and K. Teguh-Pripadi.

Sainsbury, D. (1993), Dual Welfare and Sex Segregation of Access to Social Benefits: Income Maintenance Policies in the UK, the US, the Netherlands, and Sweden, *Journal of Social Policy*, Vol. 22, No. 1, pp. 69–98.

Sainsbury, D. (ed.) (1999), *Gender and Welfare State Regimes*. London: Sage.

Chapter 2
Social Work in Japan

Hubert Liu

As with most other Asian countries, in Japan modern social work as a professional concept was introduced by Western countries. In Japan, a modern concept of social work was introduced with the 'movement of civilization' that occurred in the late nineteenth century.[1] For more than 100 years, Japan's social work followed Western models, and then after World War II, Japan gradually completed its welfare institution in pensions, health insurance, and medical services. Through these efforts, Japan became the first pioneer of the welfare state in East Asia. But, even though the model of the Japanese welfare state was recognized by many scholars, its substantial function was disputable because of the unbalanced developing welfare system and shortage of professional social workers (Ito, 1995).

The lack of balance can be observed in terms of the government's welfare expenditure. Japan's welfare institutions, education, and health care are the dominant parts in welfare expenditure, yet the amounts spent on social welfare services and public assistance are less than in other welfare states. Another difference between the Japanese welfare state and Western welfare states is that the total welfare expenditure of the former is largely lower than the latter. Therefore, in this sense, Japan's welfare institution is a prototype of the 'welfare society', rather than a Western model of 'welfare state' (Takahashi, 1997).

This argument was popular during a period of time, especially when the traditional European welfare states faced a so-called crisis of the welfare state since the 1980s. However, essentially, Japan's lower welfare expenditure led to its limited financial resources being distributed to certain departments of the welfare system in order to pursue as much 'productivity' as possible. As a result, the model of welfare state in Japan follows the features of welfare productivism, and the development of the social work profession must be seen against this background.

In addition, we have to keep in mind that Japanese social work is not the same as that which can be seen in Western countries. This is because the development of the social work profession is always embedded in a society which, with its specific culture and social context, may be different from one place to another place. Furthermore, the maturity of the social work profession in a society also

---

1   The movement of civilization in Japan took place in the late nineteenth century and was known as the 'Bunmeikaika', which meant a gradual process whereby the Japanese accepted Western culture, including the institutions, instruments, and ways of thinking. In 1868, Emperor Meiji promoted Meijiishin, which was seen as the official launch of the movement of civilization that greatly improved the progress of modernization.

relates to the timing of its introduction and length of development. Meanwhile, the government's and the public's attitude toward the profession are also crucial to the professionalism of social work. Therefore, in order to examine the development of professionalism of social work in Japan, it is necessary to explore the theme according to a historically analytical viewpoint.

In this chapter, we will firstly review the initiation of modern social work in Japan, and then describe the reestablishment of social work after World War II. Moreover, several changes and reformations of Japanese social work will be explored, particularly focusing on the rise of accreditation in social work. After rethinking the development of professionalism of social work in Japan, the conclusion looks at the challenges and possibilities for the future.

The Initiation of Modern Social Work in Japan

The beginning of a modern concept of social work in Japan can be traced to 1874, when the *Jiukyu Kisoku*[2] was implemented. The implementation of the *Jiukyu Kisoku*, on the one hand, was a symbol of the centralization of political power from local governments to the central government. Meanwhile, welfare administration could be formalized and institutionalized. Although the Japanese central government intentionally circumscribed its role and function in the poor relief system, *Jiukyu Kisoku* clearly showed the responsibility of poor relief was shared by both local governments and voluntary organizations. In general, *Jiukyu Kisoku* is compared with the Poor Law Amendment Act of 1834 (New Poor Law) because they shared the same concepts, including the emphasis on families' responsibility, division of service districts, and some parts of government's finances. But still, *Jiukyu Kisoku* was essentially different from the New Poor Law in many ways.

Firstly, instead of the institution-based relief provided under the New Poor Law in Britain or America, voluntary organizations took responsibility. Regarding residential care, the mechanism of co-dependence between the statutory sector and voluntary sector was clearly shown (Ito, 1995). In this sense, the government mandated the voluntary organizations delivering welfare services, whereas the voluntary organizations could be legitimized by the government's authority.

Secondly, the original concepts of poor relief were different from the *Jiukyu Kisoku*. The New Poor Law resulted from the tradition of the sixteenth century whereby, due to the Reformation, conflicts between the state and religion also expanded to the realm of social welfare. Conventionally, particularly in Britain, the Church took the main role in providing social welfare or poor relief. The Poor Law of 1601 (43 Elizabeth) was the first legislation that made the state officially involved

---

2 *Jiukyu Kisoku* means that a social system controls the poor people. As the original concept of social welfare, *Jiukyu Kisoku* categorized the poor into 'deserving' and 'undeserving'. Public relief mainly focuses on the deserving poor, including the handicapped, the elderly, children, etc. But social controls accompanied public relief to the 'deserving' poor. In brief, the *Jiukyu Kisoku* system inherits the idea that the causes of poverty have to be imputed to individual problems rather than social problems.

in social welfare. But the *Jiukyu Kisoku* was not a product of conflicts between state and religion. Rather, the *Jiukyu Kisoku* can be seen as an approach wherein the state cooperated with voluntary organizations in providing welfare services.

In Japan, the spirit of cooperation between the government sector and the voluntary sector cannot only be seen in the social welfare legislation, but the social work services. The Japanese *Homen-Iin* system was a typical model of cooperation between the government and voluntary organizations for providing social welfare services. Unlike the *Elberfeld* system,[3] where voluntary citizens cooperated with the statutory service provisions under the Poor Law in terms of service effectiveness, the *Homen-Iin* provided services directly from donations (Ito, 1995); however, the *Homen-Iin* system was also different from the Charity Organization Society (COS).

COS adopted scientific methods to categorize paupers into 'deserving poor' and 'undeserving poor', but the *Homen-Iin* system did not attribute the cause of poverty to the individuals' responsibility but rather to 'fate', and approached the poor in a paternalistic way (Ito, 1995). The *Homen-Iin* system was not only employed in the Japanese motherland, but also eventually expanded to Taiwan to enhance Japanese power in its colonies (Liu, 2011).

Given the fact that Japanese social work was not completely similar to that in Western countries, modern social work in Japan was recommended by the West and in order to explain the causes resulting in the uniqueness of social work in Japan, it is necessary to examine the development of Japanese social work in terms of a longitudinal viewpoint. Table 2.1 shows the predominant Japanese social work legislation and relevant social welfare policies before World War II .

Table 2.1   Japanese Social Welfare Policies and Legislations before World War II

Year	Social Welfare Legislations and Relevant Policies	Effects or Features
1874	The *Jiukyu Kisoku* system was implemented	Modern social work was introduced into Japan
1897	The first settlement was built	The public relief expanded to in-door relief, which required the recipients entering a settlement (workhouse).
1908	The Central Council for Charity was established.	A semi-government organization, which concerns the charity affairs for the public with its semi-official functions. This mechanism firmed the structure of public-private cooperation for providing welfare services in Japan.
1918	*Homen-Iin* system spread all over Japan	*Homen-Iin* system was deemed an innovation of social services.

---

3   The Elberfeld system was a plan for poor relief that originated in 1800 in Elberfeld, Germany. This system divided a city into several districts for effectively conveying poor relief.

Year	Social Welfare Legislations and Relevant Policies	Effects or Features
1921	The Central Council for Charity changed its name to the Central Council for Social Work	The beginning of the training courses for adult students to conduct social work services.
1927	The first national congress of the *Homen-Iin* was held.	More than 15,000 members participated in the system in Japan, and proactively participated in the enactment of the Poor Relief Law in 1929.
1929	The Relief and Protection Law was implemented	Japan took the first steps towards an institutionalized welfare state, yet this social legislation was mainly meant to stabilize society during the war.

Ito (1995) states that social work development in Japan came to a halt in 1933 when the Japanese invasion of Manchuria took place. Because of militarism, social work was suppressed and the function of the *Homen-Iin* system was changed in order to support nationalism and colonial governance. Moreover, social workers were seen as associates of the communists because of their left-wing political inclinations. The Japanese militarist powers regarded the profession of social work as a herald of communism, which threatened the ruling power of the Japanese Empire. Therefore, the Japanese nationalists suppressed the development of social work during World War II.

During the time of imperial expansion, Schaede and Nemoto (2006) argued that the main focus of social welfare was on supporting soldiers and their families, rather than the poverty issue per se. The function of social work was changed to motivate the morale of the military, and welfare benefits to the public became an exchange for obtaining Japanese people's allegiance to the Japanese royalty. Consequently, the profession of social work in Japan could not be regenerated until its surrender in 1945.

The Reestablishment of the Social Work Profession

After the collapse of the Japanese Empire in 1945, Japan was transformed into a democratic state with a revised democratic Constitution of Japan. During the post-war period, Japan underwent dramatic economic growth characterized by the US–Japan Alliance in the political aspect. The changes, both in the economic and political aspects are significant to the development of social work in Japan. Firstly, the Japanese government perceived that there was a gap in social services between Japan and the United States through the American General Head Quarters' (GHQ) occupation from 1945 to 1951.

GHQ, in order to alleviate extreme poverty, introduced several social programs between 1945 and 1951. These followed the conventional ideas of American social work since the 1930s, which dichotomized the target groups and focused on the needs of the 'deserving' poor, such as children and physically handicapped persons.

Regarding the *Homen-Iin* system, the GHQ deemed it was an Imperial Japanese government because it cooperated with the military during the war. Even though the *Homen-Iin* took the role of providing social services and gave relief to the public, they worked more for promoting the Imperial Japanese government's policies. Moreover, during the war, the *Homen-Iin* also took responsibility for educating militarism and recruited numerous resources for supporting the war. Therefore, the *Homen-Iin* system was compelled to change on GHQ's demand. Consequently, a new system, *Minsei-Iin* was introduced. Although *Minsei-Iin* worked between the social welfare officer and citizens, they did not have any decision-making rights (Ito, 1995).

In this sense, the *Minsei-Iin* system could not be seen as a professional social work system because its function was circumscribed to the accessory role of the social welfare officer. In fact, regarding the development of professional social work, both the *Homen-Iin* and *Minsei-Iin* systems made limited contributions: The only difference between them was the change of authority.

The *Homen-Iin* system provided a mechanism that combined the function of supervision and direct services; however, the *Minsei-Iin* system played the role of broker, in which their authorized power from the Japanese government was diminished. Consequently, the GHQ's policy, which intended to separate the statutory and voluntary sectors, could be achieved.

In addition, GHQ introduced American social workers to supervise newly employed workers in the Social Welfare Office and several social relief agencies. These American social workers came to the front line and worked with the Japanese social welfare personnel, bringing a new vision regarding social work to their Japanese colleagues. According to Ito (1995), the atmosphere of these agencies was active and the workers were highly motivated. From 1946 to 1952, even though they had endless work because of a lot of needy people, they actively worked and gave public assistance without political propaganda.

In spite of the fact that the eminently positive effect could be seen, since American social workers ushered in the Japanese welfare system, it could not fundamentally change the social work system in Japan. There were two main weaknesses regarding this arrangement: Firstly, the American social workers were too few to deal with direct social work services and indirect social work services at the same time. That is, the American social workers had to supervise the work of social welfare officers on the one hand, and deal with the various needs of starving people, homeless children, and the handicapped on the other.

The American social workers paid more attention to supervising the direct social work rather than the indirect social work services, such as social welfare staff training and social welfare education. As a result, basic reform of social work education and its professionalization could not occur during this period. Secondly, the American social workers were not expected to set up a new model for Japanese social work; they were required to be practical workers, rather than tutors for training Japanese social workers.

Therefore, they did not concentrate on the social workers' training in practical concepts although they had a high standard of professionalism. The Japanese government, during the US occupation, paid more attention to military relief rather than public relief in non-military sectors (Yoshimura, 2009). Sugamuna (2005) analyzed the reasons for the Japanese government's emphasis on military relief: After the war, the Japanese government faced such fiscal difficulties that it could not offer relief for the general population. On the contrary, the existing nongovernmental social service organizations, which had a pro-military background, such as the Veteran's Associations (*Zaigo Gunjin Kai*) and Association of Relief for Militaries (*Gunjin Engo Kai*) had relatively abundant resources for providing public assistance after the war so they were inclined to put higher priority on providing military relief.

Moreover, the Japanese government established the Association of Relief for Nationals (*Doho Engo Kai*), integrating the Association of Relief for Militaries with other major organizations in order to utilize their financial and human resources to give public assistance. However, these quasi-military organizations and other small-scale volunteer organizations largely depended on subsidies from the government in order to escape financial shortages. Hence, under this system, the voluntary institutions became subcontracted organizations of the Japanese government.

All in all, during this period, the Japanese government relied on the quasi-military organizations providing public assistance; meanwhile, the voluntary organizations were gradually controlled by the Japanese government. Most important of all, these organizations still could not develop the professional skills for social work, and the subcontracted system could not cultivate the professionalism of social work either.

Nevertheless, the GHQ's occupation facilitated the germination of social work education in Japan during 1946–1952. The Japanese School of Social Work was set up in 1946 for providing modern training courses for social workers. However, this education system could not be continued after the occupation finished because the Japanese government tried to keep their own autonomy in education.[4]

In 1950 the Japanese government implemented the School Education Law in order to abolish the pre-war educational system. The Japan School of Social Work was divided into Japan Junior College of Social Work (*Nihon Shakai Jigyo Tanki Daigaku*) and Japan Advanced Vocational School of Social Work (*Nihon Shakai Jigyo Senmon Gakko*).

This reform downgraded the Japanese School of Social Work, rather than reorganizing it into a four-year college (Japan University of Social Work, 1996). In this way, the Japanese government did de-professionalized the in field service of social work.

---

4   During the occupation, the relationship between the GHQ and the Japanese government was not the absolute relation described as superordination and subordination. Yet, sometimes the Japanese government could selectively decide if the GHQ's directives should be obeyed or not. The Japanese government could obtain more autonomy because it had a submissive attitude towards the American occupation. Moreover, in the following period of the Cold War, the Japanese government cooperated with the United States and became its firmest partner in East Asia.

In addition, the professionalism of social work, particularly the concept of casework, was not developed because of the administrative arrangement and the design of the lower educational level.

This fact resulted in social welfare policies being mostly directed to the modification of the social security system during the 1950s and the 1960s. Both central government and local governments ignored the public social services (Anderson, 1993). Furthermore, the Japanese government applied the placement system (*Sochi Seido*) to solve the problem of the lack of direct social workers (Kitaba, 2005).

Under the placement system, all the clients were firstly examined by the welfare offices, which were the sole agent to determine who should receive what types of social services, and usually provided institutional services. Nakamura (2003) argues that the placement system implies the exclusive authority of public servants to determine the flow of social welfare services. Therefore, the professionalism of social work was not the Japanese government's main concern.

For delivering welfare benefits, the Japanese government relied on the official clerical workers with lower educational requirements to examine the clients. Social workers with independent working skills were unable to work in or for the Japanese government – most worked in hospitals and the private sector with lower salaries and work status.

In conclusion, before the 1970s the professionalism of social work in Japan could not be developed successfully even though American occupation had brought some training courses and established a professional school of social work. The Japanese government, including both central government and local governments, ignored the development of professionalism within social work, such as the skills of counselling and psychotherapeutic abilities. Therefore, the social workers looked like social welfare administrators and carried out various clerical duties without full professional social work training.

The Rise of Accreditation of Social Work

According to Peng (2002) throughout the 1950s and 1960s, because economic growth was rapid and the population was still relatively young, the conservative social welfare policies were not criticized by the Japanese people.

In 1971, Japan became an aging society as the proportion of elderly people reached 7 per cent of the total population. In addition, because of the oil crises in the 1970s, Japan faced its first economic recession since the end of World War II during this period. In response to the decline in economic growth, the Japanese government curtailed social welfare expenditure and asserted that the development of the Japanese welfare state should be different from the Western countries' style.

This conservative welfare regime of the 1980s is often referred to as the Japanese-style welfare society regime (*Nihongata Fukushi Shakai* Regime), which is based on individual self-help and mutual aid between families, neighbors, and the local community. According to the Economic Planning Agency (1979), the welfare society provided welfare provisions by an efficient state as accorded by the principle of the liberal economic society.

The idea of a welfare society with this policy orientation could be seen as the concept of welfare pluralism. Welfare pluralism or the welfare society, in the Western countries, is a synonym for denoting an arrangement blending both public and private sectors. That is, a 'public-private mix' in industrial society, though the boundary separating the public and private sectors is often fuzzy and indeterminate (Rein and Rainwater, 1987).

However, in Japan the welfare society was proposed mainly for the retrenchment of the government's role in the provision of social welfare. Under the political directive of welfare society, Peng (2002) argued that the Japanese government substantially curbed the rate of the rise of social security expenditure from 1980 to 1990 (from 12.4% to 13.6% of the national income). In regard to the tiny increase during the 10 years, she said,

> This modest increase, despite tremendous expansionary pressures from pension and health care, was achieved by keeping down the cost of social welfare and by shifting public care and personal service responsibilities back to the family. (Peng, 2002: 416)

Therefore, corresponding to the changes in the demographic structure of Japan, the familialistic welfare regime not only showed the extent of the family's financial and care responsibility but also that the care burden may have increased rather than decreased over time. This fact sets the context for the political and economic dynamics that led to a new settlement in the social work system that followed.

Since the term 'welfare society' had been proposed in the 1970s, the Japanese government had attempted to establish a model based on the minimum security provided by the government plus the spirit of self-help (Goodman and Peng, 1996).[5]

Figure 2.1 shows the original concept of welfare society, which is different from the concept of welfare state and mostly relies on resources from the voluntary sector and the family.

Yet, the role of professional social workers was not taken into account under the propaganda of welfare society. On the contrary, the Japanese government proposed the slogan 'welfare society with vitality' in 1979. The objectives were to create strong and stable individuals and communities, as well as a free and energetic private sector where a secure livelihood could be obtained (Shiratori, 1985: 216). Takahashi (1997: 195) argued that the overall strategy was to create a new type of community on the basis of non-hierarchical solidarity and spontaneous participation.

---

5   The debates of social work in Japan have to expand to the welfare model and its relevant ideas. In order to avoid the 'over-Westernization' of social welfare, in which workers would become lazy and the family institution would deteriorate as a result of excessive investment in social security systems (Anderson, 1993; Takahashi, 1997), the Japanese government introduced the 'Japanese-model welfare society' in the mid-1970s. The core concept of welfare society is that the self-help of citizens was regarded as primary and central in ensuring welfare, while public welfare would be only supplementary (Chan et al., 2004).

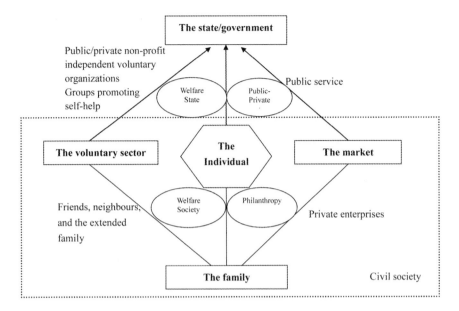

Fig. 2.1   The Welfare Diamond

Source: Revised from Firdberg (1997).

This idea, which could be found in the White Paper of the Ministry of Health and Welfare, persisted into the 1980s. Therefore, even though the Japanese government deemed the welfare society as a new strategy that surmounted the problems that occurred in the Western welfare states, it was actually a return to the traditional mode of welfare provision, relying on the family and local communities (Maruo, 1986; Goodman and Peng, 1996; Tsukada, H., 2002; Chan et al., 2004).

Chen (1996) criticizes the aspiration to a welfare society, sometimes called a caring community, as appearing somewhat idealistic, and the term 'welfare pluralism' often serves rhetoric in policy debate. In this sense, there is no doubt that the professionalism of social work could not be emphasized, and the overwhelming majority of the welfare officers on the front line were seemingly general public servants without professional training in social work.

Ito (1995) analyzed the causes for why welfare officers lacked professional training in social work. Firstly, the several policies of de-professionalization in social work made the welfare officers becoming inactive. New social work practice or theory was found in neither the statutory sector nor the voluntary sector.

In addition, the *Minsei-Iin* system lost its enthusiasm and was not very popular among citizens. Thirdly, there was much confusion in social work education. Field practice was not seen as an important part of education and, in several universities it was not included in the curriculum. Furthermore, the placement system caused a split between social work education and social work practice because social welfare officers were not required to be graduates of social work colleges (Yoshimura, 2009).

The gap between school training and the practical work was filled in the late 1980s with the rise of accreditation of the social work system. In 1987 the national, licenced social work system, which emphasized the linkage between social work education and field practice, was launched by the Minister of Health and Welfare.

However, the newly created licence, Certified Social Worker (CSW), could not guarantee the development of professionalism of social work in Japan. In fact, the launch of CSW was mainly decided by the Japanese government and was not the product of collective movements by social workers' organizations. In this sense, rather than the awakening of social work professionalism, the promotion of the CSW was like the central government's administrative decision. Moreover, according to the Certified Social Worker and Certified Care Worker Law (CSW-CCW Law), neither employees in welfare offices nor hospital social workers needed to obtain the CSW.

In fact, in the late 1980s, CSW was a profession in name only because it had no formal jurisdiction. Hence, CSWs do not have a monopoy in the field of social work, and other professionals can do the same work without a social work licence.

Ito (1995) pointed out that the CSW Law was enacted to reflect the transitional situation in the development of professionalism of social work, yet, the more fundamental change in the basic power relationship between bureaucrats, professionals, and citizens was an imperative theme. Wolferen (1993) argues the necessity of changing the power relationship in order to develop the professionalism of social work:

> The Japanese government bureau has extraordinary power of awarding licenses and other permissions for commercial pursuits, and of withholding advantages like subsidies, tax privileges or low-interest loans at their own discretion. Ministries can resort to 'administrative guidance' to force organizations in their realm of endeavor to adopt 'voluntary measures'. (Wolferen, 1993: 58–59)

Indeed, the Japanese government played a significant role in enacting the CSW-CCW Law. Instead of responding to the strong claim from the third sector, the CSW-CCW Law was legislated successfully by the Japanese bureaucrats' efforts. Usually it takes a long time to enforce a law in Japan, yet the CSW-CCW Law was enacted extraordinarily fast (in only four months).

There were several reasons behind the Japanese government promoting the accreditation of social work as a profession. Firstly, demographic changes brought new social problems affecting Japanese society, in particular the issue of an aged society and the huge number of the elderly attracted the Japanese government's attention. However, after the 1970s the Japanese government's role was retrenched in public services in order to cut down social welfare expenditure. In other words, relying on the social workers in the non-bureaucratic sector for dealing with the increasing social problems was unavoidable. Therefore, to employ a basic line of social workers in the non-bureaucratic sector became an imperative issue to the Japanese government. This was the backdrop explaining why the Japanese government actively enacted the CSW-CCW Law.

Secondly, Yoshimura (2009) explained the reasons why the Japanese government hastened the enactment of the CSW-CCW Law. According to his study, before 1987, the social worker national licence was handled by the General Affairs Section in the Bureau of Social Affairs. But, because of the Japanese government's organizational reformation in the end of 1980s, the Ministry of Health and Welfare (MHW) planned to establish a new bureau, which combined both the welfare clan and the health clan. In this way, the new bureau subsequently might manage the national licenced social workers, and that meant the Bureau of Social Affairs might lose jurisdiction over social work human resources. Therefore, the welfare officers attempted to integrate the national licence legislation of social workers with that of careworkers and to locate it under the General Affairs Section (Yoshimura, 2009: 242). As a result, this arrangement also impacted social work education.

Sakaguchi and Swepaul (2011) point out that there are some identifiable peculiarities in social work education in Japan, especially with the combining of care work and social work education. Essentially, the requirements for doing the CSW and the CCW are different in many ways. For example, the CSW emphasizes empathy, keen observation, and the ability to connect social resources under various powers; however, the CCW training places more emphasis on the proficiency of caring and communication skills.

Table 2.2   The Comparison between CSW and CCW

	Certified Social Worker (CSW)	**Certified Care Worker (CCW)**
Legislation (Year)	**CSW-CCW Law (1987)**	
Monopolization	**Nominal monopolization**	
Aims of working	• to use knowledge and professional skills to assist the people who are disabled and have difficulties in daily life through consultation, advice, instruction, and welfare services, etc. • to work with doctors and other professionals to connect and coordinate the resources for helping people.	• to use knowledge and professional skills to assist people who are disabled and have difficulties in daily life in order to provide proper care services. • to provide instructions to the clients and the relevant caretakers for the proper care services.
Contents of working	• providing synthetic and proper welfare services and relevant health services. • performing innovative work in the communities in order to ensure cooperative relationships with relevant welfare providers.	• providing synthetic and proper welfare services to people with dementia and who have other physical and mental problems. • ensuring cooperative relationships with relevant welfare providers.

Nevertheless, the CSW-CCW Law, which amalgamates two different professions in the same legislation, results in the mixture of social work and care work education. In this regard, the education in either social work or care work is not able to be professionalized because it is difficult to be make the training specialized. This is a fundamental cause hampering the development of professionalism of social work in Japan.

At the same time, paradoxically, the CSW-CCW Law describes the aims of working and contents of working for both certified social workers and certified care workers in similar terms. Even though they are describing different professional functions, the aims and contents of working overlap and are confused. Table 2.2 shows the comparison between the CSW and CCW in terms of the CSW-CCW Law.

Consequently, even though the rise of accreditation in social work could be observed by the enactment of the CSW-CCW Law in 1987, it is still hard to say that social work in Japan has become an independent profession. On the one hand, the social worker in Japan has a monopoly on the name, but not in the work. On the other hand, the nature of the social worker was still under the shadow of the Japanese government's control, rather than the awakening of social work professionalism. In conclusion, the development of the professionalism of social work was not yet fully-fledged in Japan during this period.

Rethinking of the Professionalism of Social Work in Japan

Yoshimura (2009) points out that although there was no national social worker licence before 1987, Japanese social welfare legislation had many titles for defining the status of social work employees. Table 2.3 shows the major titles of social work employees before 1987.

As above, we can find that the labor market of social work in Japan was composed of less-educated workers. In addition, a social welfare director might not have any background in social work training: As long as they can pass the competitive national exams, laymen can become welfare officers. This is another reason why the Advisory Council of Social Welfare in Tokyo City severely criticized poorly qualified workers in social welfare agencies and insisted on the introduction of accreditation for the social work field (Yoshimura, 2009).

After the 1990s, the rise of accreditation of social work continued and expanded to other welfare fields. The enactment of the CSW-CCW Law in 1987 encouraged psychiatric social workers in hospitals and psychiatric institutions. The Psychiatric Social Work (PSW) bill was proposed by the Mental Health Section, the Department of Welfare of Handicapped Persons, MHW, and was eventually enacted in 1997 but not without controversy. Even though the enactment of the PSW Law was highly disputed, the law itself was accepted by many hospital social workers and this legislation marks a further step towards professionalism in social work in Japan.

However, even though the certification of social work has increased since the end of the 1980s, the professionalization of social work still faces various challenges. Firstly, as mentioned above, the social worker who takes the national exams in order to obtain a social work licence has not necessarily studied in the college of social work. Moreover, knowledge about social work and social welfare is of no use when taking the national exam for licenced social work: English and law are more important. Secondly, the social worker, who is supposed to be trained in a professional way, is not preferred by the peculiar Japanese bureaucratic system.

Table 2.3   Major Titles of Social Work Employees before 1987

Titles of Social Work Employees	Social Welfare Director (*Shakai Fukushi Shuji*)	Welfare Officer (*Fukushi Shi*)	Counseling Worker (*Sodan In*)	Guidance Worker (*Shido In*)
Legislation	Social Welfare Service law in 1951	1. Child Welfare Law in 1947 2. Law for the Welfare of Mentally Retarded Persons in 1960 3. Law for the Welfare of Physically Handicapped Persons in 1949	1. Law for the Welfare of Mothers and Children in 1964 2. Law for the Welfare of Physically Handicapped Persons	MHW Ordinance No.18 in 1966 (The Minimum Requirements about the Equipment and Administration of Relief, Correctional, Rehabilitation, and Sheltering Institutions)
Status	Government officers who are constituted the core of social welfare workers in government sector	The welfare officers were allocated to welfare offices at prefecture governments to treat hard-to handle cases with highly technical treatment (Bureau of Social Affairs, 1981; Kuroki, 1951: 117–18)	The counseling worker seems to correspond to caseworker in contemporary American terminology (Yoshimura, 2009)	Japanese legal statements are quite ambiguous to the guidance workers. Even though the social service institutions have to employ guidance workers for helping client's behavioral corrections, they cannot utilize public resources or have formal jurisdiction over the clients.
Requirements (One of the following)	1. Accredited three subjects in college education 2. Short-term in-service training 3. Accredited continuing education	1. Special educational programs accredited by the MHW 2. BA in sociology, education or psychology 3. Physician 4. Two-year work experience as SWD	None	1. Accredited three subjects in college 2. Short-term in-service training 3. Accredited continuing education

Source: Compiled by the author

In Japan, the rotation system, which is practiced among Japanese civil servants, is a crucial personnel policy. Under the rotation system, all Japanese officers on the basic level are trained as a part of the clerical sector in order to exchange to other sectors in the future. Usually clerical workers are reassigned to other sections every three to five years and these exchanges sometimes take place between extremely different sections. For example, a government officer may be relocated from the social welfare section to the civil affairs section. Okouchi (2000) argues that the personnel administration in Japanese government organizations presupposes the employment of laypersons.

Therefore, workers in Japanese bureaucratic organizations are not supposed to be experts in specific fields. Instead, they are expected to have high degrees of flexibility so as to fit into any section in the organization (Yoshimura, 2009). Because of this a professional social worker may not be the proper person for working within this personnel policy. It is more likely than not that a professional social worker would resign because their career cannot be continued under the rotation system. Undeniably, this personnel policy is a disadvantage to cultivating the professionalism of social work in Japan. Thirdly, the career development within social work is segmented and enclosed. There is a gap between the government and private sectors and mobility beyond sector boundaries is almost completely non-existent (Yoshimura, 2009).

Although a licenced social worker may have practical experience in the private sector, such as hospitals or corporations, the only way for them to work in the public sector is to pass the uniform recruitment examination which has an age restriction. In addition, the rigid personnel administration policy constrains mobility between local governments in the public sector. Consequently, social workers and welfare officers are enclosed in the internal labor market, which is divided into numerous segments. This is also the fatal point at which social work practitioners in Japan failed to develop an integrated organizational movement, as well as failing to form the profession across the public sector and the private sector.

Conclusion

Even though the rise of accreditation of social work can be found in Japan since the late 1980s, the professionalism of social work is still developing. The different working statuses between certified social workers and certified care workers remain despite them obtaining their jurisdictions from the same legislation.

In this sense, it is difficult to determine how many social workers in social welfare services are 'professional social workers' (Japanese National Committee, 1986). This is because, firstly, in Japan social work as a profession has not received full recognition until very recently. Secondly, bureaucratic dominance over the social work profession has negatively influenced the education, employment, and qualifications of social workers (Ito, 1995).

Before 1987, the Certified Social Workers and Certified Care Workers Law (CSW-CCW Law) had not been enacted, so it was hard to clarify the number of practical social workers on the one hand and to judge their quality of services on the other. The legislation in 1987 promoted official certification for social workers in Japan, and afterward certified social workers gradually came to be accepted by Japanese society. However, at the same time bureaucratic dominance over the social work profession distorted the welfare market and interfered in social workers' professional autonomy.

Therefore, the development of professionalism of social work in Japan is decided by the relationships between the public and private sectors, and their interactions may affect the transformation of Japanese social work education. In effect, the development of professionalism of social work in Japan was a unique process in which the role of government, the political situation, and cultural factors amalgamated.

Appendix 2.1

Year	The Development of Welfare Legislation
1874	Relief Ordinance
1909	Reformatory relief work, organizing mutual assistance
1911	Grace foundation Saiseikai labor movement
1917	Rice riot, Social Work introduced (reforming houses, child care on a small scale)
1922	Health Insurance Act
1932	Relief Act, unemployed excluded
1934	Reform of Health Insurance Act
1937	Military Assistance Act, protection of mother and children
1938	National Insurance
1941	Pension Insurance for Workers
1944	Welfare Pension Act
1946	Livelihood Protection Act
1947	Workmen's Accidents Insurance Act, Unemployment Insurance Act, Children's Welfare Act
1949	The Disabled Welfare Act
1959	National Health Insurance Program was implemented
1961	National Pension Law was implemented
1963	Welfare for the elderly
1973	Free Medical Care for the Old
1975	Council for Fiscal Institutions: 'already caught up with western levels,' recommending restriction of social welfare
1987	The enactment of the CSW-CCW Law
1997	The enactment of the Psychiatric Social Worker Law

Source: Compiled by the author

References

Anderson, S.J. (1993), *Welfare Policy and Politics in Japan: Beyond the Development State*. New York: Paragon House.

Bureau of Social Affairs (1981), *Sekatsu Hogo Sanjyu-nen*. Shakai Fukushi Chosa-Kai.

Chan, R.K.H., Cheung, C.K., and Peng, I. (2004), Social Capital and Its Relevance to the Japanese-Model Welfare Society, *International Journal of Social Welfare*, Vol. 13, pp. 315–24.

Chen, S. (1996), The Chinese State and the Socialist Welfare Pluralism, in *Social Policy of the Economic State and Community Care in Chinese Culture: Aging, Family, Urban Change, and the Socialist Welfare Pluralism*. Aldershot: Ashgate.

EPA, Economic Planning Agency (1979), *Shin-Keizaishakai 7-kanen Keikaku*, Tokyo: EPA.

Firdberg T. (1997), *Hvem løser opgaverne I fremtidens velfærdssamfund?* Copenhagen, Socialforskningsinstituttet.

Goodman, R. and Peng, I. (1996), The East Asian Welfare States: Peripatetic Learning, Adaptive Changes and Nation-Building, in *Welfare State in Transition: National Adaptations in Global Economies*, edited by G. Esping-Andersen. London: Sage.

Ito, Y. (1995), Social Work Development in Japan, *Social Policy & Administration*, Vol. 29, No. 3, pp. 258–68.

Japan University of Social Work (JUSW) (1996), *Nihon Shakai Jigyo Daigaku Gojyu-nen Shi*, Japan University of Social Work.

Kitaba, T. (2005), *Sengo Sochi Seido no Seritsu to Henyo*. Horitsu Bunka-sha.

Kuroki, T. (1951), *Gendai Shakai Fukushi Jigyo no Tenka*. Central Board of Social Welfare.

Liu, H. (2011), Winding Route to Consensus Building: Democratisation and Taiwan's National Pension Scheme, PhD Dissertation, Graduate School of International Cooperation Study (GSICS) of Kobe University, Japan, Kobe: Kobe University.

Maruo, N. (1986), The Development of the Welfare Mix in Japan, in *The Welfare State East and West*, edited by R. Rose and R. Shiratori. New York: Oxford University Press.

Nakamura, Y. (2003), *Nakamura Yuichi Chosaku-shu: Shakai Fukushi no Genri*. Tokyo: Jyunpo-sha.

Okouchi, S. (2000), *Gendai Kanryo-sei to Jinji Gyosei*. Yuhikaku.

Peng, I. (2002), Social Care in Crisis: Gender, Demography, and Welfare State Restructuring in Japan, *Social Politics*, Vol. 9, No. 3, pp. 411–33.

Rein, M. and Rainwater, L. (1987), From Welfare State to Welfare Society, in *Stagnation and Renewal in Social Policy: The Rise and Fall of Policy Regimes*, edited by M. Rein, G. Esping-Andersen, and L. Rainwater. New York: Armonk.

Sakaguchi, H. and Sewpaul, V. (2011), A Comparison of Social Work Education Across South Africa and Japan in Relation to the Global Standards for Social Work Education and Training, *International Journal of Social Welfare*, Vol. 20, pp. 192–202.

Schaede, U. and Nemoto, K. (2006), Poverty and Politics: Evaluating Public Assistance in Japan, retrieved 30 June 2013, cpe.ucsd.edu/assets/001/6214.pdf.

Shiratori, R. (1985), The Experience of the Welfare State in Japan and Its Problems, in *The Welfare State and Its Aftermath*, edited by S. Eisenstadt and O. Ahimeir. London: Croom Helm.

Sugamuna, T. (2005), *Hi Senro-ki Shakai Fukushi Bunseki*. Tokyo: Minerva.

Takahashi, M. (1997), *The Emergence of Welfare Society in Japan*. Aldershot: Avebury.

Tsukada, H. (2002), *Economic Globalization and the Citizens' Welfare State: Sweden, UK, Japan, US*. Aldershot: Ashgate

Yoshimura, H. (2009), The Formation of Social Work Professions in Japan, PhD Dissertation, Department of Sociology, Chicago: University of Chicago.

Chapter 3
Social Work in Mongolia

Oyut-Erdene Namdaldagva

This chapter will discuss professional social work developments in Mongolia, and the context and background for social work education and practice. In Mongolia social work is a relatively new professional discipline and field of practice, though elsewhere in the world the social work profession has been in existence for more than 100 years.

Professional social work development in Mongolia dates back to the mid-1990s after the country made the transition from a centralized economy to a market economy, from a one-party political system to a parliamentary democracy, and from a socialist society to a democratic and pluralist society. The democratic change laid a strong foundation for promoting social justice, human rights, and development of a civic society in the country and new political, economic, and social environments created both opportunities and challenges for its people. The challenges in all spheres of society – including service infrastructure breakdown, inflation, budget cuts, job losses, increase in poverty – necessitated professional interventions helping people and families to deal with the personal and social problems triggered and made worse by the transitional difficulties.

This situation led to the introduction of professional social work in Mongolia. In addition to these nationwide factors, international factors influenced the development of social work as a profession and a service system. Child rights and humanitarian aid organizations contributed to introducing social work from the Western world. This chapter outlines developmental milestones in Mongolian social work, describing its scope, policy, and domains. The progression and developmental process of Mongolian social work is discussed through four phases: the pre-professional period (before 1996), the launching and professionalization phase (1996–2001), the capacity-building years (2001–2007), and lastly, the further institutionalization of social work education and practice (2007–Present). This chapter concludes with ideas for future developments of social work in Mongolia.

The Country Context for Development of Social Work

Mongolia is well known for Chinggis Khan, a founder and a ruler of the Mongolian Empire in the thirteenth century. Mongolia is a large, landlocked country with a territory of 1,564,100 square kilometers, inhabited by about 2.8 million people. It borders with Russia in the north and with China in the south. Its population structure marks Mongolia as a young country due to the fact that 67 per cent of the population is under the age of 35 and 27.3 per cent is below 15 (NCS, 2011). Little more than half of the total population are women and the elderly population over 60 makes up 5.5 per cent. Life expectancy at birth is gradually increasing and reached 68 in 2010. Mongolia is divided administratively into 21 provinces called *aimags* and the capital city is Ulaanbaatar. *Aimags* are comprised of *soums* and the capital city Ulaanbaatar consists of nine districts. The smallest administrative units in Mongolia are called *baghs* and *khoroos* in provinces and districts, respectively.

Of the total population, urban residents increased to 67.9 per cent in 2010 and of these urban residents, 43.6 percent live in the capital city Ulaanbaatar. Currently, the net migration rate of Mongolia is -1.2 migrant per 1,000 population (PD, 2012) showing an excess of persons leaving the country. Many Mongolians, predominantly men, are leaving for better salaries and lives.

In the twenty-first century, the population structure of many countries is changing due to the increase in the number of older people, and this trend is also evident in Mongolia. There is an estimation that the number of Mongolian people over 65 will double by 2020 (GM, 2009). The growth of the older population challenges government to improve a country's social protection and population development policies, taking into consideration population ageing and its social and economic effects.

One of the biggest social problems is that there is a striking difference between urban and rural lives. Traditional livestock production dominates the agricultural sector and 25 per cent of households still live a nomadic and semi-nomadic way of life. Mongolia is perceived as a nomadic country with agricultural industry, and the main religion is Tibetan Buddhism. Mongolia ranks 108 out of 186 countries of the world in the 2012 Human Development Index. According to the World Bank (2012), Mongolia is among the lower middle income countries with GNI per capita $3,160 USD. However, modern Mongolia is characterized by rapid information technology development, and an increase in the service sector.

The strongest social indicator for Mongolia is its high literacy and school enrollment rates: The literacy rate among adults is high (97.6%) compared with other developing countries and there is universal compulsory education.

The Mongolian economy is largely dependent on mining exports, commodity prices on the global market, and commodity demand. Although the country is experiencing some economic growth, challenges remain in terms of its economic instability, fluctuation of exchange rate, increase of inflation, instability in government, and poor infrastructure (energy, road, health, and education). Another constraint affecting the lives of the people is the very harsh winters: The temperature ranges from -30° Celsius in the winter to 30° Celsius in the summer. On average, herders lose 53 per cent of their herds due to a winter natural disaster called *dzud* (NHRC, 2012).

One of the influential contextual factors of livelihood in Mongolia is the strong family network. However, as a consequence of demographic changes the family structure is changing and the number of extended families, where children and parents live together, is decreasing. Today there are more and more families where older people live on their own and the implications of this change are manifold. In Mongolian society, families are the main source of support for its dependent people – children, persons with a disability, and the elderly. With the changes in family structure, the role that government is taking in the care of dependent persons is gradually increasing.

The poverty headcount ratio at the national poverty line is 27.4 per cent of the total population (NSC, 2012). Poverty remains a serious problem with multiple consequences for single-parent headed households with many children, rural households with less than 100 head of livestock, the unemployed, and the vulnerable population including children, people with a disability, and older people. People with a disability constitute 4.3 per cent of the population.

According to a Ministry of Social Welfare and Labor (MSWL) report, 88 per cent of people with disability live below the poverty line and their employment rate is only 13 per cent (Ministry of Social Welfare and Labor, 2011). There are six special schools for children with disabilities and one national rehabilitation centre.

One of the distinctive features of the social work profession is that it is rooted and defined by culture and traditions, history, people's mindset and lifestyles, and the social fabric and environmental conditions. The country's economic, social, cultural, geographical, and demographic contexts define the situation of social work services in Mongolia, and relevant regulations governing social work are set forth by the government.

Overview of the Mongolian Social Security System

Social work is a contextual professional practice as Hugman (2010: 8) states,

> … the form of social work that is possible in any particular location is structured by the type of welfare regime in that country. Thus it can be argued that the possibilities for social work are circumscribed by national borders ….

The social security system in Mongolia is regulated by the Constitution of Mongolia (1992), Family Law (1999), Civil Health Insurance Law (1993), Law on Social Insurance (1994), Law on Social Welfare (1995), Law on Social Security for the Elderly (1995), Law on Social Security for people with a disability (1995), and Labor Law (1999), Law on Protection of Children's Rights (1996), and so on. The social protection policy in Mongolia aims to improve the quality of life of the population including children, the elderly, women, persons with disabilities, and unemployed people by increasing their health and income security and reducing poverty.

The Economic Growth Support and Poverty Reduction Strategy (2003), Social Security Master Plan (2003), Millennium Development Goals of Mongolia (2005), Millennium Development Goals based on Comprehensive National Development Strategy (2008), and Action Plan of the 'Reform' Government (2012–2016) identified strategies for the country aimed at promoting social and human development and reducing poverty. In 2004 Parliament approved the State Policy of Mongolia on Population Development. It included policies for children, youth, families, older people, women, people with a disability, and families.

Moreover, there are numerous National Programs of Action related to issues of population groups and social problems such as combating human trafficking, HIV/AIDS, unemployment, domestic violence, and promoting gender equality. In 2009 Mongolia endorsed the National Strategy on Ageing which encourages multi-sectoral responses to ageing. The current framework of social security policies and programs is enforced by the Social Security Master Plan approved in 2003. It declared the establishment of a social security system with objectives for better community-based social care, better access to services and information, sustainable livelihood, greater community involvement, cooperation with nongovernmental and government organizations, and research on solutions to existing social problems.

Similar to the popular international scheme, the social security system of Mongolia consists of policies and programs on social welfare, social insurance, and service provisions for all population groups. Social security policy implementation is governed at the national level by the Ministry of Population Development and Social Welfare. There is no regional structure even though Mongolia consists of five regions: Western, Central, Khangai (Highland), Eastern regions, and Ulaanbaatar as an independent region. Local governments, at *aimag* and *soums* in provincial areas and in districts and *khoroos* in Ulaanbaatar, are responsible for implementing national social security policies in their respective areas. A Livelihood Support Council which is responsible for identifying and selecting beneficiaries for social welfare assistance, benefits, concession, and other services is operated in each local community. Social workers serve as a focal person in this structure.

The government policy framework for social protection of its people consists of three main components: prevention (social insurance system), community-based care, and residential care reform. Mongolia has a relatively new system of social assistance and insurance targeted at needy population groups. According to the Laws on Social Insurance, the contributory pension is given to people to protect them from contingencies of retirement and disability and to provide social guarantees for workers, considering their years of work, average wage, contributions to pension insurance, and working conditions. The implementing body is the General Authority for Social Insurance. According to the Laws on Social Welfare, poor and vulnerable people are entitled to a social pension and assistance and this scheme aims to provide social protection for vulnerable groups such as elderly, women who are head of a household, children in difficult circumstances, homeless people, and people with a disability. The implementing body is the General Office of Social Welfare Services. Beneficiaries of social pensions and other assistance are identified on the basis of assessment of livelihood circumstances.

This livelihood assessment includes measurements of household capability such as whether a person lives in an urban or rural area, their education level, number of household members, their employment status, housing conditions, and measurements related to the economic situation of a household. These can include property ownership, number of livestock, use of transportation, receipt of social assistance, other benefits and services, and the vulnerability of the family – for example, if there is disabled member, orphan child, female head of household, bed-bound member in the family. Categories of social pension, concession, and pecuniary aid include social pension; monetary allowance to caretaker; discount in housing rent, fuel, wood and coal; provision of prosthetics, orthopedic aids, hearing appliances, wheelchairs, walking sticks,and so on; residential care; and cash benefit for the honored mother who has four and more children. According to the MSWL annual report (2011), the MSWL distributed allowances of 27.6 billion MNT (Mongolian national currency, *tugrug*) to 56,700 people in 2010. The amount of monthly social welfare allowances was raised 3.8 times between 2004 and 2010.

In addition, community-based welfare services are provided to vulnerable people, including services such as rehabilitation services, home care, awareness and skills training, and liaison for involvement in the labour market. Along with the government, international and domestic nongovernmental organizations play a vital role in meeting people's needs and enhancing their well-being. Food, clothing, shelter, micro credit loans, skills training, domestic violence victim counselling services, and small financial grants are provided to vulnerable people and families.

Trajectory of Social Work Development in Mongolia

In order to describe how social work is being developed in Mongolia, it is essential to know how this profession is defined and understood by its people. The process of how to define social work has been an ongoing project among Mongolian social workers. There is no national definition operationalized and agreed upon by local professionals. Despite differing viewpoints, the definition by the International Federation of Social Workers (2000) is used in Mongolia as a reference for social work education and practice. It is a strategic decision for Mongolian social work professionals to introduce and popularize the social work profession in the country due to the novelty of professional practice in the social service system.

Today's society recognizes social work as one of the forms of social services and there is an increase in understanding of the roles of social workers. However, the public and clients interpret social work in many different ways – the nature and scope of social work services are still not clear for many people. To date, social workers' roles are perceived as community leader, activity director, *khoroo* coordinator, inspector of living conditions, and counsellor of relationship problems. At the grass-roots level, some people still think that a social worker is a person who is responsible for distributions of common welfare goods including flour, rice, and clothes and making referrals to goodwill agencies. The 2004 study 'Current Situation of Mongolian Social Work' (DMTC and MUST, 2004), showed that 40 per cent of people surveyed responded that they 'do not know about social work' or had 'just heard about it' and only 20 per cent of them had a good understanding of the profession.

The Mongolian government has played a significant role throughout the social work profession's development process. Since its beginning, the government provided effective leadership that ensured a conducive mechanism and legal environment, providing education and training of social workers, encouraging the assimilation of foreign practices and developing local initiative, and establishing service infrastructure: The Social Security Sector Master Plan identified the development of professional social work as one of the reform elements of the social welfare subsector's 10-year strategy, stating that 'the objective is to establish a nationwide national system of social workers at the professional level' (26).

The definition of social work and the role of social workers is outlined in the Social Welfare Law, which prescribes the required professional qualifications and integrity and professional ethics for the social work profession (Parliament of Mongolia, 2006).

Other laws, the Law Against Domestic Violence and Laws on Education, have been in force since 2004. Social workers' roles and duties are reflected in these policy documents, however, the provisions of these laws are not integrated. Each law has defined the roles of a social worker within the command of that law. Because of these differences, a process of the development of social work as well as professional values, ethics, and obligations of social work has been hindered.

In order to give an overall understanding of the development of the social work profession in Mongolia, we outline four interfacing periods: the pre-professional (before 1996), the launching and professionalization phase (1996–2001), the capacity-building years (2001–2007), and lastly, the further institutionalization of social work education and practice (2007–Present) (Namdaldagva et al., 2010).

Phase 1: Pre-Professional (Before 1996)

The first phase of Mongolia's social work development covers a vast historical period from ancient times to modern days. This phase is characterized by the nonexistence of the concept of social work as a professional discipline; although Mongolia has had a long tradition of social welfare. The helping traditions of Mongolia's nomadic peoples have served as a rich foundation for the profession's development. For centuries, herders and families relied on each other to overcome the everyday problems they faced. Strong family networks have been an advantage to facilitate this helping process.

On the other hand, because of factors such as an extreme climate, a sparsely populated land mass, and dependency on the land for food and survival, people have become resilient, independent, and learned to solve problems. They had to as there was no alternative. Additionally, spirituality and religion as well as ideology during the period of Russian communism have impacted the lives of Mongolians, while influencing their perception and mindset as to what is good and bad, what is worthwhile, and what is to be expected. All of these factors combined have given Mongolians a largely unquestioned sense of fatalism.

Historically, the Mongolian government was genuinely concerned about the disadvantaged people in society. For example, according to the *Secret History of the Mongols*, rules and regulations of the Mongolian Empire included some types of social provisions and protective and rehabilitative services to people such as war veterans, their dependents, and poor families. Social services were centralized and became ideological in nature during the social regime from 1921 to 1990 and mass population-based organizations such as the Mongolian Pioneers Organization, Mongolian Revolutionary Youth League, Mongolian Organization for the Elderly, and the Mongolian Trade Union provided social services to the target populations of children, youth, elderly, and workers, respectively.

In 1990, the Republic of Mongolia made the peaceful transition to a multiparty parliamentary system and a market-driven economy. During the 1990s, legislative reforms took place and the social welfare system was newly restructured with the establishment of an independent social welfare system (Ogborn and Humphries, 2002). The Social Welfare Laws approved in 1995 became the first legislation for social welfare and social work services and the beginning of a professional helping system for needy people and their families.

Children were the most disadvantaged group in this transitional society. Following the collapse of the socialist system because of an abrupt end to monetary aid and subsidies coming from the socialist bloc (countries with communist orientation) and Russia, the social services sector experienced huge cuts in expenditure. According to the UNDP Human Development Report between 1992 and 1998, as a proportion of GDP, government spending on health, education, and social security dropped from 16.2 to 14.8 per cent. Consequently, support for child welfare deteriorated. The previously unknown phenomenon of street children emerged. As well, other social problems such as unemployment, child neglect, school dropouts, youth crime, and working children started increasing.

In the mid-1990s the National Children's Organization began to collaborate with the United Nations Children's Fund, Save the Children UK, Norway's Save the Children, World Vision, and so on. International organizations came forward to redress the transitional difficulties affecting children and their families. Professional social work interventions familiar in the Western world were seen as needed to tackle the child welfare issues present in Mongolia. A situational analysis was undertaken with the intention of launching social work education (CSD, 1996; Tuvshintugs, 2009) and according to this analysis, social work education and interventions were appropriate and necessary in Mongolia to promote individual and community well-being (CSD, 1996).

Phase 2: Launching and Early Years (1996–2000)

This phase is characterized by the birth of social work as a professional discipline and practice. With the initiatives and contributions of Save the Children, UK social work education and practice in schools has been commenced and supported in Mongolia (Batkhishig, 2001).

The need for social work professional services has increased due to rapid changes in the political, economic, and social environments of the country. The issues drawn from the social problems, including the increase in numbers of children living without parental care; people engaged in illegal mining; working abroad; affected by human trafficking, prostitution, and HIV/AIDS; a widening gap between the poor and the rich; and stresses aggregated by family dysfunctions and other negative social problems, are creating the need for new types of social work. A legal environment for social work services has been introduced by the enforcement of laws in education and the protection of children's rights.

Social work education programs were first offered to professionals working with children and families and they became 'child social workers' (Tuvshintugs, 2009). In the fall of 1997, the Mongolian State Pedagogical University (SPU), with financial and consulting support from Save the Children Fund UK, launched the first formal university undergraduate degree for social workers in Mongolia. An undergraduate degree to train social welfare specialists also commenced at the Mongolian University of Science and Technology in 1997.

The first National Seminar on Social Work was organized in 1997 to learn from the experiences of other countries where the social work profession was well established. Social work and social development practitioners and academics from the United States, the United Kingdom, China, and Russia shared their experiences and provided their expertise (Social Work Resource Center, SPU, 1997). Through subsequent consultations and workshops, Mongolian professionals declared that the most appropriate model for social work in Mongolia (through university education and professional development and training) was that of social development and preparation as a generalist social worker.

Social work educators provided leadership in the development of the social work profession in Mongolia and their initiatives led to the foundation of professional associations, the first of which was named the National Association of Social Workers, established in 1997 and soon thereafter becoming a provisional member of the International Federation of Social Work.

Social work was introduced through numerous seminars, workshops, and training to various professionals and at different levels of education and expertise. Topics ranged from child rights and child protection, school social work, social welfare and assistance, social policy, program planning, community development, and poverty reduction to domestic violence.

Social work teachers immersed themselves in the profession through short-term, intensive training with academics from the United States, India, Australia, Russia, Denmark, Scotland, and Japan, 'train the trainer' models, and co-teaching with international colleagues. In the summer of 1997, the first group of social work teachers attended two weeks of social work training in Russia. These academics played an essential role in the further preparation of instructors to teach social work, developing social work curricula and methodology, and teaching and learning resources.

A pilot program in two urban schools implemented by the Mongolian Child Rights Center during 1998–1999 served as groundwork for the introduction of school social work in secondary schools. By virtue of its successful implementation, the Mongolian government approved the position of school social worker in 2000 (Batkhishig, 2001).

Social work positions emerged in local government organizations, and in government and nongovernmental organizations working with children, youth, and families. Unfortunately, these new social work positions were just renamed 'social work' and filled with the previous occupants of the positions – people who had responsibility for children, youth, and family affairs.

The development of civil society in Mongolia at the time led to favorable conditions for the emergence of social work in the country. Since the 1990s, many nongovernmental organizations became established in the social sector to fill the gap in the provision of social services to needy people and families in order to tackle the social problems adversely affecting them. National NGOs such as the Center for Children's Rights, the National Center Against Violence, the Center for Social Development, the Danish-Mongolian Training Center, and the Methodology and Research Center served as field practicum places for social work students.

In addition, learning opportunities for social work practice were provided through programs and projects run by international NGOs. During the 1996–2000 period, a solid foundation of social work education was established as well as the formal recognition of the social work profession.

Phase 3: Capacity Building (2001–2007)

Between 2001 and 2007, the number of universities offering a bachelor of social work or masters of social work (MSW) degree increased sevenfold across Mongolia. By 2007, a total of 877 bachelor of social work degrees and 90 master of social work degrees were awarded from more than 14 universities and institutes. The number of social work educators with a degree in social work increased by 40 per cent compared to not one educator with a degree before 2001 (Enkhtuya et al., 2008). Social work degrees expanded into specializations such as school social work, health social work, direct service, and community organizing, social work in detention centres, and so on. Social work professionals with an MSW from well-known universities overseas such as Columbia University, Pennsylvania University, and Washington University in St. Louis in the United States joined the social work community in Mongolia. Moreover, Mongolian social workers expanded their networking and collaboration nationally and internationally by forming professional associations, exchanging information and experiences with colleagues abroad, participating in conferences and forums, and becoming affiliated with international social work organizations. Thus, the third phase of the development of social work in Mongolia was characterized by capacity-building processes that would lead to the institutionalization of the profession (Namdaldagva, 2009).

Milestones of the social work developments in the third phase were the emergence of social workers in different sectors, sustainable improvements in the social work education system, and so on.

Since 2003, the community of social work practitioners has extended in range from the public service and education sectors to other sectors of society. To date, 1,200 social workers are employed in public service agencies. Six hundred and twenty-four of them are school social workers. Social welfare agencies employ 798 people; 510 of them are *soum* or *khoroo* social workers and 102 *soums* and *khoroos* with a dense population now have two social workers; law enforcement agencies have about 70 social workers, and hospitals of third ranking have begun to hire health social workers.

Contributing developments were that professional associations grew rapidly during this period, including the Mongolian Association of School Social Workers (2001), the Mongolian Association of Social Work Educators (2002), the Mongolian Association of Professional Social Workers (2002), and the Mongolian Association of Health Social Workers (2006). These associations provided guidance for social workers in their professional development and experience enrichment, networking and collaboration, and promoted public awareness of social work and increasing the status of social workers.

The Mongolian social work profession and social work degrees have benefited from structural reforms by the government and international programs to foster educational reforms in higher education in former socialist countries.

The government approval of the Social Security Sector Master Plan in 2003 contributed to the rapid development of social work across the country. It highlighted the importance of capacity building of social protection workers and establishing a structure for social work services in the social welfare sector (MSWL, 2003).

The role of social worker in the newly established social welfare structure was expanded into nearly all administrative areas from a grass-roots level to nationally. At a grass-roots level, social workers were pivotal in the Livelihood Support Council, which made all the decisions regarding social assistance and welfare program provision for needy people and families. During the implementation of the strategy, more than 720 social workers completed social work training and obtained a certificate. A professional development training program was established for social workers in the social welfare sector on topics such as introduction to social work, social work ethics, community organization, social policy, social development, case management, social work with children, people with a disability, child protection, social work with families, and groups and special populations. Among social work practitioners, however, the number of social work professionals holding a degree remained at very low levels, comprising only 20 per cent of the social welfare workforce (Enkhtuya et al., 2008).

The Open Society Institute (OSI) Social Work Fellowship Program, the Higher Education Support Program, and the Network Scholarship Program contributed enormously to furthering social work in Mongolia. With OSI support, social work summer schools were organized and run annually. The summer schools trained a core group of Mongolian social work academics teaching in the various universities. In addition to developing a social work pedagogy, one particular key achievement of the summer school program has been the contribution to building a common ground for social work education throughout Mongolia (Oyut-Erdene, 2009).

Topics that drew early attention included 'Development of a Code of Ethics', 'Development of Social Work Research', 'Collaboration among Social Work Schools and Teachers', and 'Core Curricula for Social Work Programs'. The issue of a core curriculum was deemed a priority, as many schools were offering social work education programs, but there was no consensus on minimum standards of basic knowledge and skills or on what content should be core to the professional curriculum (Ogborn and Humphries, 2002; Oyut-Erdene, 2004).

In addition, through the OSI scholarship program, 15 social work professionals were awarded MSWs from two US universities (Columbia University and Washington University in St. Louis), becoming the first cohort of internationally trained social workers in Mongolia. They have provided vital leadership in establishing professional associations, enhancing networking, and sponsoring professional activities. They have also been instrumental in developing a professional code of ethics, promoting professional development for practitioners, and improving field education.

The main challenge during this phase was improving the quality of social work education and increasing public understanding of the social work profession. Social work in Mongolia needed a suitable service infrastructure as well as well-formulated strategies and goals. Studies defining issues and problems in school social work (Enkhtuya, 2006) and *khoroo* social work services (Erdenechimeg and Amarjargal, 2007) and in social work developmental process in general (Enkhtuya et al., 2008) underscored the integrated and coordinated efforts to improve the provision of social work services, to increase the understanding of the profession by the government and the public, and the revision and refinement of regulations governing social work roles and functions, improving the social work curriculum and the integration of theory and practice.

Phase 4: Institutionalization (2007–Present)

The fourth and final phase of the development of social work education in Mongolia to date has been characterized by the further institutionalization of the profession. The main achievements of this period were the approval of social work education standards by the Ministry of Education and Mongolian Agency on Standardization and Measurement in January 2010. During these years, social work education became more systematic, more rigorous, and more specialized. The latter included curricula on, for example child protection, domestic violence, human trafficking, HIV/AIDS prevention, child labor, and advocacy (Namdaldagva et al., 2010).

Significant gains were achieved during this period in the areas of faculty development (regular training, more graduate social work degrees); curriculum development (in alignment with international standards; enhanced collaboration with local, national, and international colleagues and professional organizations; development of curricular materials; schools; and departments preparing for accreditation); field education (training/retraining of faculty and field supervisors, academic-practice partnerships strengthened); community relations and service (cooperation with the social service community for field education, research projects, and training with manuals); awareness and interest (growth in the number of programs and student enrollment); and network building (establishment of professional teachers' community; expanded foreign partnerships; and teacher and student participation in local, regional and international conferences). The number of social work students and teachers increased to 1,600 and 70 respectively.

In addition, standards for practice in shelters, child protection services, and social work in community centres for older adults have been developed by professionals in the field (MSWL, 2011). Field education has also been developing rapidly, due to collaboration with social work colleagues from Australia, Japan, America, and the Czech Republic.

The working relationship between universities and practice organizations continues to be enhanced by the steady flow of graduates into government and nongovernmental organizations, some of whom have become field supervisors. The fourth phase of social work has also seen improvements in resources and facilities. The *Mongolian Social Work Journal* was inaugurated in 2009.

Social Work Practice

Social work is a growing field in Mongolia and the state takes the main responsibility for the social services. To date, there are social work positions in five publicly funded settings: secondary schools, local administrative units called *khoroo/bagh*, court-decision implementation agencies, social welfare agencies, and hospitals. The first social work position sanctioned by the government was that of school social worker. Since 2000 the number of school social workers has grown to 689 employed at 775 schools (Mongolian Association of School Social Workers, 2012). More than 700 social workers are grass-root social workers in the social welfare system. Social workers at *khoroos* and *baghs* – local administrative units – perform the functions of community social workers. School social workers became a part of the teams committed to building child-friendly schools, and social workers started to work in detention centres under the Court Decision Implementation Agency in 2004. Workers in the social welfare sector have committed themselves to the better provision of community-based services shifting from just providing direct social welfare benefits and assistance to people and families. This change was necessitated by the Social Security Development Master Plan adopted by the Mongolian government in 2003, which set forth a policy promoting the development of community-based social services. Health social workers started working in family clinics and specialized hospitals, such as those providing palliative care.

Social workers are employed in NGOs specializing in promoting human rights and child protection, combating domestic violence and trafficking as well as supporting poor and homeless people. Social workers from the nongovernmental organizations fill the service gaps where the government cannot reach. Social workers in some NGOs are dedicated to prevention, crisis intervention, and rehabilitation services; some of them provide child protection services and conduct training on behaviour changes. The opportunities to access these types of services do not exist in rural settings or remote districts/*khoroos* where particular NGOs are not operating. A small number of private social service agencies provide health care, legal assistance, and counselling and care services; however, limited types of services and poor quality are attributed alike to governmental, nongovernmental, and private services.

Mongolian social workers are predominantly female; for example, more than 70 per cent of school social workers are female. While in developing countries social work is practiced by professionals with a master of social work degree and a licence for providing social work services, in Mongolia the professional criteria for social workers are different. The criteria include minimal requirements such as having a bachelor of social work degree, and working experience in the public or service sectors.

Many Mongolian social workers began their careers by practicing social work before they formally studied for a degree or certification. Mongolian social work practitioners as well as teachers gain professional experience through their experience at work. The majority of practitioners who hold social work titles in Mongolia are professionals from other backgrounds who became 'social workers' through certified training programs. As a result, social work graduates in these fields are mainly employed in NGOs or in other sectors. Many teachers became social work teachers shifting from other disciplines such as philosophy, language, art, and psychology.

Social workers have many kinds of roles in order to deliver social services. They are involved in program development, advocacy, program evaluation, policy development, and social work as educators, brokers, case managers, community organizers, and counsellors. Today Mongolian social workers provide the following services:

1. Community-based services,
2. Resources and information,
3. Liaison with health care and other social services,
4. Supportive services,
5. Referral to jobs and training,
6. Home care,
7. Family and individual counselling,
8. Crisis intervention,
9. Health education and services,
10. Food and shelter services for the homeless,
11. Rehabilitation services,
12. Protective services,
13. Awareness raising,

14. Gerontology or social work with the elderly,
15. Child protection services,
16. Psychosocial and socio-educational services,
17. Case management,
18. Group work,
19. Employment services,
20. Social work services with offenders, and
21. Shelter services for victims of human trafficking

Children and family issues are the focus of social services in Mongolia and a multidisciplinary approach to services for children and families is the framework for social workers who work toward protecting children who are abused or neglected and provide services to meet their developmental and social needs, such as participation in educational and social activities. Child protection and child welfare services are provided in shelters and drop-in centres. Monthly financial support is provided for people who are looking after orphans or children living in difficult conditions.

Moreover, the Mongolian government approved policies and programs to eliminate the worst forms of child labor. Social workers work in programs protecting children from participating in child labor, especially working in the mining sector and at dumpsites on the list of prohibited jobs for minors, and ensuring they enroll at school.

Community services are mainly targeted to functionally independent people. Since 2003 community-based service centers for children and families run programs consisting of various developmental activities and protection services. Within the supportive services, social workers help find employment for the poor and unemployed people who seek a job. In Mongolia people have problems finding employment due to, for example, a poor employment history, lack of working skills, and age discrimination.

In addition to services in child protection, care, and other welfare services for the elderly and the disabled, the roles of social workers are increased in all areas of the social sphere, including children without parental care; rehabilitation services for victims of domestic violence, crime, and perpetrators; behaviour change training for alcoholics and substance abusers; social service referrals and employment services for poor and homeless people. Mongolian social workers join efforts to protect and ensure the human rights of people, especially disadvantaged people. Social workers are engaged in the implementation of the 'National Program on Protection from Human Trafficking, Especially Sexual Exploitation of Children and Women' and a national standard on 'General Guidelines on Protection Shelter and Services to Victims'.

The Human Rights Commission report on Mongolia (2012) reported poor prison conditions, abuse of prisoners by police, and uneven law enforcement. In Mongolia, there are a total of 25 correctional facilities including one detention facility and 13 detention centres where, on average, one social worker works with 200–250 prisoners (NHRC, 2012). The responsibilities of social workers in detention centres include the protection of human rights and the provision of social and rehabilitation services.

Ratios of clients per social worker differ by sector: *Khoroo/soum* social workers in densely populated urban settlements as well school social workers have high workloads of clients. Hence, although social workers perform a wide variety of tasks, it is still unclear what services can be considered the main duties of Mongolian social workers. Many people visiting Mongolia comment that social work here is different from the Western concept and practice. Many social work responsibilities do not match the definition by the International Federation of Social Workers.

In particular, many duties of *soum/khoroo* social workers are in administrative matters. They are responsible for providing almost all public services including civil registration, social welfare entitlements, environmental cleanliness, community development, and employment support at a grass-roots level. School social workers spend most of their time maintaining order and discipline at schools and organizing extracurricular activities. Social workers in other sectors also spend a lot of time on administrative and logistics matters. Professional and workplace supervision, which play important roles in increasing the effectiveness of social work services, promoting capacity-building of social workers, and creating professional values and ethical norms for social work, have experienced slow development.

International practice shows that professional associations of social workers act as leaders of professional development and define vision and perspective for social work. Professional associations strive to improve job descriptions for social workers, and their social and occupation status, and develop the profession in line with international standards. Six professional organizations uniting social workers contribute to the development of social work through independent or collaborative activities. They extend training opportunities for social workers and provide them with learning resources, and with the support of these organizations, social workers share their best practices and exchange ideas. However, only the Mongolian Association of School Social Workers has permanent staff and an office. More than 80 per cent of school social workers are members of the Mongolian Association of School Social Workers. Other organizations have few members and function occasionally. This contributes to a situation wherein their voice is weak in decision making regarding social work regulation.

Social Work Education

The current structure of social work education was established in 2001 and includes five levels:

1. Doctoral program (minimum 4 years),
2. Master's program (1.5–2 years),

3. Bachelor's program (4 years),
4. specialized training, and
5. in-service training.

The teaching and scholarly skills of social workers have increased significantly over recent years, and there are now more than 800 students in social work degree programs. In comparison to early 2000, the number of social work faculty and students has doubled. The majority of social work students come directly from secondary schools and have little or no experience in social services. Each year the number of social work students as well as the demand for quality education increase.

The first social work degree program of baccalaureate level was accredited in 2010. Mongolian social work curricula have been adapted primarily from the American, Russian, and German models, depending on the mission and goals of the university and department (Oyut-Erdene and Ulziitungalag, 2004). For example, the Mongolia State University of Education curriculum is modelled on the US scheme with input from Japanese and Indian programs. In addition to the curriculum being a good fit, MSUE obtained resources such as textbooks, visiting lecturers, and training materials from the Unite States. The Mongolian University of Science and Technology, on the other hand, is influenced by the Russian model, and the National University of Mongolia's model has mainly been German-influenced since the German Academic Exchange Service funded the curriculum development and continuing education project from 2001 to 2009.

In-service training opportunities for social workers differ by sectors, rural or urban settings, as well as capacities and other specific features of a particular agency. Training, retraining, and professional upgrading systems for social workers are waiting on more developments. The Ministry of Social Welfare and Labor (newly structured as the Ministry of Population Development and Social Welfare since 2012) has coordinated the training activities including short-term training for the preparation of social workers and retraining of previously prepared social workers. Social welfare sector social workers have had multistage training and received a social work textbook and other resources.

However, social workers lack social work resources including handbooks, guidelines, and professional newspapers or journals to facilitate their in-service training efforts. The development of teaching and learning resources that reflect Mongolian conditions is seen as crucial.

Conclusion: Challenges and Issues, and Future Trends of Mongolian Social Work

In 2012 Mongolian social workers celebrated the fifteenth anniversary of the professional establishment of social work. Developments in Mongolian social work to date were mainly responsive in nature and are characterized as multidimensional. Development processes required political, legal, cultural, social, educational, and structural changes and commitments. Looking back over the last 15 years, we can conclude that the current system of social work in Mongolia is developing in line with international developments.

Nationwide and international factors influence the development of social work as a profession and service system and transitional changes in Mongolian society during the 1990s established the background for professional social work development in the country. Economic, political, cultural, and social factors caused changes favoring the birth of the social work profession. Currently, there are social workers in education, social welfare, child protection, local government, the detention system, and humanitarian and voluntary organizations. Provisions on social work services and social workers are embedded in laws including the Law on Social Welfare, Law on Education, and Law Against Domestic Violence. However, the challenge still remains to distinguish between social welfare and social work, and psychology and social work. Charity is perceived as social work by some people. In other words, there is a need to educate people's understanding of which professional social work offer is necessary.

Conceptual understanding is the key for proper social work development in the country – developmental social work was defined as a main conceptual framework for the development of social work in Mongolia in 1997 – however, concepts on developmental social work have been reflected poorly in training and service programs (Askeland, 2004). The field is in demand for social work job opportunities and qualified professionals. There is a need to expand services for special target groups including persons with severe forms of disabilities, the elderly without family support, unsupervised children, prostitutes, victims of trafficking, domestic violence and child abuse, persons with mental health problems, alcoholics and substance abusers, and persons affected by HIV/AIDS and to train professionals to work with these vulnerable groups.

Mongolian social workers are striving for better recognition of their roles in the processes of poverty reduction, promoting social equality, and fostering social development in the country. While there are an increasing number of social workers, social problems are not reducing by much. Each year about 200 social work graduates enter the labor market and thousands are working as social workers. People expect that since there are professionals to deal with social problems then they should solve all the social problems; however, social problems can be addressed in a number of ways. Providing more social workers alone will not solve many problems. There is a need to change legislation, public attitudes, and the structure of organizations. Adequate interventions require addressing problems such as insufficient cooperation of social workers from different sectors, lack of official mechanisms on referral and networking services, and a high unemployment rate among graduates of the social work schools, and so on.

Social workers in Mongolia are criticized for mainly performing administrative and supervisory duties but the agencies responsible for supervision of social workers have low capacities to perform this task because senior level officers have no or little knowledge and skills in social work, and the effectiveness and quality of social work has not been evaluated properly. Development of national standard requirements on social work practices for working with various groups of clients, and introducing a range of social work assessment tools that can enhance decision making and provide consistency in service delivery is deemed important (Verdi, 2003). Namdaldagva et al. (2010) call for development of evidence-based practices for the Mongolian context underscoring:

> There is a great need to systematically analyze a variety of social, economic, emotional, and health-related problems in order to determine the appropriate interventions and policies needed to effectively address these needs and improve the overall quality of people's life. (Namdaldagva et al., 2010)

Although social workers have a high load of clients, social work as a profession is among the lowest-paid. On the other hand, provisions for social welfare recipients are also low and the social welfare allowances are not raised to come up to inflation levels. Thus, the government works for improvement of policies and programs to consider inflation factors and the market price as well as to address issues of work compensation and benefits for social workers.

The Mongolian social work community has been actively cooperating with international social work communities and universities and schools towards strengthening the capacity of social workers, improving service provision and teaching and curricula. Further, the institutional capacity of Mongolian social work professional associations needs to strengthen to foster professional development in the country as well as to keep up with international developments in the field. Their collaboration is essential to promote the development of this profession, solve common problems faced by social workers, identify values and ethics of Mongolian social work, and improve the integration of different sectors.

Although social work professional services are new to Mongolia, they have been expanded with new forms. Social work services in Mongolia range from direct services to vulnerable groups of people, delivering social welfare services entitled by existing laws, providing people with opportunities to improve their quality of life using community resources and services to running advocacy and awareness raising activities among communities and people in order to change policies and structures leading to violations of human rights and vulnerability.

Social work became a common profession in Mongolia over the past 15 years. Today professional associations and social workers and researchers face the need to engage more in discussions on the development of social work in Mongolia. These discussions involve broad areas from enhancing public understanding of social workers and increasing professional identity and reputation in the country to other social work education and practice issues.

In order to foster national social work developments, Mongolian social workers emphasize the importance of learning from the international developments of the profession through collaboration with social work colleagues from countries of the Asia and the Pacific region as well as other parts of the world.

References

Askeland, G.A. (2004), *Feedback on the Revision of Social Work Program at State Pedagogical University*. Ulaanbaatar.

Batkhishig, A. (2001), *Development of Social Work Education of Mongolia: Lessons from American Social Work Education,* Ulaanbaatar: LST.

Center for Social Development (CSD) (1996), *Situation Analysis to Launch Social Work in Mongolia: Study Report.* Ulaanbaatar: Save the Children, UK.

Danish Mongolian Training Centre (DMTC) and Mongolian University of Science and Technology (MUST) (2004), *Study Report: The Current Situation of Mongolian Social Work.* Ulaanbaatar: Munkhiin Useg.

Enkhtuya, S. (2006), *Situation Analysis of School Social Work in Mongolia: Study Report.* Ulaanbaatar: Save the Children, UK.

Enkhtuya, S.; Olonchimeg, D., and Oyut-Erdene, N. (2008), *Review of Social Work Development in Mongolia.* Ulaanbaatar: Save the Children, UK.

Erdenechimeg, T. and Amarjargal, T. (2007), *Situation Analysis of Khoroo Social Work from the Perspective of Child Protection: Study Report.* Ulaanbaatar: Save the Children, UK.

Government of Mongolia (GM) (2003), *Social Security Sector Master Plan.* Ulaanbaatar: Government of Mongolia.

GM (2009), *National Strategy on Aging.* Ulaanbaatar: Government of Mongolia.

GM and UNDP Mongolia (2011), *Human Development Report.* Ulaanbaatar: Government of Mongolia.

Hugman, R. (2010), *Understanding International Social Work: A Critical Analysis.* London: Palgrave Macmillan.

Ministry of Social Welfare and Labor of Mongolia (MSWL) (2008), *List of Prohibited Jobs for Minors*, Decree #107. Ulaanbaatar.

MSWL (2011), *2011 Program Report.* Ulaanbaatar: MSWL.

Mongolian Association of School Social Workers (MASSW) (2012), *Introduction of 'Oyuny Gegee'*, Mongolian Association of School Social Workers. Ulaanbaatar.

Namdaldagva, O.-E. (2009), Ten Years of Capacity Building Efforts and Development of Social Work Education in Mongolia, paper presented at *Seoul International Social Work Conference*, Korean Association of Social Workers and IASSW. 15–18 April, 2009, Seoul, Korea.

Namdaldagva, O.-E. and Ulziitungalag, K. (2004), Challenges of Social Work Education in Mongolia, paper presented at *Reclaiming Civil Society: International Federation of Social Workers Conference*, 2–5 October. Adelaide, Australia.

Namdaldagva, O.E., Myagmarjav, S., and Burnette, D. (2010), Professional Social Work Education in Mongolia: Achievements, Lessons Learned, and Future Directions, *Social Work Education*, Vol. 29, No. 8, pp. 882–95.

National Human Rights Commission (NHRC) (2012), *The 11th Report on Human Rights and Freedoms in Mongolia.* Ulaanbaatar: NHRC.

National Statistics Committee (NSC) (2011), *2010 Population and Housing Census: Main Indicators.* Ulaanbaatar: NSC.

NSC (2012), *Statistical Yearbook 2011*. Ulaanbaatar: NSC.

Ogborn, K. and Humphries, P. (2002), *The Development of Professional Social Work in Mongolia*. Manila: Asian Development Bank.

Population Divisions (PD) UN Department of Economic and Social Affairs (2012), *World Population Prospects: The 2012 Revision*. New York: UN.

Parliament of Mongolia (PM) (1995), *Laws on Social Insurance*. Ulaanbaatar.

PM (2005), *Laws on Social Welfare*. Ulaanbaatar.

State Pedagogical University (SPU), Social Work Resource Center (1997), *Report of the First International Social Work Conference*. Ulaanbaatar: State Pedagogical University.

Tuvshintugs, T. (2009), The Development of Social Work in Mongolia: The Beginning of Professional Training: Dairy, *Mongolian Social Work Journal*, Vol. 1, available at www.caritas.mn/index.php?id=247.

Verdi, G. (2003), Situation of Unsupervised Children of Mongolia: Report,. Ulaanbaatar: UNICEF.

World Bank (WB) (2012), Human Development Index 2012, www.worldbank.org.

Chapter 4
Social Work in Taiwan

Huang Pei Jie and Ku Yeun Wen

The article 'Is Social Work a Profession?' by A. Flexner (1915) has triggered widespread discussions regarding this issue ever since its publication, with those conditions of professionalization forming 'profession' as the centre of such discussions (Carr-Saunders and Wilson, 1962; Vollmer and Mills, 1966; Hughes, 1971; Freidson, 1994). It is believed that once certain conditions, defined by profession, are met with a development following such conditions, the process of professionalization can be completed and achieves 'profession' (Carr-Saunders and Wilson, 1962; Parsons, 1954; Caplow, 1954; Wilensky, 1964; Larson, 1977). However, the definition of profession proposed by professionals might only be a strategic allegation to obtain legitimacy of profession privilege, instead of the authentic nature of a professional. There is no connection between the degree of professionalization and problem-solving abilities (Johnson, 1972; Collins, 1979). The appearance of professional autonomy is inevitable in any society and politics (Freidson, 1970). Parry and Parry (1975) indicate that professional organizations wish to establish a monopoly with legal effect (legitimacy) and control the market by manipulating education and professional skills, yet the intension is to maintain the collective upward flow of profession, not the flow in society ('collectiveness', as proposed by Parsons, where professionals in a certain field can obtain social status and prestige much higher than in other professions). Similarly, this situation has happened in Taiwan.

Since 1970, professionalization has also been at the centre of various discussions in Taiwan's social work society (Yang, 1998; Lin, 1994, 2002a, b; Tao and Chien, 1997). The contractual system is an issue always mentioned in these discussions.[1] The social worker contractual system caused unstable labor conditions and brought a survival crisis on basic-level government social workers. The call for 'professionalization' eventually contributed the certification system of the social work profession and initiated the establishment of professionalization. Green Wood's five professionalization qualities and the United States's certification system indicators can determine whether a professionalization process has been completed. The legislation on certification in 1996 saw the beginning of the establishment of the social work profession; however, along with the inauguration of the Social Worker Act, all sorts of development crises under Taiwan's social work professionalization started to provoke disputes. These crises are as follow:

---

1 Contracted social workers are those not officially employed in government agencies. Normally a working duration will be specified and the contract will be terminated by the date noted in the contract.

- the massive expansion of social work-related university faculties;
- multitrack social work education training channels;
- the profession positioning issue of social work caused by the similarity and overlapping of related professions;
- the adoption and autonomy of social work education, localization, and glocalization under the waves of globalization;
- the structural gap between the partnership of academic and practical fields;
- inspection and evaluation of the professional social worker certification exam;
- lack of openness of professional social work organizations;
- massive and complex workload in both administrative affairs and social work practices;
- insufficient indemnification in the local social work system; and
- the accountability and performance of social work relying on the manageability of data and an unequal power structure, lacking a related balance mechanism. (Wang, 2002; C.S. Wang, 2003; Li, 2005; Hsu, 2004; Chen et al., 2005; Huang and Hsiao, 2006; Huang et al., 2002; Hsiao, 2005; compiled from Wang, 2008)

This shows that instead of the professionals' practical qualities, it is the professional privilege legitimacy strategies, backed by state power, that define the social work profession in Taiwan. Professional organizations expect to create a legal monopoly and take advantage of education and skills manipulation as means to control the market. The intention is to maintain the profession's collective upward flow, yet the profession here is becoming irrelevant in terms of problem-solving skills and the degree of public recognition.

Tables 4.1 and 4.2 show a contradiction in professionalization. It can be seen that throughout the years covered, 2,799 people obtained a social worker certificate, the indicator of profession; however, less than one-third of these professional social workers actually undertook social work services in local areas. The data from 2006 to 2008 reveal that in these three years only 639 out of 1,036 people who obtained a certificate offered services in cities and counties; in other words, 40 per cent of these professional social workers did not get involved in social work practices. This issue highlights not only crises but also the difficult situation in Taiwan's social work profession whereby the status of the profession is achieved by strategies instead of skill/environment maturities. This chapter would like to elaborate how, since 1970, certification strategy, highlighting merely legitimacy and monopoly, has been applied through state-power intervention in Taiwan's social work development. Besides, a collective myth has formed where 'profession' seems to be realized by the establishment of a certification system, despite the fact that it is a state-led profession.

Table 4.1   Number of Social Welfare Personnel from 2001–2008

	Administrators	Social Workers	Professional Social Workers	Specialists	Others
2001	2,759	1,231	–	5,486	–
2002	3,032	1,185	–	5,770	3,544
2003	3,146	1,159	–	6,153	3,733
2004	3,211	1,229	–	6,184	3,606
2005	3,192	1,180	–	5,900	3,689
2006	3,301	1,405	238	5,864	3,801
2007	3,442	1,791	191	5,814	3,612
2008	3,582	2,110	210	5,506	3,962

Sources: Municipalities and local governments, National Statistics, R.O.C (Taiwan)

Note: This graphic covers current employees who are in charge of social welfare related affairs for the Ministry of Interior, Municipalities and offices within local governments.

Table 4.2   Admission of the Civil Service Special Examination for Social Welfare Workers from 1997–2010

	Number of Applicants	Number of Candidates on Spot	Admission Number	Admission Rate (%)
2010	4,080	2,924	333	11.39
2009	5,790	4,561	246	5.39
2008	3,307	2,419	615	25.42
2007	2,601	1,923	200	10.40
2006	2,871	1,995	221	11.08
2005	2,898	2,119	195	9.20
2004	2,626	1,672	25	1.50
2003	2,275	1,571	266	16.93
2002	1,888	1,209	77	6.37
2001	2,031	1,468	95	6.47
2000	1,931	1,189	191	16.06
1999	1,962	1,206	193	16.00
1998	2,146	1,308	211	16.13
1997	3,114	2,196	264	12.02
Total	35,440	24,836	2,799	

Source: Compiled from the data of the Ministry of Examination, Taiwan.

Overview of Taiwan's Social Work System

Although not perfect, a social work system has long existed in Taiwan, dating back to the Ming and Ching dynasties,social welfare introduced in the Japanese colonial period became the root of Taiwan's social work system. In the following section, three phases, defined by the degree of completion, will be introduced to explain the development of the social work system in Taiwan. The three phases are (1) Under-Construction, (2) Pre-Professionalized, and (3) Professionalized Social Work System.

Under-Construction Social Work System

Japanese Colonial Period
The social welfare introduced by the Japanese authority after colonization in 1895 is the root of Taiwan's social work (Lin, 2002a), and its measures and development were heavily influenced by Japan's colonial policies, with Japan's own benefits and developments as the foundation. In the early period of colonization, social welfare was ignored because of frequent revolts and the Japanese government's repressions. During the 1920s' Kominka movement and the 1930s' 'period of expansion', when Taiwan was used as Japan's Southern base, social welfare measures underwent a huge growth. This was not only a continuation of the disaster-relief methods of the Ching dynasty, but contributed to social welfare with expansibility (Lin, 2002a; Huang, 1988).

Owing to changes in governing policies, influences from the West, and the hierarchical diffusion of the colonial government, social welfare then could be seen as an embryo of the social welfare system today. Although Japanese people accounted for most of the personnel involved, this social welfare system had gone beyond disaster-relief affairs with more progressive ideas and structures (Chuang, 2004). Other social welfare areas were also gradually promoted during the same period, for example: the probation system, reformatory education, community centres for poor families, and kindergartens (Lin, 2002a).

To conclude, the Japanese colonial government's implementation of social welfare–related affairs targeted mainly systems and regulation constrictions. On the one hand, this can be seen as post-protest appeasement with the goal of achieving legitimacy for the Japanese government's political power; on the other, during Japan's capitalization development, the implementation of these measures was important for capital accumulation (Lin, 2002a; Huang, 1988).

The Period of Kuomintang Government. In this period, the Kuomintang government continued working on social work affairs based on the thoughts and experiences from mainland China.[2] At that time social work was considered a

---

2   In 1949, the Kuomintang government migrated to Taiwan. Lin Wan Yi (2002a) and Huang Yan Yi (1988) thought that in this period, the development of the economy and national defense were the emphasis of government policies, social welfare was less important. During that period the social welfare services covered merely disaster-relief and

political affair and the base of revolution to retake mainland China, in the hope of achieving social consensus and political control. Despite the fact that social welfare was not the top priority of the government, insurance laws regarding labor (1950), soldiers (1950), and civil servants (1958) were introduced during the 1950s, along with the implementation of land reform. These measures are believed to be means of political power, reassuring and appeasing citizens.

1965 'Current Social Policy of the Principle of People's Livelihood' Period.
The Kuomintang started to promote social policies that could meet the needs of the local environment, specifying that community development was one of the seven measures of social welfare, marking the first step in the development of a professional social work system. Although this policy diminished into a political slogan due to the military- and economy-led policymaking focus, it took the promotion of professional social work system one step forward. Community development started to be proactive after the Ministry of Interior drew up the 'Regulations on the Work of Community Development' and the Social Affairs Bureau of Taiwan Province published the 'Eight-Year Community Development Project in Taiwan Province' in 1968. In 1970, with guidance from the UN Development Plan, the Ministry of the Interior established the 'Republic of China Research and Training Center for Community Development', which governed the research and dissemination of related affairs (Lin, 2002a; Huang, 1988).

In the 'Under-Construction Social Work System' phase, social work in Taiwan transformed constantly and became more in line with local needs although, with some pivotal regulations established, the legitimacy of the nation's power was still the main function of Taiwan's social welfare system during this time.

Pre-Professionalized Social Work System

Post–World War II Period
Between 1949 and 1977, the United States's economic assistance of 8 billion USD, together with development of the national infrastructure, had facilitated Taiwan's industrial transformation and economic development, with the latter further boosting Taiwan's social welfare development (Lin, 2002a; Huang, 1988; Yang, 1997). Although Taiwan's withdrawal from the UN in 1972 saw the end of

---

education institutions; for example, the Social Relief Act promulgated in 1943 governed health services for the poor covering all public and private hospitals. On the other hand, many ongoing projects regarding medical social work continued to progress; for example: the Provincial Taipei Hospital (Now Taipei City Hospital Chung Hsing Branch) the Department of Social Services in 1940; in 1951, the Social Service Office of the National Taiwan University Hospital was established with the assistance of the chair of the UN Emergency Foundation—Taiwan Affairs. Later on the Social Service Department was established in Mackay Memorial Hospital (1956), Changhua Christian Hospital (1963), Taiwan Sanatorium (now Kai-Suan Psychiatric Hospital, 1966). Children's social welfare was also given high importance, owning to UNICEF's influence.

such economic assistance, community development continued (Huang, 1988; Lai, 2002). This development also unexpectedly had a critical influence on Taiwan's social work system.

Period of the Forming of a Social Worker Employment System
Although the Executive Yuan had once mentioned the establishment of a social worker system in the 'Republic of China Social Construction Project Phase I',[3] it was not until 1972, when the Taiwan Provincial Government promulgated the 'Experimental Project of Social Workers' Placement in Taiwan Provincial Cities', that social work was included in government policies – this project also clearly specified the service targets of social work – and in 1973, Keelung, Taichung, Tainan, and Kaohsiung started the placement of social workers. Although after two years the results were evaluated as ineffective, with the Chair of Province Hsieh Tung Min's positive attention being focused on the Taichung Dali Township experiment,[4] this method of social work continued to be adopted in another project: the 'Well-Off Family Project'. This project, in conjunction with community development, aimed at terminating poverty. In chapter 6 of the 'Economic Constriction Six-Year Project of the Republic of China', published by the Executive Yuan in 1976, the establishment of a social worker system was mentioned for the first time; in 1980 there were 17 cities and counties with social workers.

The Period of Increasing Social Worker Replacements with Graduates from Related Departments
By 1982, the social worker apparatus was nearly finished, and the alliance of social work organizations was growing gradually. During this phase the social worker system applied to the whole nation,[5] yet this project remained experimental; although with the number of the contract social workers growing, group pressure for incorporating social workers developed.

Professional Organization Developing Period
In the late 1970s, Taiwanese scholars started to promote the establishment of a nationwide professional social work organization to boost collective strength and consensus. Under the pressure of professional medical groups, the Taiwan Medical Social Services Association[6] was founded in 1983 with the objectives of taking over medical social worker training and increasing medical service quality. Following the abolishment of martial law, the Republic of China Association of

---

3   The content mentioned that the ratio of residents to social worker should be 200:1, while that of poor families to social worker is 500:1.

4   Taiwan's withdrawal from the UN suspended funds from UNICEF, the Taiwan Children's Social Welfare Research Center also faced a crisis of funding withdrawal. In 1974, the Social Affair Bureau of Taiwan Province transferred research centre employees to Dali, Taichung, for the Well-Off Family Project that the government was promoting.

5   In 1988, social workers existed in 21 cities and counties.

6   Later, this association changed its name to the Association of Medical Social Work.

Professional Social Workers[7] was founded, in spite of countless obstacles.[8] In the early period of its inception, this association took as its top tasks the assisting of social worker incorporation and the upgrading of the hierarchy of social welfare organizations. After the Executive Yuan published the incorporation plan, in reaction, this association held several seminars and discussions and even launched protests (Lin, 2002a; Yang, 1998).

During this period, the professional social worker system was established under the government's experimental project and regulations, yet the service areas and service details were still restrained by government policies. The establishment of professional organizations and their action plans were often ignored by the government. The 'professional system' in this period was still confined by the ideology of government agencies and laws/regulations without considering the construction of a local social work system.

The Professionalized Social Work System in Taiwan

According to Lin Wan Yi (2003) and Yang Mei Ying (1998), in the 1970s there were already a number of scholars calling for the establishment of professional social worker organizations, in order to boost professional influence and enhance communication between social workers (Chang, 1978; Li, 1980). In the 'How to Establish Professional Social Worker System' and 'Reminiscences and Prospects of Social Works' seminars, the need to establish a professional social work organization was emphasized; academia had started to realize that to achieve a professional social work system, the establishment of a nationwide professional organization must be made a priority (Hsa and Lin, 1984; Chang, 1991; Tsai, 1989; Chien and Tao, 1993).

In 1990 when the incorporation plan was finalized, the crisis of social workers' labor conditions was not solved, and calls to legislate social work certificates arose. In 1991 two professors, Hsu Chen and Lin Wan Yi, drew up the first version of the Social Worker Act; in 1992, this draft was proposed by legislators such as Chu Feng Chih in the Legislative Yuan. In 1993, legislator Huang Ching Kao drew up the Professional Social Worker Act Draft. Proposed jointly by legislator Pan Wei Kang and Hung Jui Che, this draft adopted the previous version as its basis, adding parts regarding employment and the management of social workers. In 1994, the Legislative Yuan authorized Professor Lu Kuang and Professor Lin Cheng Chuen to compare and evaluate Chu Feng Chih and Pang Wei Kang's versions of the draft and propose another version based on their evaluations. In the same year, the Ministry of the Interior authorized the 'Republic of China

---

7   In 2000, this association changed its name to the 'Taiwan Association of Professional Social Workers'.

8   According to the 'Law of Citizen's Organization in the Period of Mobilization for the Suppression of Communist Rebellion', only one organization with the same properties can be established. At that time the existing China Association of Social Workers hindered the founding of the Republic of China Association of Professional Social Workers.

Association of Social Workers' to undertake the drafting, with Professor Lin Wan Yi as convener and expert participation from the academic and practical fields. In 1995, Lin's version of the Social Worker Act was completed and was proposed by commissioned legislator Huang Chao Huei. The 'Republic of China Association of Social Workers' later commissioned legislator Lin Chih Chia to propose another version that amended five articles in the draft version.

Although the social worker community proactively compiled and edited the 'Social Worker Act' and obtained assistance from several legislators on the matter of proposal between 1991 and 1995, the 'Social Worker Act' was not submitted to the Legislative Yuan for examination. With social worker communities' efforts on a series of strategies and campaigns, including a march on 26 October 1995, the 'Social Worker Act' was eventually taken into the discussion agenda of the Legislative Yuan on 31 December 1995 and passed the third reading on 11 March 1997. On 27 July 1998, the promulgation of 18 items of social work ethical principles by the Ministry of Interior saw the completion of constructing a professional social work system (Lin, 2002b).

The process of professionalization started with the necessity of professionalization proposed by academia, yet during the process political backing (the legislators' support) was needed in order to pass the 'Social Work Act' and a subtle relationship between government and profession emerged and was even enhanced during this process. As specified in the 'Social Worker Act', one must pass the Civil Service Special Examination for Social Welfare Workers to gain a licence, or a special exam to obtain the Professional Social Worker certificate. This shows that the power of decision over qualification as a professional social worker lies with the government, pushing the government and development of the social work profession into a difficult situation where a tug of war never ceases.

The Social Work System Abroad

The certification system for this special profession includes three methods:

1. 'Certification' – the authorities of examination, professional associations, or government agencies examine the professional knowledge and skills of a candidate. Once qualified, they will be awarded a certificate and allowed to use a professional 'title'.
2. 'Licence' – granted by the government through application. With such a licence, one can provide professional services. The government has the right to enforce a ban on discovering a case of non-licenced professional service or business activity.
3. 'Registration' – which can be further divided into 'Voluntary Registration' and 'Obligatory Registration'.

Practitioners who are qualified with certain basic requirements can register in a designated institute. Among these three methods, the one with the strictest rules is 'Certification', followed by 'Licence' and 'Registration'. Therefore, most professional social workers preferred 'Certification' or 'Licence' methods to ensure their professional status (Li, 1996: 25).

Looking at the professional social worker certification system of various countries, it can be seen that every country has its own rules . The United States, Canada, Japan, Taiwan, and Korea use the examination system, while the United Kingdom and Hong Kong use the registration system and different countries have different examination systems. For example, in the United States, there is a professional organization in charge of the examination while the government is responsible for awarding a licence; however, in Japan, Korea, and Taiwan, the government is in charge of both examination and licence (Lin and Shen, 2008).

The General Social Care Council (GSCC), founded in 2001, is responsible for the candidature, registration and application, in-service training, and advanced certification of professional social workers in the United Kingdom.[9] Regarding candidature, applicants must provide certificates of their bachelor or master's degree from social work–related faculties. Normally, high school students in the UK who wish to enroll in a social work–related faculty have to obtain credits from at least five AP subjects (English and math included), as well as for third-level subjects in vocational school such as hygiene, social service subjects, and so on. Those faculties the students enroll in must be approved by the GSCC, so that students can register as social workers in the future. Currently, there are more than 40 universities with approved social work faculties. The duration of study at the undergraduate level is two years, and students must look for internships in a registered Social Care Institute, working full-time for at least 200 days. Students whose major at the undergraduate level is not social work have to complete a two-year postgraduate course to become qualified as a social worker.

Once all of the above-mentioned documents are presented, one can registers as a qualified social worker. The GSCC provide social work practice principles and in-service training courses for renewing a licence, which is required every three years.

In Hong Kong, the registration system is under the governance of the Hong Kong Social Welfare Personnel Registration Council and the Social Workers Registration Board. The following two types of candidate are qualified for registering:

1. Holders of a certificate or diploma approved by the Social Workers Registration Board. Generally, this includes certificates or diplomas from the social work–related faculties of the six Universities and Colleges in Hong Kong, or those in foreign countries such as Singapore, Taiwan, Australia, the United Kingdom, Canada, and the United States.

---

9 Information source: Cheng Li Chen (2008), 'The Dialogue between the Profession Development of Social Work and Professional Social Worker Certificate', *National Elite Quarterly*, Vol. 4.

2. Those who are currently social workers without a certificate or diploma
   from a related faculty: To register candidates must study and pass the five
   essential subjects in a related faculty and complete an internship of at
   least 800 working hours (for undergraduate course, 700 hours for diploma
   course) and obey the practice principles and guidelines specified by the
   Social Workers Registration Board.

There is no regulation over continuing education, since the system in Hong Kong
values the approved diploma/certificate the most; once a social worker succeeds
in registration, they can extend this status by following the laws on regulations
and fees.

In the United States[10] there exists the 'double-track'[11] social worker qualification
exam system, where the licence is authorized by each state government and the
certificate is approved by the National Association of Social Workers (NASW). All
independent professional social workers must obtain membership in the NASW,
which provides 10 certificates in 10 specialized fields to differentiate closely
related social work fields (Lin and Shen, 2008). Social worker certification within
government agencies is led by the Association of Social Work Boards (ASWB),
which was reformed in 1999. The examination designed by the ASWB covers
four degrees. Despite certain special rules required by some state governments,
the regulations on candidature in these four degrees are as follows: For bachelor's
and master's levels, social workers must hold a bachelor's or master's certificate
approved by the Council of Social Work Education (CSWE); advanced generalists
must obtain a master's degree followed by two years of work experience; clinical
social workers must obtain a master's degree followed by two years of clinical
work experience. The CSWE developed the Standards for Accreditation and
Curriculum Policy Statement in 1973 to examine the faculties who apply for
approval and determine whether their taught course conforms to the professional
knowledge and skills a practitioner would need. Regarding the application
procedure, applicants must prepare all documents needed along with a candidature
examination form; after ASWB approval, the candidates are able to attend the
exam. A multiple-choice test is applied, focusing on both theoretical and practical
principles that a practitioner would frequently come across and real life cases are
sometimes employed as questions in such tests. There are 170 questions in total
with a difficulty corresponding to each different type of exam – 20 out of the 170
questions are not scored, serving as effectiveness testing. Those who pass this
exam can be awarded a licence. The ASWB is also responsible for continuing
education and verification of certificate renewal, yet the renewal regulation varies
by state. Once a social worker obtains the certificate, they can register to become a

---

10   Information source: Cheng Li Chen (2080) 'The Dialogue between the Profession
Development of Social Work and Professional Social Worker Certificate', *National Elite
Quarterly*, Vol. 4.

11   To become a practitioner one must obtain a license issued by the state. The NASW
certificate cannot replace such license as a substitute.

member of the ASWB and periodically receive information on professional skills, continuing education, licence renewal, and so on.

In Japan, there are multiple ways to become a professional social worker, even without the requirement on education background:

1. Students in a short-term program, as well as the two- or three-year course at social welfare scheme-related universities or colleges, after completing 13 subjects and 35 units (non-credit internship included) as designated by the Ministry of Health, Labor and Welfare and working at least one year in social welfare institutes, are qualified candidates for the National Examination for Social Worker.
2. Social workers with more than five years of work experience (including both administrative personnel and practitioners, as specified in the Children, Disability and Senior's Social Welfare Act) are also qualified candidates.
3. Students in a four-year course at social welfare scheme-related universities or colleges, after completing the designated six subjects and 16 units and six-month training course from an training institute, are qualified candidates.
4. Students from a two- or three-year course at social welfare scheme-related universities or colleges, who completed the designated six subjects and 16 units, have to obtain one year's (three-year course students) or two years (two-year course students) of work experience in institutes designated by the Ministry of Health, Labor and Welfare. On top of that, they must pass a six-month training course in an training institute to become qualified for the exam.
5. Students from a four-year course in an ordinary university who did not select the designated subjects (as previously mentioned) can complete at least one year of an education training course from an training institute to become qualified candidates.
6. Students form a two- or three-year course at an ordinary university or college who did not select the designated subjects can obtain their candidature after working at least one year (for three-year course students) or two years (for two-year course students) in institutes designated by the Ministry of Health, Labor and Welfare, and passing at least one year of an education training course at an training institute.
7. Those who work in institutes designated by the Ministry of Health, Labor and Welfare for more than four years and have passed at least one year of an education training course from an training institute are qualified candidates. All candidates with qualifying scores can register to become an official professional social worker. (Chiang, 2002)

There are 150 multiple-choice questions in the exam, divided into a total of 13 groups of general and special subjects. Local social work organizations serve as examiners in such examinations.

From the social worker certification system of the United Kingdom, Hong Kong, the United States, and Japan, it can be seen that there is no significant difference between the registration or examination system of each one, only different designs due to cultural factors or laws. However, we should pay special attention to who dominates the system and its development. In the United Kingdom, the United States, and Hong Kong, it is the professional organization in charge of its development and related affairs, while in Taiwan and Japan, it is the government that dominates from the examination system to the test questions. The history of the development of social work in these countries reveals the fact that problems vary according to who dominates the field.

Phenomena after Promulgation of the Social Worker Act

Although the promulgation of the Social Worker Act is one of the important indicators of the professionalization of social work in Taiwan, several challenges emerged, including doubts over the professional role, contradiction between the professional system and professional autonomy, and constant controversy regarding the professional social worker examination, all leading to the demand for amendments.

Doubts over the Professional Role

During the events of the abolition of prostitution in Taipei City and the demolition of Taipei's Nos 14 and 15 Parks, the grass-roots social workers realized that they were stuck in a dilemma and eventually 'betrayed' the latter (Fang and Cheng, 1999). Those who became professional social workers after the promulgation of the Social Worker Act suffered from the contradiction between reality and their ideology and started to develop doubts. Fang Ya Li (1999: 33) once said,

> I wonder what my role is in these two incidents? Am I a righteous policy executer or the one to clean out suffer from the unpleasant situation for the government? During the process … . On one side, there are vulnerable people ignored in the society, and there are professional social workers on the other, authorized with power from the nation. Both sides all struggle for their own living, yet for the latter this means to expel those vulnerable people from the world where they are no longer tolerated. This process is rather ambiguous and will definitely create an opposing situation for the bureaucracy and professional autonomy.

There are more doubts about the role of the profession. Yang Mei Ying posed the problem that the object of service might change – from disadvantaged groups to the upper level of society. This is against the genuine meaning of the profession and causes an issue of professionalization positioning. Chou Yueh Ching (2002) thinks the Social Worker Act has brought about a crisis where the profession is controlled by the system and academia and is facing the fact of being homogenized. Through research on case management in social work fields, Wang Tseng

Yun (2003) analyzed the process of 'skill/knowledge transmission', mapping out the professional position of social workers, who have become the players of social control during the process of professionalization. Also, during the earthquake of 21 September 1999 (known as the 921 Incident) and the SARS period, the social workers' role was questioned because they were not able to be effective in time and later faced the mess of government withdrawal of subsidies[12] and unemployment. The above facts reveal a question about whether social workers offer services to disadvantaged groups based on their profession or whether they are, in fact, stuck in this professional position and do not know how to define their professional role. Or do they lose their identification with their profession due to being stuck in their professional position? The discussion and controversy over the role of social workers and their responsibility continues.

The Contradiction of the Professional System and Professional Autonomy

The controversy generated by doubts over the role of the profession further triggered discussions on the professional system and the contradiction of professional autonomy. Tao Fan Ying (1999) was the first to mention that institutionalization does not equal professionalization. Institutionalization tends to walk side by side with, or even cling to, the government system; in professionalization, the degree of professional autonomy increases, enhancing control over the working field. Hence, institutionalization and professionalization are like two paths leading professional development in completely different directions. He also believes that the Social Worker Act is like institutionalization for the social work profession, leaving an illusion of professionalization but in truth reducing the freedom of professional autonomy.

Under this institutionalization in Taiwan, the autonomy of basic-level social work was gradually impaired with social welfare organizations drawing close to the government and the academic groups full of power and knowledge; it is the government that decides what to do, and the scholars/experts determine how to do it and evaluate the results (Wang, 2006). Some social workers felt that the professional system equated to deserting the object of service, as described by Fang Yu (2004: 77):

> The profession I am facing is actually one that requires efficiency, effectiveness and performance, self-aggrandized and controlled by power and politics; it can never stand side by side with the ones to be concerned.

Besides the professional system and professional autonomy, the impact of managerialism on professional personnel was also discussed. This indicates that social work is now in the quasi-market stage. It is necessary to break down the traditional hierarchical management, with a certain degree of professional

---

12   Please refer to the Community Life and Society Reconstruction Promotion Task Force website at http://921.yam.org.tw/workstation/swact/index.htm.

Social Work in East Asia

autonomy being sacrificed, to accomplish social workers' role in the competitive market (Huang, 1999: 202).

To conclude, these discussions and analysis of institutionalization, power structure, or the applying of new management tools all highlight the contradictory and complex relationship between professional autonomy and the professional system. Among them, weakened professional autonomy and the paradoxical relation with clients are significant questions found in every aspect of social work.[13]

The Controversy over the Examination for Professional Social Workers

Several defects of the examination at this time were pointed out: it was not effective, lacked validity, and disqualified those without a social work educational background. Also, there were other issues such as controversies over candidature, low admission rates, non-flexible test questions, and the qualification and ratio of examiners. Besides, the licence system was not working smoothly and this problem was ignored (Chou, 2002; Ho, 2004, Hsiao, 2005; Huang, 2006; Huo, 2007). Following these issues, questions arose regarding the examination system, candidature, classification of licence, professional continuing education, professional social workers in private practice, ethics, self-discipline, and so on (Lin, 2002b; Chou, 2002; Hsiao, 2005; Lin and Shen, 2008), yet the situation where the old system did not work and caused disagreement in the social work field persisted.

In other words, the certification system is just like a screen, the function of which is to tell the 'qualified' from the 'unqualified' (C.S. Wang, 2003). It also causes stratification, and conflict between these two types of social workers (Lin, 2001). Hsiao Huei Ju (2005) thinks the disunion appeared between those who are for and against the examination, qualified or unqualified, with or without related educational background, and so on. Some scholars also think that the examination system not only fails to bring about the expected positive effects, but makes social workers spend their time studying for exams in order to transfer to government positions, leaving behind their promises to the mission of social worker (Chou, 2002). This system will very likely just create a dependency on examinations (Yu, 1998; Chen, 2003).

Also, the controversy showed the conflict between the academic and practical fields. Currently, those who are given the right to design the exams are scholars recognized by the national system; in other words, practitioner social workers have to pass an examination designed by academics to qualify for certification. The gap and paradox between the practice and theories of social work has become evident. Moreover, the exam-led system was discovered to have dominated not

---

13   Please refer to the master's thesis from the Department of Sociology, Ching Hua University, 'Formation of Consensus or Setback for Imagination? An Inspection of Professional Sociology Regarding the Social Work Issue in the Society' by Hsiao Hsin Bing, 2006.

only academia but also the practical aspect of social work in that the academics possess the products of legal knowledge such as 'credits', 'courses' and 'degrees'. Such products grew to form a sort of 'power' which increasingly commercialized the nature of the social work profession, and knowledge products such as 'in-service studies' and 'continuing studies' were promoted to the practical fields, with practitioner social workers as the main consumer (Wang, 2006).

Following are several thoughts from professionals in the fields of social work in Taiwan:

> The promulgation of [the] professional Social Worker Act can't necessarily elevate professional social workers' professional status, neither does it ensure the right of the clients. (Lin, 2001)

> [The] Profession Social Worker Act has negative influence on social work's environment. (Chou, 2002)

> The rapid expansion in the social work education will ... impact and influence ... the profession of social work. (Lin, 2002a)

> The 'skill adapting and knowledge passing' stage during professionalization is gradually becoming a competition over the inner power of profession. (C.S. Wang, 2003)

> The low admission rate of social worker has caused the opposition of the academia and the practitioner. (TASW, 2004)

More worrying issues were presented including the following: the over expansion of social work–related faculties in universities and colleges; the underdevelopment of academic models and research communities of social work; the profession-positioning issue of social work (brought about by the similarity between and overlapping of related professions); the structural gap in the partnership between the academic and practice fields; the evaluation and inspection of the professional social worker examination; the lack of openness in the professional social work organizations; the massive and complex workload in both administrative affairs and social work practices; and insufficient indemnification in local social work systems – the accountability and performance of social work relies on the manageability of data and an unequal power structure, and it lacks a related balance mechanism (Wang, 2002; C.S. Wang, 2003; Li, 2005; Hsu, 2004; Chen et al., 2005; Huang and Hsiao 2006; Huang et al., 2002; Hsiao 2005; compiled from Wang, 2008).

It has been concluded that amendments to the Social Worker Act are necessary in order to solve the crisis mentioned above and realize an authentic professionalization. Professional continuing education will allow social workers to provide specified services with professional quality.

In effect, these arguments highlight several issues: the disparity between the law and the real world, which unexpectedly triggered a series of controversies in the social work field; the heterogeneity among social work–related parties;[14] criticism of phenomena such as exam subjects dominating school education; school education transforming to align with cramming for exams due to the certification exam system, and the decline of professional autonomy in social work, which is becoming dependent on the government (Kao, 2003; Tao, 1999; Chen, 2003; Hsiao, 2005).

Amendments of the Social Worker Act

The amendment issue brought about by the controversy mentioned in the last chapter triggered the question 'Who is dominating Taiwan's social work education?' along with a series of actions[15] that accelerated amendment of the Social Worker Act.

In 2005, the Ministry of the Interior commissioned the Taiwan Association of Social Workers, the Taiwan Association of Medical Social Work, the National Union, and the Taiwan Society of Mental Health Social Work to project-manage the drafting of the Social Work Act amendments.[16] According to the draft submitted to the Ministry of the Interior, it is hoped that quality of services and professional competence will increase and the rights of both worker and service target can be assured through controlling candidates' qualifications and broadening the aspects of service, securing working conditions and the compilation of the according penal code (TASW, 2005). The procedure to amend the Social Worker Act was scheduled as follows: (1) organize the task force to gather information, (2) analyze the findings, and (3) organize public hearings. Once the public hearings had been held, social worker communities would be invited to share their feedback and come to a consensus on the proposed amendments.

Ideas for the amendments originated from Taiwanese laws regarding lawyers, accounting, psychology, occupational therapy, and nursing; social work law from New York State, California, and British Columbia, Canada; the definition of social work/social work practices from NASW, BASW, IFSW, the United Kingdom, the United States, and Hong Kong; the operational details of California, British Columbia, and the Social Worker Registration Board of New York State.

Regarding the establishment of a Social Worker Classification System, the classification systems of British Columbia, New York State, Texas, and the NASW in the United States were referred to along with those of specialists, nurse

---

14   See Hsiao Hsin Bing (2006), 'Formation of Consensus or Setback for Imagination? An Inspection of Professional Sociology Regarding the Social Work Issue in the Society', master's thesis, Tsinghua University, Hsinchu, Taiwan.

15   Cf., e.g., the demonstration led by Lin Wan Yi, Lu Pao Ching, and Chen Wu Tsung, who requested installation of a Social Work Education Board; in June 2004 the Social Worker Department of the National Taiwan University held the 'Competence of Social Workers and Social Work Education' seminar; the 'Diagnosis of Taiwan's Social Work Profession Education' public hearing was held during August 2004; seven sessions of 'Seminar of the Examination, Training and Employment System of Professional Social Workers' were held in 2004 by the Taiwan Social Worker Association.

16   Also referred to as the four families.

practitioners, social workers, and laws regarding the professional behaviour of other professionals, for example, lawyers, psychologists, and so on in British Columbia, and California.

As to the practice regulations, the professional social worker regulations of British Columbia and operational details governing clinical social work in California were discussed.

The necessary tasks were divided between the four professional organizations:

- The Taiwan Association of Medical Social Work was responsible for managing the scope of the exercise, defining 'professional' social worker and assuring the rights of social workers;
- The Taiwan Association of Social Workers was responsible for qualifications, both the obtaining and withdrawal of;
- The National Union was in charge of the inspection mechanism and organizing; and
- The Taiwan Society of Mental Health Social Work was responsible for task scoping.

Situations that the four groups expected after the amendments would be

- Regulations being made to introduce specialized professional social workers, to provide services in specific areas;
- Professional, continuing education, which would enable social workers to provide specified services to a professional standard; and
- The expansion of an exemption list for the post-filling of social workers can ensure the rights of both clients and social workers, including their personal safety.

The four professional organizations contributed a final draft of the amendment that was proposed and underwent a series of legislative negotiations and consultations before passing the third reading on 19 December 2007, and the new Social Worker Act was inaugurated.

Taiwan's Social Work Profession Development: Professionalism vs. National Professionalism

The beginning of this chapter claims that Taiwan's social work profession was brought about merely by means of strategies rather than by the accomplishment of skills or the maturity of the social work environment. However, through the process of compiling the developmental history of Taiwan's social work profession it can be seen that government plays an indispensible role in the profession. Throughout history, government was sometimes the leader that protected benefits, sometimes the object to fight against, and sometimes an ally. On the one hand, the social work profession serves as a key element during the forming of a nation (e.g., the

Japanese colonial period and the Kuomintang government period); on the other, the establishment of the profession also requires acts such as the incorporation of social workers and the legislation from the government.

Since 'certification' is employed in Taiwan within the social work system, its effect of regulation inevitably divides those who are competent from those who are not. On the basis of law, the competent ones provide specialized services based on their specialized knowledge and skills; although the certification system proposed by the government is supposed to protect professional service personnel and consumers, in fact it allows professional groups to maintain their economic power and elitism in education and society. Thus, the certification system has become a regulatory captive or is controlled by professional organizations (Wilson, 1984). However, the government is, in law, the power that should control these organizations.

Following the above arguments, we believe that to discuss the development of social work as a profession in Taiwan, it is necessary to look into its relationship with government. In Taiwan, ever since the application of national examinations, the development of social work as a profession in Taiwan has always wandered between professionalism and national professionalism. This is a unique phenomenon: Looking at the development of Taiwan's social work profession from the perspective of both the government and the profession, it can be seen that in the early stages, collective power of an alliance urged for the birth of the Social Worker Act, yet professional autonomy was later set back and weakened by the government intervention. Apparently the professional organizations resumed control during the period of amendments when means such as negotiation and public hearings were applied to make voices in the community heard. Nevertheless, the outcome emerged, hinting at the unbalanced situation whereby academics eventually became the representatives of the profession and the government, with social workers being clients.

The development of social work as a profession in Taiwan appeared to be a process wherein a single service provider could manage to form and control the 'market' of 'profession'. When the buyer was the government or vested interest groups, 'profession' was forced to face the buyer-dominated market and transformed into national professionalism. This chapter shows the phenomenon and emphasizes the connection between professionalization and national professionalism, yet it is not possible to point out which party is more superior. What is the ultimate outcome of the two parties' inter-influence? The answer is left to time to reveal.

References

Caplow, T. (1954), *The Sociology of Work*. Minneapolis: University of Minneapolis Press.

Carr-Saunders, A.M. and Wilson, P.A. (1962), The Emergence of Professions, in *Man, Work and Society*, edited by S. Nosow and W.H. Form. New York: Basic Books.

Chang, S.C. (1978), The Idea of Social Work Professionalization in Taiwan, *China Forum*, Vol. 6, No. 10, pp. 8–11 (in Chinese).

Chang, Y.H. (1991), Review and Prospect of the Social Work Profession System in Taiwan, *Social Work Journal*, Vol. 1, pp. 1–14 (in Chinese).

Chen, C.C. *et al.* (2005), Social Workers Working Conditions Survey, *Community Development Journal Quarterly*, Vol. 109, pp. 475–86 (in Chinese).

Chen, W.T. (2003), Between Name and Reality: Reflect Professional Development Education after Social Worker National Examination, Paper presented at the Role of Social Workers and Social Work Education Seminar, Taichung: Tunghai University (in Chinese).

Cheng, L.C. (2008), The Dialogue between Social Work Professionalism and Social Work License, *National Elite Quarterly*, Vol. 4, No. 4, pp. 127–40.

Chiang, L.Y. (2002), Japanese Social Work Education, Training and Social Welfare Worker, *Community Development Journal Quarterly*, Vol. 99, pp. 156–65 (in Chinese).

Chien, C.A. and Tao, F.Y. (1993), Taiwan Social Work Professional Development, paper presented at the *Conference of Social Work Profession System*, Taipei, Taiwan (in Chinese).

Chou, Y.C. (2002), The Crisis and Turning Point of the Development of Taiwan's Social Work Profession: Reflections on Social Work Education and Practice, *Community Development Quarterly*, Vol. 99, pp. 90–125 (in Chinese).

Chuang, H.M. (2004), Taiwan's Social Welfare and Social Works during the Japanese Colonial Period, *Soochow Journal of Social Work*, Vol. 10, pp. 1–33.

Collins, R. (1979), *The Credential Society: An Historical Sociological of Education and Stratification.* Academic Press: New York.

Fang, L. and Cheng, L.C. (1999), The Inquiry of Social Work Professional Autonomy—For Example in the Event of Taipei Licensed Prostitutes, *Community Development Journal Quarterly*, Vol. 86, pp. 208–15.

Fang, Y. (2004), The Action and Narration of "Qing-Shui-Gou": My Community Work Practice and Criticism of Professional Social Work. Unpublished Master's thesis from the Department of Social Work, Soochow University, Taipei.

Fang, Y.L. (1999), The Government's Social Work Dilemma in the Event of Taipei Licensed Prostitutes: A Reflection of Action Research, thesis, Department of Social Work, National Taiwan University, Taiwan (in Chinese).

Flexner, A. (1915), Is Social Work a Profession? *Research on Social Practice*, Vol. 11, No. 2, pp. 152–65.

Freidson, E. (1970), *The Profession of Medicine.* University of Chicago Press: Chicago, IL.

Freidson, E. (1994), *Professionalism Reborn: Theory, Prophecy and Policy*, Polity Press: Cambridge, UK.

Ho, T.Y. (2004), A Study on Career Transfer of Social Worker: An Example of Qualified Social Worker in Local Government, thesis, Department of Social Policy and Social Work, National Chi Nan University, Puli, Taiwan.

Hsa, J.C. and Lin, W.I. (1984), *Contemporary Social Work.* Wu Nan: Taipei.

Hsiao H.J. (2005), Reflections on Taiwan's Social Work Certification System, Based on the Comparisons of Taiwan and the USA's Social Work Certification System, thesis, Department of Social Work, National Taiwan University, Taipei (in Chinese).

Hsiao, H.B. (2006), Formation of Consensus or Setback for Imagination? In Inspection of Professional Sociology: The Social Work Issue in Society, thesis, Dept. of Sociology, Ching Hua University: Hsinchu, Taiwan.

Hsu, C.Y. (2004). Social Work Education in Taiwan: Testing Development of Degree Theses, 1990–2003, thesis, Department of Social Policy and Social Work, National Chi Nan University, Puli, Taiwan.

Huang *et al.* (2002), *Overall Survey of the Social Welfare System.* The Control Yuan: Taipei (in Chinese).

Huang, Y.H. (1999), New Managerialism, Community Care and Social Work, *Community Development Journal Quarterly*, Vol. 85, pp. 200–213 (in Chinese).

Huang, Y.S. (2006), Construction of Long-Term Care Quality Management System, *Community-Based Long Term Care Quarterly*, Vol. 3, pp. 19–44 (in Chinese).

Huang, Y.S. and Hsiao, W.K. (2006), *Social Policy and Social Legislation.* Yeh Yeh Book Gallery: Taipei (in Chinese).

Huang, Y.Y. (1988), Research on Taiwan's Social Work Development (1683–1988), thesis, Department of Sociology, National Taiwan University, Taipei.

Hughes, E.C. (1971), *The Sociological Eye.* Aldine-Atherton: Chicago, IL.

Huo, C.H. (2007), Research on Social Workers' Mindset Southern Taiwan Towards to the Certification System of Social Work, thesis, Institute of Interdisciplinary Studies on Social Sciences, National Sun Yat-Sen University, Kaohsiung, Taiwan (in Chinese).

Johnson, T. (1972), *Professions and Power.* Macmillan: London.

Kao, T.L. (2003), Professional Certification Examination System of Social Work, Paper presented at the Role of Social Workers and Social Work Education Seminar, Tunghai University: Taichung, Taiwan.

Lai, L.Y. (2002), The Historical Development and Function Transformation of Community Work in Taiwan, *Community Development Journal Quarterly*, Vol. 100, pp. 69–80.

Larson, M.S. (1977), *The Rise of Professionalism: A Sociological Analysis.* University of California Press: Berkeley, CA.

Li, T.L. (1980), The Development Trend of Social Work Supervision, *Community Development Journal Quarterly*, Vol. 52, pp. 9–11 (in Chinese).

Li, Y.C. (2005), Development of Medical Social Work in Taiwan, *Community Development Journal Quarterly*, Vol. 109, pp. 165–70 (in Chinese).

Li, Z.P. (1996), Discuss Social Worker Certification and Approval System, *Community Development Journal Quarterly*, Vol. 76, pp. 24–33 (in Chinese).

Lin, W.I. (2002a), The Historical Development of Taiwan's Social Work, in *Social Work and Taiwan Society*, edited by P.C. Lu (ed.), Chu-Liu Publishing: Taipei (in Chinese).

Lin, W.I. and Shen, S.H. (2008), The Road Towards Specialization: The Next Step of Social Work in Taiwan? *Community Development Journal Quarterly*, Vol. 121, pp. 199–233 (in Chinese).

Lin, W.L. (1994), *The Welfare State—Analysis of Historical Comparison*, Taipei: Strong Current (in Chinese).

Lin, W.L. (2001), Looking for the 21st Century Social Work in Taiwan, *Social Work Journal*, Vol. 7, pp. i–xv (in Chinese)

Lin, W.Y. (2002b), *Contemporary Social Work: Theories and Methods* Wu Nan: Taipei.

Parry, N. and Parry, J. (1976), *The Rise of the Medical Profession: A Study of Collective Social Mobility*, Croom Helm: London.

Parsons, T. (1954), *The Professions and Social Structure*, in *Essays in Sociological Theory*, edited by T. Parsons (ed.), The Free Press: New York.

Taiwan Association of Social Workers (TASW) (2004), *Work Report*, Taiwan Association of Social Workers: Taipei (in Chinese).

TASW (2005), *Work Report*, Taiwan Association of Social Workers: Taipei (in Chinese).

Tao, F.Y. (1999), The Analysis and Prospect of Social Work Development, *Community Development Quarterly*, Vol. 88, pp. 190–96 (in Chinese).

Tao, F.Y. and Chien, C.A. (1997), The Review and Prospect of the Development of Social Work Profession, *Social Work Journal*, Vol. 4, pp. 1–25.

Tsai, H.H. (1989), *Establishment of Social Work Profession System: A Cornerstone of Welfare Policy*, Social Research Center: Taipei (in Chinese).

Vollmer, H.M. and Mills, D.L. (1966), *Professionalization*. Prentice-Hall: Englewood Cliffs, NJ.

Wang, C.S. (2003), Research of Social Work Profession Development in Hong Kong: 1950–1997, thesis, Department of Social Welfare, National Chung Cheng University, Taipei.

Wang, Frank T.Y. (2003), Between Care and Control: Discursive Practices of Case Management in Social Work, *Taiwan: A Radical Quarterly in Social Studies*, Vol. 51, pp. 143–83 (in Chinese).

Wang, S. (2002), Comparing Social Worker and Psychological Counselor Ethics, in *Social Work Ethics*, edited by J.C. Has and M.C. Li (eds.). Wu Nan: Taipei (in Chinese).

Wang, S. (2006), From Push to Resist: My Action in the Process of Institutionalization of Counseling Psychology, *Research in Applied Psychology*, Vol. 30, pp. 21–36 (in Chinese).

Wang, S.M. (2008), The Humanistic Thinking of Social Workers Law Changed, *report*, National Policy Foundation, Taipei, February 4 (in Chinese).

Wilensky, H. (1964), The Professionalization of Everyone?, *The American Journal of Sociology*, Vol. 70, No. 2, pp. 137–58.

Wilson, G.K. (1984), Social Regulation and Explanations of Regulatory Failure, *Political Studies*, Vol. 32, No. 2, pp. 203–25.

Yang, D.C. (1997), *Michel Foucault*. Sheng-Chih Book: Taipei (in Chinese).

Yang, M.Y. (1998), Research on Social Work's Professionalization in Taiwan: Analysis of the Establishment of Professional Social Worker System, thesis, Department of Social Work in Soochow University, Taipei.

Yu, H.Y. (1998), Social Research Ethics, in *Dangerous and Secret: Research Ethics*, edited by S.R. Yan. Taipei: Sun Min (in Chinese).

Chapter 5
Social Work in Hong Kong

Ernest W.T. Chui

Hong Kong is essentially a Chinese community with a great majority (95%) of its population being ethnic Chinese. However, with more than 150 years of colonial history, and also located as the gateway to mainland China, Hong Kong has been characterized as a place where 'East meets West', and is probably the most Westernized city in China. As social work is essentially a 'Western' discipline, it would be interesting to analyze how this 'foreign' academic discipline and profession finds its root and develops in this Westernized Chinese city. This chapter firstly provides a brief introduction of the city of Hong Kong, as above, and then gives a review of the historical development of the social work profession in the context of social welfare development. It then provides a brief account of the evolution of and recent developments in the professional training and education in social work, as well as the professional community, and ends up with highlights of the upcoming challenges facing the profession.

The Context of Social Work Practice: Social Welfare in Hong Kong

Similar to the experience of other advanced countries in which the social work profession flourishes, Hong Kong's social work practice is also working within the context of social welfare. It is therefore essential to have a contextual understanding of the evolution of social welfare in Hong Kong.

In 1842, when Britain took over Hong Kong as her colony, she merely regarded it as a stepping stone for entering the huge mainland China market. Thus, the colonial regime maintained a minimal administration and was not keen on welfare provision for the then sparse population. Welfare provision for the indigenous people was left to the pre-existent traditional philanthropic associations and local community and clansmen organizations. This minimal welfare stance had been maintained before World War II. When Britain resumed governance after the Japanese occupation during the war, the colonial administration still relied on international relief organizations to provide help for the poor and the Chinese refugees coming across the Chinese border. Thus, local academics commented that the social welfare system at that time was essentially a residual model, and the government's stance on social welfare was passive and discouraging (Chow, 2008) and non-interventionist (Aspalter, 2006; Chui, 2007; McLaughlin, 1993).

This could be seen from the government's first White Paper on social welfare in 1965, in which the British colonial administration claimed that excessive social welfare provision would break down the family and its traditional functions (HKG, 1965). The government had refrained from developing a welfare state that would cost it money. Furthermore, it was believed that welfare provision could breed dependence and jeopardize people's incentive to work, which resembles the neoconservative tenet of 'moral hazard' (Barry, 1999; George, 1997). The priority of the colonial regime had been on developing the economy. Given that Hong Kong was not naturally endowed with resources, and had a relatively small internal market, these apparently provided the rationale for the government to maintain relatively low tax rates and adopt laissez-faire policies to provide a favorable business environment for local and foreign investors. Thus, social development was subordinated to economic development, which made Hong Kong resemble such East Asian states as Korea, Singapore, and Taiwan, to become a 'developmental state' (Ramesh, 2004; Tang, 2000).

Apart from economic concerns, there was also the pervasiveness of a normative order that sustained anti-welfarism in Hong Kong. As Hong Kong is a Chinese community, there is the influence of traditional Chinese culture, in particular familism, which regards the family as the basic entity that plays the crucial role of caregiving for its members. The traditional virtue of filial piety in particular specifies the younger generation's duty of care for older family members (Chow, 1992). On the other hand, there is also an emphasis on the traditional virtues of self-reliance and self-sufficiency and denigration of dependence on others. Seeking help, to a large extent, should be avoided, or at most, confined to immediate family members or clansmen. There is thus a subtle stigmatization of the concept of seeking welfare from others (Mak and Cheung, 2008), especially with the prevalent Chinese norm of avoiding 'loss of face'.

As a result, there appeared to be concurrence in welfare ideology between the government and the general public in heralding self-reliance and minimal state provision. All in all, government's provision of social welfare had been kept to a minimum and welfare had never been seen as a right for citizens, but rather benevolent acts of the government that people should be thankful for (Tam and Yeung, 1994).

A major 'paradigm shift' in the government's stance on welfare came in the 1970s, which marked the beginning of progressive development, or the 'golden era', of social welfare in Hong Kong. After a major social riot in 1966–1967, the colonial regime began launching massive programs on public housing, health care, free education, and welfare.

This, nonetheless, was made possible by the post-war economic growth that had bestowed on the government sufficient revenues to improve people's living conditions. By the early 1980s, the social welfare system had secured a basic standard of living for all Hong Kong people, and the wide range of service provisions was said to be comparable to other developed societies (Chow, 2003):

> It is also in the 1970s that there was a marked change in the government–NGO interface in local welfare provision. When Hong Kong had gradually become prosperous, there came the gradual shrinkage of overseas funding to the NGOs.

Then, the NGOs had to turn to be reliant upon government funding. It is also in this context that the NGO welfare sector had engaged in a "partnership" relationship with the government in which the government provided funding to the NGOs which delivered professional social work services to the Hong Kong citizenry.

However, times were changing, especially with the rise of neoconservatism worldwide, set against the background of the 'rolling back of the welfare state' in the 1980s with the ascendancy of the Conservative Thatcher administration in the United Kingdom and the Republican Reagan administration in the United States. The Hong Kong government had started to adopt more neoconservative notions in welfare policy and this had significant repercussions in the social work profession as practitioners became subject to pressure from the government through its financial subsidy. Specifically, commencing from the late 1980s, the then colonial administration began adopting privatization strategies, following the British sovereign regime that practiced neoconservativism in social policies. In welfare, the government had started to exercise more stringent control over expenditure. In particular, with the pervasive trend of managerialism, more 'market-oriented' principles had been adopted; these included such notions as the 3Es (i.e., economy, efficiency, effectiveness) and the 3Ms (i.e., market, management, measurement).

Such a trend had been carried over after the turnover of political regime in 1997, when the inaugural administration had basically followed its predecessor in adopting such neoconservative welfare ideology. With respect to its working relationship with the NGOs, the government had assumed an even more predominant role over the nongovernmental welfare sector. The previous scenario in which the government and the NGOs could basically work collaboratively under a 'partnership' relationship turned to be one characterized by the service purchaser–provider dyad. Specifically, the government introduced contracting-out of welfare services in 1999, which aptly manifested such a changed relationship. In fact, the breaking up of the government–NGO collaboration was signified by the abrupt halt in 1998 of the Five-Year Program Plan Review exercise that originally was a platform for NGOs and the government to negotiate and plan in accordance with systematic review of demand and shortfall of welfare services.

Moreover, in 1999, the government also commenced the 'Service Performance Management System' for the NGOs. This reflects the government's adherence to the tenets of 'New Public Administration', especially that of emphasizing 'accountability' in the usage of public funds. In 2001 the government introduced the 'Lump Sum Grant' subvention system in its provision of subsidy to NGOs. This new funding regime signifies the government's shift of monitoring the NGOs from 'input' to 'output' to ensure delivery of quality services. Under this funding system, NGOs are bound by a contractual 'Funding and Service Agreement' to deliver specific service outputs. The emphasis on quantitative output indicators has affected the daily delivery of social services, exerted much pressure on social work practitioners, and to a certain extent affected the professional practitioners' performance of their duties, thus undermining professional autonomy. In another instance, this new funding mode was meant to enable NGOs to have more flexibility in their resource allocation, especially in staff salary and manpower establishment. However, this results in the formal uncoupling of social workers' salaries from the civil service salary scale, which in practice is a reduction of the overall remuneration package for the social workers serving in the NGO. This has resulted in considerable demoralizing amongst the nongovernmental social work community.

Also in 1999, the government instituted a system of competitive bidding in which NGOs have to compete for service contracts from the government. This contracting mechanism has brought instability to service delivery as contracts are usually short-term. In addition, it has spurred intense competition and thereby induced hostility amongst the NGOs, which turned out to be divisive for the welfare sector. It has been commented that the introduction of these managerialist doctrines into the welfare sector could be viewed as the government's attempt at containment of welfare expansion and control over the NGO sector, which could be regarded as operating under a 'statist–corporatist regime' (Lee and Haque, 2006, 2008).

The above review serves to provide the changing context in which social workers perform their professional duties in serving the Hong Kong community. In the following, various pertinent issues related to manpower, service scope, training and education, and development of professional organizations, will be discussed.

Social Work Manpower

Given that Hong Kong has achieved considerable economic development and the government could generate sufficient revenue to finance its social policy provisions, there is a wide range of welfare services in which social workers perform their duties. Thus, there are quite a sizeable number of professional social workers in Hong Kong – as of April 2009, there are a total of 14,460 Registered Social Workers. Similar to other places, there is a majority of female – 71.7 per cent (as compared to 28.3% male) – practitioners, apparently substantiating the usual claim that social work is a 'feminine' occupation. There are more practitioners with degree level of training: 57.7 per cent, while sub-degree level constituted 41 per cent and others 1.3 per cent. A majority of practitioners worked in the NGO sector (58.6%), some 13.1 per cent in the government, and another 28.3 per cent with no information provided. It should suffice to clarify that, some registered social workers may not be actually practising, but they only want to register to acquire such a qualification. Such a distribution should be understood against the background that the Hong Kong government assumes responsibility for providing statutory services – for example, probation and some specific family services – which only take up a relatively small proportion of the entire welfare sector, and that social welfare services are largely provided by NGOs.

Although there is quite a critical mass of social work practitioners in Hong Kong, with the constant supply from training institutes, there have been considerably high wastage and turnover rates over the years, which can be seen in the reports of the Social Work Manpower Requirements System. This system originated from the efforts of a Joint Committee set up in 1987 comprising representatives from the government's Social Welfare Department and the Hong Kong Council of Social Service (2010). The committee provides a platform in which both government and the NGO sector work together in devising a Social Work Manpower Planning System, which from 2005 onwards has been renamed the Social Work Manpower Requirements System.

In fact, social work manpower planning has been a formidable task in Hong Kong. In the first place, the Hong Kong economy is rather volatile as it is subjected to regional and global economic environmental changes, given its small scale of economy and its external-oriented nature. Thus, the labor market is subjected to the booms and bumps of economic performance, which has implications on drawing away trained professional social workers, especially those fresh graduates who might aspire for a more adventurous careers in the business (especially financial) field.

To illustrate, during the late 1980s – when many social work graduates did not enter the profession, leading to a manpower shortage – the government injected money to local training institutes to implement the temporary measure of increasing annual intake to training programs. However, upon the completion of the program, the large number of graduates faced a contracted market in the welfare sector due to reduced manpower wastage (due to economic downturn) and stagnant government expansion of social welfare services. On the other hand, the supply of social work manpower is also subject to the development of higher education. Upon the 1997 handover, the inaugural administration embarked on an ambitious expansion of tertiary education, thus leading to the proliferation of various self-funded, post-secondary programs, including professional social work training degrees and sub-degrees. Thus, although there has been a manpower planning mechanism instituted since the 1980s, there is no mandate for the system to coordinate and control 'demand' (i.e., the government's welfare services and the NGO sector) and 'supply' (i.e., the training institutes). It thus renders the recurrent mismatch of social work manpower demand and supply.

Upon closer examination, it can be seen that the turnover rate of social workers is much higher in the NGO sector than the government's Social Welfare Department, to the magnitude of 10 times in the 2000s (Law, 2009).

One of the possible reasons for this pattern would be the introduction of the Lump Sum Grant system in 2001 that had exerted considerable pressure upon the NGO workers in meeting service requirements in both quantity and quality. This new funding mode has adversely affected the job satisfaction and morale of social work practitioners precipitated by the constellation of such challenges as inadequate resources, heavy workload, long working hours, high staff turnover within agency, and job insecurity (Lai and Chan, 2009).

A local study (Lee, 2008; cited in Lai and Chan, 2009) reveals that job satisfaction is correlated to job security among social workers. Amongst the 1,077 social workers surveyed, those having permanent terms of employment or holding more senior positions indicated higher levels of job satisfaction. The introduction of competitive bidding and contracting of services has resulted in the instability of services as well as job insecurity. Such a situation echoes overseas findings that lower job satisfaction amongst social workers would result in a higher turnover rate (Barak et al., 2001). In turn, high turnover of social workers would adversely affect service quality and elicit service recipients' dissatisfaction (Powell and York, 1992; Fung, 2008).

Scope of Services and Clienteles

Social workers in Hong Kong serve a wide array of clientele: With respect to age, it could range from children, to youth, adults, and the elderly; in terms of the type of problem, it could span family, rehabilitation of people with physical and mental challenges, behavioural problems like addiction and substance abuse, criminal offences, poverty, community disorganization caused by physical dislocation (e.g., urban renewal), and the like. In the mode of operation, social workers may practice in a centre-based, community-based, or 'outreaching' mode, or most recently, an integrated model that incorporates various modes. Nonetheless, most services are still operated in a specialized mode with their respective clienteles, for example, a centre for the elderly. It is only the 'community centre' that provides an integrated arena in which social workers may address community needs holistically and serve a wide spectrum of clients with diverse needs.

With respect to the actual practices, professional social work practitioners in Hong Kong adopt a wide repertoire of practice competencies, including casework, group work, and community work. From the mid-1990s onwards, the government has commenced promoting integrative practices by revamping some preexisting services and setting up integrated service centres. Thus, there has been an increasing trend for social work practitioners to adopt holistic and integrative practices. On the other hand, with the increasingly complex social condition and newly emerged social problems, social work practitioners have to equip themselves with more innovative practices and models. Specifically, with the greater economic and social interface between Hong Kong and China, there are more services catering for the needs of migrants coming from mainland China.

In addition, as Hong Kong is also a cosmopolitan city, there is also increasing ethnic diversity in the population. In this regard, there are also new services tailored to the ethnic minorities in Hong Kong, mostly migrants from South and Southeast Asia. There are also other new, emerging social problems; for instance, addictive behaviours on soft drugs, gambling, the Internet, and the like, that pose challenges to social work practitioners in developing new intervention models and skills.

Development of the Social Work Professional Community and Professional Organizations

Hong Kong has quite a well-established social work professional community, though it only evolved after the change of regime in mainland China in 1949. Before that, traditional philanthropic organizations had served a remarkable function in providing mostly relief services to the local Chinese community.

Upon the communist takeover of the mainland, many of the social service agencies with Western missionary backgrounds moved to Hong Kong, which kickstarted Hong Kong's professional social work development. With a view to achieving better coordination amongst the various voluntary welfare organizations and thus the provision of welfare services, a Committee on Voluntary Emergency Relief Council was established (HKCSS, 2010), which in 1947 became the Hong Kong Council of Social Service (HKCSS), incorporated in 1951. The council has served as a solid foundation for subsequent development and consolidation of the social work profession in Hong Kong, by providing a platform for coordination of welfare services and even a united front for the NGO sector to negotiate with the government in the formulation of welfare policies that have direct implications on social work practice in the territory. As of 2009, the council has more than 370 member agencies that collectively provide over 90 per cent of the social welfare services for the community through their 3,000 service units all over Hong Kong (HKCSS, 2010).

The setting-up of the council also provided an impetus for practicing social workers to form a professional body, the Hong Kong Social Workers' Association (SWA), which was set up in 1949. Unlike the HKCSS, which embraces both agency and individual membership, the SWA only recruits individual members based on their status as practicing social work professionals. However, while the two professional organizations were set up with a view to promoting service provision and professional development, the setting-up of a labor union for the social workers in Hong Kong was coincidental. In 1980, when some social workers, or more accurately, community organizers, were arrested and prosecuted for illegal assembly while they were leading a procession of service recipients carrying petition to the government office, great uproar was aroused within the social workers community. Consequently, the Social Workers' General Union was formed that year to pave the way for fighting for the rights of professional social workers, complementary to the other two professional organizations.

On the verge of the 1997 handover, urged by the Chinese government's pledge that professional bodies established before the handover would be recognized afterwards, the Social Workers' Registration Ordinance was enacted in 1996 and the Social Workers' Registration Board was set up in 1998 to formally commence the licensure of professional practitioners. The board is vested with the authority to oversee matters related to the recognition of professional qualification pertinent to registration, including the power to lay down standards and criteria for accreditation of academic qualifications and professional training programs offered by training institutes both local and overseas.

Before the gradual formalization of the social work profession signified by the sequential establishment of the various professional bodies, social welfare services had previously been provided by charity organizations manned mainly by missionaries, clergymen, expatriate volunteers, and non-trained government officials (Leung, 2010). Since the early 1970s, when the government took over primary responsibility for relief work and social assistance (e.g., the launch of the cash payment of social security), and more significantly, proactively launched various social provisions (e.g., in housing, education, health, and not least, personal welfare), there arose a trend where trained social workers were increasingly employed to provide professional services in a various welfare service settings (ibid.). More crucial still, in 1972 the Hong Kong government first made professional training an entrance requirement for its social work officers. This marks the official recognition of professional training as a prerequisite for performing social work duties. Furthermore, this policy also linked the salary scales of social workers employed in NGOs with their counterparts in the civil service. Thus, this was generally regarded as one of the most important milestones in the professional development of Hong Kong social workers (Chow, 2008).

Social Work Education and Professional Development

Social work education in Hong Kong began in 1950 when the University of Hong Kong began offering the Diploma in Social Studies (postgraduate program) and the Certificate in Social Studies (post-secondary program). The colonial government set up its Social Welfare Department in 1958 and began providing short-term, in-service training programs for its staff. Subsequently a Social Work Training Advisory Committee and the Social Work Training Fund were set up respectively in 1960 in 1961, the latter became the Social Work Training Institute in 1973.

From the 1980s onward, before the 1997 handover of sovereignty, the British colonial administration embarked on large-scale expansion of tertiary education as an attempt to forestall the public's dwindling confidence in the departing regime. As a result, there followed the setting-up of new universities or the conversion of polytechnic colleges to universities. Some of these also expanded their previous sub-degree programs to become degree programs. Currently, as at 2010, there are six universities and nine post-secondary institutes in Hong Kong offering a wide range of professional social work training programs, ranging from sub-degree to undergraduate and postgraduate levels.

While universities in Hong Kong have their own self-accreditation in academic standards, the post-secondary colleges have to be accredited by the Hong Kong Council for Accreditation of Academic and Vocational Qualifications (HKCAAVQ). However, all social work training programs, including both degree and sub-degree levels, have to be accredited by the Social Workers Registration Board. The board will review and accredit (or otherwise) new and existing programs according to its Principles, Criteria and Standards for Recognizing Qualifications, which is constantly reviewed by the board. Graduates of accredited programs from local (and overseas) training institutes could be eligible for registration and thereby use the title of 'registered social worker' (RSW) and practice in Hong Kong. Holders of overseas social work training qualifications have to provide information to the board for ascertaining whether the curriculum of such education programs meet with the aforesaid Principles, Criteria and Standards.

In an attempt to boost social morale upon the historic political transfer of sovereignty, the inaugural regime had to institute policies that could inject elements of stability and the long-term development of the Hong Kong economy. It is also primarily based upon the administration's embracing of a pro-productivist social policy (Holliday, 2000), as well as its recognition of the local Chinese community's emphasis on education, which is conceived as useful to social investment and thus the economy (Chui et al., 2010).

Against such a background, there came the ambitious plan of setting a target of 60 per cent of school-leavers having the chance to pursue post-secondary education. However, the strategy adopted by the government was not one of injecting more money into the higher education sector, but instead one of promoting the opening of self-financed programs by universities and colleges. As a result there has also been a mushrooming of professional social work training at various levels, ranging from associate degree programs to undergraduate and even postgraduate ones. With the increased number of providers and programs, or 'education products' available in the 'education market', this aptly reflects the embracing of neoconservative tenets by the administration in adopting privatization and marketization strategies in the provision of public services including higher education (Mok and Tan, 2004; Chui et al., 2010). This situation could also be conceived as a brand of marketization or even 'Macdonaldization' in higher education (Mok, 1999).

With respect to the evolution of a curriculum, before the setting-up of the Social Workers Registration Board (SWRB), all the training institutes had autonomy in curriculum design and self-accreditation. Following the SWRB's establishment, all training programs aimed at enabling their graduates to be eligible for registration with the SWRB had to be accredited by the board. Thus, each curriculum has to comply with the criteria and standards set by the board. Broadly speaking, all programs, ranging from sub-degree to undergraduate as well as some postgraduate programs, tailored for non–social work first degree holders, have to put in place a curriculum that covers policy, research, social science subjects (including sociology, and psychology at least), social work practice, management, law, and most important of all a prescribed length of supervised practicum.

Basically, all these programs have a 'generalist' orientation or adopt a 'generic' approach that provides basic training to students and prepares them to serve a wide range of clients. This has the merit of enabling the graduates to enter a wide range of service fields.

Furthermore, as many of the social services have adopted an integrated approach, frontline practitioners are actually expected to be able to perform the full range of social work practice, including casework, group work, and community work, and render services at the micro, mezzo, and macro levels. On the other hand, in view of enabling continuing professional development and specialization, local training institutes also offer quite a wide range of postgraduate programs, ranging from diplomas to master's degrees. For instance, such programs may cover special clienteles or service fields, like mental health, gerontology, family, and children; or specific interventions, like family therapy, counseling, social service management, and the like.

As professional social work has originated from a Western, especially largely Anglo-American cultural background, there is a need to address the issue of differences between Western and local Chinese cultural structures. As aforementioned, professional social work education commenced in the late 1960s, teaching staff and materials were very much largely 'imported' from Western countries, especially the United Kingdom and the United States. Over the years, local social work educators and trainers have endeavored to achieve indigenization of the curriculum with the awareness that the Western heritage of social work knowledge and practice has to be localized in the Chinese community of Hong Kong.

As revealed from earlier documentation, the awareness of the need for indigenization originated in the mid-1980s, the impetus of which came from the APASWE (Asia Pacific Association of Social Work Education) Conference in Tokyo in 1986. The conference resolved to set up a Working Group on Relationship with China that was to be based in Hong Kong. This served to kickstart efforts in engaging in exchanges and collaboration between Hong Kong and China that reaffirmed the need for indigenizing social work (Chau, 1995). However, some critical observers cautioned about the possible limitations of merely developing local social work literature written in Chinese, and the mere mechanical adoption or translation of concepts and theories found in overseas (mainly English) literature (Kwong, 1996). Kwong (1996) proposed his notion of developing 'local knowledge' and 'indigenous practice' rather than merely transplanting or translating Western theories that are grounded upon Western cultural normative paradigms that are distinct from Chinese ones. This echoes Midgley's (1981) seminal work that called for the attention and critical awareness of the possible incidence of 'professional imperialism' when Western theories and practice models are mechanically adopted and applied in non-Western countries. Lam (1996) took a sceptical stance on the nature of and efforts towards indigenization in Hong Kong, questioning the ambiguous understanding of 'Chineseness' in Hong Kong's culture and social fabric, upon which discourse on indigenization had evolved. Finally, Tsang (1997) reiterated the need for social work practitioners and educators to be self-critical and reflective in their attempts at using Western theories in the local (Hong Kong Chinese) context.

The local academia also engaged in collaborative efforts with the service sector in their exploration of and efforts towards indigenization. These were grounded on an emphasis on evidence-based practice and research-led teaching. In actual practice, local social work educators have actively collaborated with local NGOs in conducting program evaluation in which such programs are guided by and designed with reference to Western theories and concepts. This vividly illustrates the close partnership between training institutes and service providers in evaluating local services and practices, that in turn is channelled into curriculum design and teaching, thus achieving better indigenization.

In another instance, local social work training institutes, motivated by the mission of serving China as well as expanding their scope of activities, have been venturing into providing professional social work training courses or even degree programs on the mainland since the early 1990s. This may also be conceived as a further step towards indigenization that contributes to enabling Hong Kong social work professionals to serve a much larger Chinese community; that of mainland China.

Apart from the curriculum and issue of indigenization, there are also concerns about pedagogy. This is particularly evident with the mushrooming of professional social work training programs at various levels offered by the training institutes. With the increasing number of academics and trainers, forming a critical mass and constituting positive competition amongst themselves, there are tremendous efforts made and resources deployed in exploring innovative pedagogy. For instance, there have been successful applications of the problem-based learning (PBL) mode of teaching and learning – which has been adopted in the fields of medicine, architecture, and dentistry – in the teaching of social work practice. There is also the popular utilization of information technology or Web-based teaching. Some even explored international collaborative teaching via the Internet.

Furthermore, with the pervasive trend of globalization, there arises the phenomenon of 'homogenization of social policies' (Healy, 2001) in which policies successfully implemented in one country are learned by and adapted in other countries. As a result, local social work training institutes have also ventured into a greater degree of internationalization by engaging in more international collaboration in research and teaching, recruiting overseas academics, and more spectacularly, arranging overseas placements for students. In this latter case, students are exposed to the challenges of multiculturalism and thus enhance their cultural sensitivity for their future practice.

However, though there is a wide spectrum of pre-service professional training programs offered by educational institutes, as well as the provision of in-service training by the government's Social Work Training Centre and NGOs, there is no formal requirement for continuing professional development (CPD) for practitioners in Hong Kong. This is to be contrasted to both other local professions, like doctors, engineers, and lawyers as well as overseas social work counterparts. In the absence of any requirement regarding CPD in the Social Workers Registration Ordinance the Registration Board, which oversees professional registration, does not have a mandate to enforce CPD as a prerequisite for registration or renewal of registration. In fact, the board has launched surveys and forums to solicit views from the professional social work community about the desirability of introducing a mandatory or voluntary CPD scheme. However, repeatedly, there has been an overwhelming majority indicating resistance to mandatory CPD. This is attributable to various reasons, the most significant of which might be the heavy workload and pressure experienced by the frontline practitioners. In fact, the board's study in 2009 reveals that while social workers objected to having mandatory CPD, most of them had actually been engaged in CPD activities on their own initiative (SWRB, 2010).

Diffusion of Hong Kong's Social Work into Mainland China

From the 1990s onwards, even before the handover in 1997, local NGOs had already ventured into exploring service provision in mainland China. The author's earlier study in 1999 found that some 17 NGOs had set up service units or commenced collaborative projects with either the government at various levels or NGOs in 16 provinces in China (Chui, 1999). Amongst the 12 agencies that were interviewed, one commenced its service in China in the 1970s, three in the 1980s, and eight in the 1990s. Most recently, with the increasing awareness and recognition of the indispensable role of a professional social work service in tackling emerging social problems, there could be a potential demand for some 3 million social workers in the whole country (CASW, 2008).

There has been a burgeoning of setting-up or reinstituting social work schools or departments at universities. Some municipal governments even made bold attempts, probably modelled on the Hong Kong government's strategy of 'purchasing' services from, or providing subsidies to, Hong Kong NGOs, to commence service provision in various cities. For instance, after the Sichuan earthquake in 2008, a Hong Kong NGO was invited to set up a centre in Sichuan to provide rehabilitation services for the victims who suffered from various kinds of physical injury. In another instance, the city of Shenzhen, the city with the second highest GDP in China, commissioned a Hong Kong NGO to provide a community mental health project in 2009, largely using the 'Hong Kong model' of service delivery.

It is to be reckoned that, through the author's contact with government officials and service operators throughout the years, there appears to be a perception amongst the policymakers and operators that, since Hong Kong is a Chinese community that has already experimented with localization and indigenization of Western, empirically proven models of professional social work practice, China should embrace the Hong Kong model of social work readily.

Nonetheless, with years of experience in providing training in China, the author takes a sceptical view of this perception and would hope that colleagues in mainland China will leave sufficient room for further indigenization of Hong Kong's model with due consideration of China's own specific context; especially in view of the great diversity exhibited amongst the urban and rural, as well as coastal and inland regions.

Roles and Image of Social Workers

The classic literature on the roles of a social worker, contains a wide range of roles, from activist, advocate, counselor, enabler, and facilitator, to mediator, organizer, and trainer. However, from the more critical social work literature, there can be seen a dichotomous role differentiation between a 'social control agent' and a 'social change agent'. The former denotes the conventional roles of social workers in welfare provision to the destitute, thus largely playing a remedial role to alleviate the casualties of social problems. This could be seen as working on a relatively micro or individual level. The latter, on the contrary, apparently is more concerned with tackling the root causes of social problems related to deprivation, social injustice, and so on that are rooted in socioeconomic, cultural, political, or grossly institutional factors. Social workers are there to rectify social ills by inducing change at a macro level. In Hong Kong, social workers also exhibit this whole array of different roles that characterize their counterparts in other parts of the world.

Nonetheless, there is a certain degree of confusion amongst the local citizenry between 'social worker' and 'volunteer', as the Chinese words for the two appear to be quite similar. That explains why social work students at universities have been telling their teachers that they might have been subjected to their parental dissuasion regarding social work as a subject as their parents perceive 'volunteers' as generating no income.

In another instance, a social worker is highly regarded by the general public as someone doing 'good deeds' for others, again, to a certain extent due to the aforementioned confusion with 'volunteers' and also due to the general impression portrayed in mass media that social workers are committed to helping the poor, the sick, and the destitute. Thus, when Hong Kong embarked on 'democratic opening' in the 1980s with the introduction of district level popular elections, many of the candidates who happened to be social workers – or using the title 'social worker' (as it was only after the enactment of the Social Workers Registration Ordinance in 1997 that the improper use of the title was made illegal) – got elected. It should also be understood against this background that before the introduction of such local-level elections many of the social workers, especially community organizers, had assisted many clients in deprived communities to get benefits in terms of improvement in housing, social services, and the like. The social workers in general, and community workers in particular, have proven their efficacy in fighting for justice, benefiting the people and society at large, and thus won the people's general trust and confidence.

As revealed in a local study, social workers in Hong Kong generally have a positive image amongst local citizens, as a profession that looks after the deprived and disadvantaged. They are also seen as bringing hope and confidence to those being helped, enhancing their determination to tackle their problems. However, social workers could only secure the trust of slightly more than half of the respondents (53%), which was lower than doctors (76%) and nurses (63%) (Wong and Leung, 2005). There is apparently the need for the local social work community to portray a clear and positive image amongst the public that is of paramount importance for social worker practitioners to work effectively with their clients (LeCroy and Stinson, 2004).

A special note should be given to the political role played by social workers in Hong Kong that is contextualized in Hong Kong's political development in recent decades. As revealed in Chui and Gray's (2004) historical review of Hong Kong's development from the postwar period to the near present, it could be postulated that the socioeconomic and political development of Hong Kong society has provided a fertile social context for the development of social workers' participation in politics in Hong Kong. There had been a gradual shift from the service role to that of participating in informal and then formal channels of political participation.

There are three distinctive roles played by the social work community: first, social workers emerged from a service-oriented profession; then they increasingly played a policy advocacy role working through informal channels; eventually they evolved to take up a cogently political role by utilizing the formal channels of election and political representation in district councils and the legislature. These three different roles, according to Chui and Gray (2004: 179) are neither mutually exclusive nor conflicting with one another. This evolution of the 'politicization of social workers' (Chui, 1989), is essentially a manifestation of the dialectical relationship between Hong Kong's political evolution and the social functions of the social work profession, which in itself is contextualized as a natural evolution of the increasing role of government intervention in social policies, and the sudden politicization of society at large induced by the political changeover in 1997 (Chui and Gray, 2004).

Concluding Remarks

The development of the social work profession in Hong Kong is contextualized against the background of the evolution of social welfare, which in turn has been juxtaposed in the complex socioeconomic, cultural, and political changes over the span of Hong Kong's unique transformation from a British colony to a Special Administrative Region under China. Before the government took a proactive stance in welfare provision, the NGO sector, based on its lineage with overseas, charitable, and religious organizations, had been able to enjoy autonomy in service innovation. Upon the government's assumption of a benevolent state in welfare provision, albeit by no means a 'welfare state' per se, but largely under a residual or productivist model of welfare, the NGOs had increasingly been subjected to the government's control in both finance and service accountability. This is particularly evident with the ascendancy of tenets of neoconservative, managerialism, and New Public Administration since the 1980s.

As Hong Kong's professional social work community has been largely working under government subsidy, it has thus been subjected to the control and pressure brought about by such changes in funding and managerial regime. On the other hand, professional education and training has similarly been subject to the influence of marketization in which training institutes have to develop more self-funded training programs and produce more social work graduates at various levels, ranging from sub-degree to postgraduate degrees. With the greater interface between Hong Kong and China upon reunification in 1997, there is increasingly more 'Chineseness' in the social work profession.

In fact, Hong Kong has rightly served the function of indigenizing 'Western' knowledge and practices in a Chinese community. Specifically, services have to cater for Chinese migrants in Hong Kong, agencies have to venture into working in mainland China, and social work education institutes have to collaborate with their mainland counterparts in diffusion social work training in China.

The social work profession in Hong Kong is well-placed in a strategic position in serving a Chinese community that embodies a significant portion of the world's population. Building upon past successes in indigenizing a largely

Western profession, the Hong Kong social work profession could be able to enable China, an emerging world power and increasingly active member of the global community, to be better prepared in facing up to the various challenges ahead.

References

Aspalter, C. (2006), The East Asian Welfare Model, *International Journal of Social Welfare*, Vol. 15, pp. 290–301.

Barak, M.E., Nissly, J.A., and Levin, A. (2001), Antecedents to Retention and Turnover Among Child Welfare Social Work, and Other Human Service Employees: What Can We Learn from Past Research? A Review and Meta-Analysis, *Social Service Review*, Vol. 75, pp. 625–61.

Barry, N. (1999), Neoclassicism, the New Right and British Social Welfare, in *British Social Welfare in the Twentieth Century*, edited by R.M. Page and R.L. Silburn. New York: St. Martin's Press.

Chau, K. (1995), Social Work Practice in a Chinese Society: Reflections and Challenges, *Hong Kong Journal of Social Work*, Vol. 29, No. 2, pp. 1–8.

China Association of Social Workers (CASW) (2008), Professionalization of Social Workers to Tackle Manpower Problem (in Chinese), http://www.cncasw.org/sgrc/zysppj/200812/t20081203_8187.htm.

Chow, N.W.S. (1992), Family Care of the Elderly in Hong Kong, in *Family Care of the Elderly: Social and Cultural Changes*, edited by J.L. Kosberg. London: Sage.

Chow, N.W.S. (2003), New Economy and New Social Policy in East and Southeast Asian Compact, Mature Economies: The Case of Hong Kong, *Social Policy and Administration*, Vol. 37, No. 4, pp. 411–22.

Chow, N.W.S. (2008), Social Work in Hong Kong: Western Practice in a Chinese Context, *China Journal of Social Work*, Vol. 1, No. 1, pp. 23–35.

Chui, E. (1999), Hong Kong Social Service Agencies Operating Services in China, research report, Department of Social Work and Social Administration, Hong Kong: University of Hong Kong.

Chui, E. (2007), The State of Welfare in Hong Kong, in *The State of Social Welfare in Asia*, edited by C. Aspalter, A. Aldosary, A. Dashkina, and S. Singh. Hong Kong: Casa Verde.

Chui, E. and Gray, M. (2004), The Political Activities of Social Workers in the Context of Changing Roles and Political Transition in Hong Kong, *International Journal of Social Welfare*, Vol. 13, No. 2, pp. 170–80.

Chui, E., Tsang, S., and Mok, J. (2010), After the Handover in 1997: Development and Challenges for Social Welfare and Social Work Profession in Hong Kong, *Asia Pacific Journal of Social Work and Development*, Vol. 20, No. 1, pp. 52–64.

Fung, H.L. (2008), Professional Direction and Service Qualities: Reflection on Social Work Professionalization, in *Bridging Theories and Practices: Reflection on Social Work*, edited by L.C. Leung and K.F. Chan. Hong Kong: Chinese University Press (in Chinese).

George, V. (1997), The Decline of Europe Welfare State, *Hong Kong Journal of Social Work*, Vol. 30, No. 2, pp. 7–17.

Healy, L.M. (2001), *International Social Work: Professional Action in an Interdependent World*. New York; Oxford: Oxford University Press.

Holliday, I. (2000), Productivist Welfare Capitalism: Social Policy in East Asia, *Political Studies*, Vol. 48, pp. 706–23.

Hong Kong Council of Social Service (HKCSS) (2010), Brief History about HKCSS. http://www.hkcss.org.hk/abt_us/index_e.asp#.

Hong Kong Government (HKG) (1965), *Aims and Policy of Social Welfare in Hong Kong*.Hong Kong: Government Printer.

Kwong, W.M. (1996), Local Knowledge, Indigenous Practice: Linking the Cultural, the Personal, and the Professional in Social Work Practice, *Hong Kong Journal of Social Work*, Vol. 30, No. 1, pp. 22–30.

Lai, W.H.F. and Chan, K.T.T. (2009), Social Work in Hong Kong: From Professionalization to 'Reprofessionalization,' *China Journal of Social Work*, Vol. 2, No. 2, pp. 95–108.

Lam, C.W. (1996), Indigenization of Social Work Values in Hong Kong: A Brief Review, *Hong Kong Journal of Social Work*, Vol. 30, No. 1, pp. 10–21.

Law, C.K. (2009), Wastage of Social Worker Manpower: A Grave Concern, newsletter, Social Workers Registration Board, Hong Kong.

LeCroy, C.W. and Stinson, E.L. (2004), The Public's Perception of Social Work: Is It What We Think It Is?, *Social Work*, Vol. 49, No. 2, pp. 164–74.

Lee, E.W.K. (2008), *Study on the Impact of New Public Management Reform on Government Funded Non-Profit Organization*. Hong Kong: University of Hong Kong.

Lee, E.W.Y. and Haque, M.S. (2006), The New Public Management Reform and Governance in Asian NICs: A Comparison of Hong Kong and Singapore, *Governance: An International Journal of Policy, Administration, and Institutions*, Vol. 19, No. 4, pp. 605–26.

Lee, E.W.Y. and Haque, M.S. (2008), Development of the Nonprofit Sector in Hong Kong and Singapore: A Comparison of Two Statist-Corporatist Regimes, *Journal of Civil Society*, Vol. 4, No. 2, pp. 97–112.

Leung, J. (2010), An Overview, in *Stepping Up to the Challenge: Celebrating the 60th Anniversary of Social Work Education at the University of Hong Kong*, edited by J. Leung. Hong Kong: University of Hong Kong.

Mak, W.W.S. and Cheung, R.Y.M. (2008), Affiliate Stigma among Caregivers of People with Intellectual Disability or Mental Illness, *Journal of Applied Research in Intellectual Disabilities*, Vol. 21, pp. 532–45.

McLaughlin, E. (1993), Hong Kong: A Residual Welfare Regime, in *Comparing Welfare States*, edited by A. Cochrane and J. Clarke. London: Sage.

Midgley, J. (1981) *Professional Imperialism: Social Work in the Third World*. London: Heinemann

Mok, K.H. (1999), The Cost of Managerialism: The Implications for the 'McDonaldization' of Higher Education in Hong Kong, *Journal of Higher Education Policy and Management*, Vol. 21, No. 1, pp. 117–27.

Mok, K.H. and Tan, J. (2004), *Globalization and Marketization in Education.* Cheltenham, UK: Edward Elgar.

Powell, M.J. and York, R.O. (1992), Turnover in Country Public Welfare Agencies, *Journal of Applied Social Sciences*, Vol. 16, No. 2, pp. 111–27.

Ramesh, M. (2004), *Social Policy in East and Southeast Asia: Education, Health Housing and Income Maintenance.* London: Routledge-Curzon.

SWRB, Social Work Registration Board (2010), statistics, http://www.swrb.org. hk/EngASP/statistic_e.asp.

Tam, T.S.K. and Yeung, S. (1994), Community Perception of Social Welfare and Its Relations to Familism, Political Alienation and Individual Rights: The Case of Hong Kong, *International Social Work*, Vol. 37, No. 1, pp. 47–60.

Tang, K.L. (2000), *Social Welfare Development in East Asia*. Basingstoke: Palgrave.

Tsang, N.M. (1997), Examining the Cultural Dimension of Social Work Practice: The Experience of Teaching Students on a Social Work Course in Hong Kong, *International Social Work*, Vol. 40, No. 2, pp. 133–44.

Wong, Y.C. and Leung, J.C.B. (2005), *Report on Opinion Survey on Image of Social Workers in Hong Kong*, Hong Kong: Institute of Social Service Development, Department of Social Work and Social Administration, University of Hong Kong.

Chapter 6
Social Work in Thailand

Kitipat Nontapattamadul

Development of social work as a profession in Thailand is closely related to the development of social welfare. According to the Social Welfare Promotion Act, B.E. 2546 (2003) and 2550 (2007), 'social welfare' means the social services system pertaining to the prevention, remedy, development, and promotion of social security in satisfaction of the basic minimum needs of the people to enable a good quality of life and self-reliance. Furthermore, according to this act, social welfare should be a system which is extensive, appropriate, fair, and in accordance with standards in terms of education, health, housing, occupation and income, recreation, the justice process, and general social services and that takes account of human dignity and the people's entitlement to rights and participation in the provision of social welfare on every level. However, by observing the history of Thai welfare systems, various interpretations have emerged. They relate to changing social, political, and economic conditions over time. The interpretations also influence the meanings of 'social work profession'.

Residualism: A Mainstream Welfare Model in Thailand

The history of Thai social welfare reflects the fundamental beliefs of the main developmental strategies of the country. Social welfare has been determined by the development concepts that fed economic growth since 1957 when the International Bank for Reconstruction and Development (IBRD or World Bank) consultants suggested that Thailand establish a National Economic Plan. Since 1957, the main development strategies have emphasized rapid economic growth. Those who gained national administrative power expressed the very least concern for the welfare of the people. Believing strongly in the trickle-down effect, the interpretation of social welfare as well as the meaning of social work was limited for the sake of maximizing economic growth (cf., e.g., Nontapattamadul, 2011; Nontapattamadul and Cheecharoen, 2008; Sungkawan, 2002; Phongvivat, 2009).

That is why Thailand has the latest social insurance act among the East and Southeast Asian nations (Hort, and Kuhnle, 2000). The more the administrative powers believed in the notion of accelerated economic growth, the narrower the interpretation of social welfare as well as the meaning of social work became. Society at large, in addition, was shaped to understand social work roles merely as a relief function.

The narrow interpretations of social welfare and social work were accompanied by negligence of social justice. The poor were considered only when they were unable to adjust to the market economy. Lots of the poor were socially vulnerable, prone to be criminals or sex workers, but if they had been protected appropriately by the social welfare mechanism, they might be far from these difficult circumstances. If social work had a broader meaning, they might have been able to access a professional service that promoted their rights and dignities.

As a matter of fact, Thailand almost had a welfare scheme as early as 1932; proposed by Pridi Banomyong, the leader of the civilian faction in the Siamese Revolution. On 24 June 1932, 'Khana Ratsadon' the tiny People's Party carried out a lightening coup that abruptly ended 150 years of absolute monarchy under the Chakri dynasty. Pridi proposed an economic plan for the Thai nation which was intended to create an assurance of well-being for every Thai, which could have been the first step in establishing a Thai welfare state. It was unfortunate that those in power criticized the plan as a Bolshevic idea and stirred the fear of communism. The plan thus was rejected at the very beginning.

If the Thai people had really understood Pridi's intention to gradually establish a welfare state, they might by now have had a welfare state such as many European countries do. The social work profession in Thailand might have been recognized in the same way as in those European countries.

Social Welfare: The Big Burden from the Eyes of Elites

From the first national economic development plan in 1961 to today, most of Thais enjoyed an economic boom. The country even became known as the 'economic miracle' or the 'Fifth Tiger of Asia' during General Chatichai Choonhavan's government. However, the government gave little priority to the welfare of the people as most of the workforce was in the informal sector, self-employed, or worked in agriculture, and the government hesitated to protect wage-earners from insecurity. Also because of the uncertain of international trade and the world economy, Thailand could hardly have afforded social security that covered everyone. The bureaucratic elites believed that arranging social welfare would be too much of a burden on the national budget and would worsen public debt.

Thai welfare has depended mainly on the market. If the market failed to provide welfare to people, the government passed their concerns to the traditional safety nets – families and kinship, village communities, Buddhist temples, religious groups, and charities, as well as patron-client relationships were substituted as welfare providers before any government intervention (Schramm, 2003; Tonguthai, 1986). Compared to other East Asian and Southeast Asian countries, Thailand is the last to benefit from social security (Hort and Kuhnle, 2000; Ramesh, 2001).

The First Effective Step in 1990: A Long Struggle for the Social Insurance Act

In 1954, under Field Marshall Pibunsongkram's administration, the Thai Parliament approved a Social Insurance Act covering six contingencies: maternity, sickness, incapacity, childcare, old age, and death. The law was heavily attacked by different groups and never implemented (Sungkawan, 1992). Between 1981 and 1988, there were some attempts to draft a social security bill, but not strong enough to get one into Parliament. However, the economic boom and the political conditions put pressure on General Chatichai Choonhavan's government to put a draft social insurance bill to Parliament in 1988. Most of the senate opposed the law. Parliament however unanimously passed the Social Insurance Act on 11 July 1990. This was an historic event, for its long journey marked the first step of a changing trend towards institutionalized social welfare.

After the 1997 Financial Crisis: A New Move to Welfare or Just a Populist Model?

In July 1997, the financial crisis weakened the Thai economy as well as the social well-being of the people. Many lost their jobs unexpectedly and a lot of people in the middle class abruptly became poor. Unemployment benefits were supposed to provide for them, according to the Social Insurance Act, but its activation had been postponed – there was no social safety net to protect them. Moreover, the government reduced the welfare and social services budgets more than half.

The International Monetary Fund (IMF) prescribed a series of measures to make the government change its policy by increasing expenditure on education, health, and social services. People on low-incomes were provided with free medical care. The government also tried to create more jobs in the public sector, undertook infrastructure development, backed vocational training and gave financial support to small businesses. These efforts, however, were too little, too late, and the government was unable to prevent a great number of Thai from falling into poverty.

In 1998 Thaksin Shinawatra founded the populist Thai Rak Thai (TRT) party in 1998, which won a historic election in 2001. Thaksin became Prime Minister and was the country's first PM to serve a full term. He introduced a range of innovations in government policies which were highly popular because they helped reduce poverty by half in four years. He launched, for instance, the nation's first universal health-care scheme – the 30-baht scheme: village-managed microcredit development funds, low-interest agricultural loans, direct injections of cash into village development funds (the SML scheme), and the One Tambon One Product (OTOP) scheme.

Thaksin's economic policies helped Thailand recover from the 1997 Asian Financial Crisis and substantially reduce poverty. GDP grew from 4.9 trillion baht in 2001 to 7.1 trillion baht in 2006 and Thailand repaid its debt to the IMF two years ahead of schedule. From the social welfare standpoint, the Thaksin administration gave more concern to people's social well-being. Although some scholars have pointed out that he had no interest in land reform, land for small farmers programs, tax reforms, or other policies to shift the structural position of peasants within the national economy, the residual model has been less emphasized.

The King's Philosophy of Sufficiency Economy: An Alternative Welfare

Sufficiency economy is a philosophy that was invented by King Bhumipol during the Cold War and the communist insurgency in the northeastern part of Thailand. The king noted that part of the problem of Thailand's lack of unity was selfish capitalism, which lacked morality and was by nature divisive. Capitalism is dangerous since it tends to deny reward to the hardest workers or the decent people who perform their duty. It rather benefits those who take advantage of others, and this damaged the nation's unity.

The king remarked that greedy traders and land speculators who took advantage of peasants 'may be on [the] side of terrorists'. He further suggested that rural development should be carried out with a high degree of ability, wisdom, and intelligence coupled with honesty without any thought of financial gain (SEAS, 2013).

The king's remarks are reflected in the Tenth National Economic and Social Development Plan (2007–2011), which set the target of reducing poverty from 13 per cent in 2004 to 4 per cent by 2011. It also targets a ratio of the richest quintile to the poorest quintile of no more than 10 times.

Very much inspired by King Bhumipol's self-sufficiency approach, the development plan also emphasized implementation of the 'Good Living and Happiness Society Strategy', which consists of five development plans:

1. a sufficiency economy plan aimed at building up knowledge and creating occupational skills;
2. a community development and opportunity creation plan focusing on reducing household expenditure (e.g., use of organic fertilizer and vegetable home gardening) and creating market opportunities for community products;
3. a rehabilitation plan for natural resources;
4. a vulnerable people and senior citizen assistance plan; and
5. a provision plan for basic services (e.g., health, education, and vocational training).

The plans will be implemented through projects jointly designed and implemented by community leaders, local governments, provincial governments, and the central government (SEAS, 2013).

The king's philosophy of sufficiency economy is an alternative welfare practice and has implications for change as it affects the well-being of all Thais. Its emergence and practice are also relevant to what Anthony Giddens, a proponent of the New Left model of the welfare state in Europe, called 'welfare pluralism' (Giddens, 2001).

The 2009–2010 Crisis: A Reduction of Inequalities or Even More Populist?

When the Thaksin administration was toppled by the bloodless military coup on 19 September 2006, the constitution was rewritten at the generals' behest, to give

Abhisit Vejjajiva and the Democrat Party a better chance of winning. To their dismay, Abhisit lost again in the general election on 23 December 2007. He finally came to power after the Constitutional Court of Thailand's removal of (1) PM Samak Sundaravej in 2008 for 'vested interests', that is, taking a salary from a cooking show while still PM, and (2) PM Somchai Wongsawat for his involvement in the scandal as one of PPP's executive board members. *Time Online* made a comment that Abhisit Vejjajiva might be a decent man but his disreputable route to government power does not inspire confidence (TO, 2013).

Abhisit and his Democrat Party attacked the former government for its populist policies but he also promised many populist policies including free education, textbooks, milk, and supplemental foods for nursery school students, and increasing the minimum wage.

Abhisit and his government launched most of the policies in response to the crisis but they are directed towards short-term needs and shoring up the economy. Without hesitation, Abhisit injected monetary aid into the system in order to generate domestic consumption that would relieve the pain of domestic producers and consumers. Certainly, there is a degree of copycatting of the economic and social policies initiated by Thaksin and then continued by the Democrat government. However, there is no measurement nor any mechanism to sustain the fiscal injections. There is also less concern about redistribution for strengthening the well-being of the Thai people or new economic growth.

A researcher director from TDRI (Thailand Development Research Institute) who pointed out that Thai social security is used as a political gain produced evidence to back her analysis by referring to the way that some better-off people have also benefited from the elderly allowance program. During the TRT period, the number of eligible elderly rose from 400,000 to 1 million but before the TRT could extend the program to cover all elderly people nationwide, the party faced its demise. In 2009 the Democrats, took the opportunity to extend the benefits to all (TDRI, 2013).

Professor Johannes Dragsbæk Schmidt commented that in response to the 2009–2010 crisis, Abhisit came up with an economic stimulation package meant to protect its economy and stimulate the consumption rate of low-income groups but it is hardly sufficient. It appears that there are many structural problems in the Thai economy which need to be addressed. These problems are of a more long-term nature related to improved quality of education, upgrading skills, increasing taxation (particularly of the rich), and the implementation of pro-poor policies – the last could be in the form of redistribution of wealth and the establishment of social welfare entitlements (SEAS, 2013).

With scholars being sceptical of the copycat populist policy, Abhisit has expressed the need to give all Thais basic social security. He has announced universal social welfare as a national agenda and Welfare For All in 2017 is planned to cover four pillars: social security, public welfare, social assistance, and social partnership strengthening and promotion.

The Mixing Systems within Thai Social Welfare

From the Thaksin Shinawatra administration (2001–2006) to the present, the populist policies have been the significant strategies of government, from Abhisit Vejjajiva's Democrat Party (2009–2011) to Yingluck Shinawatra (Thaksin's youngest sister – 2011 to present). The populist trend might be a political gain by its nature. However, it helped to lessen residual feature of social work in Thailand. In the meantime, many scholars propose the idea of a social democratic approach; a number of NGOs and social activists have recommended alternative welfare approaches and a number of local communities now practice microfinance, self-help, and self-reliance approaches.

Thailand increasingly embraces the significance of 'social welfare for all'. The mainstream welfare services are provided by government while the alternative streams support local administrations, nongovernmental organizations (NGOs), business sectors, volunteers, and the general public's participation in social welfare arrangements. The trend is to call for 'welfare pluralism', with social work practices incorporated into all three systems of Thai social security:

1. The welfare service systems as are valued as citizens' rights, which are clearly mentioned in the Constitution of the Kingdom of Thailand B.E. 2550 (2007). These systems are, for example, Health Insurance for All, Compulsory Education for All, and so on.
2. The Social Security system which provides full social insurance, and is extending to informal workers. In addition, private insurance is also increasing its activities and there is a trend towards grass-root savings groups in many communities, many of which have moved into welfare provision for community members.
3. Social Assistance, which provides a series of services to many groups of people. These have been arranged by GOs and NGOs or even some business firms in the light of Corporate Social Responsibility (CSR).

These three main systems are expected to integrate or link to each other. Social work practices within these systems also put greater effort into increasing the use of case management. Besides, political parties express their enthusiasm about social welfare and social work practice. During the last general election in December 2007, all of the political parties paid much more attention to social welfare and social work. Some parties even announced clearly in public, 'Thai people! We need a welfare state!' A number of university scholars and former senators propose adopting a classical welfare state. Others debate 'welfare society' versus 'welfare pluralism'.

Social Work in Thai Values

The term 'social work' in the Thai language '*sungkom songkhrau*' has many layers of meaning. From the very subtle layer, it refers to 'relief', which connotes a unique set of patron–client values and the delicate hierarchical nature of the Thai social structure – the patron–client and hierarchical values of Thailand have their roots in ancient history. The deeper meanings, interpreted in Buddhist terminology, range from 'assistance' and 'solidarity' to 'integration'.

The Thai social work practitioners and educators followed the deeper sets of meaning but the majority of Thai people, unfortunately, hold to the subtle rather than the deeper one. The original intention of the social work profession was to join with the creation social welfare services as one of the political strategies of that time. Furthermore, the subtle understanding of the meaning of 'social work' is strongly compatible with the uniqueness of Thai political culture and democratic development.

As Thai social structure is hierarchical in its nature so the Thai bureaucratic system is very powerful and controls all professions: medical doctors, engineers, architects, and scientists all become bureaucrats (Mongkolnchaiarunya, 2009). Bureaucratic values often support the career achievement of an individual social work professional to a greater degree than her/his own professional strengths, and senior social workers therefore become project/office administrators rather than remain professional practitioners.

In everyday life, the patron–client system embraces every level of Thai society and influences the mentality of politicians and senior administrators who have less commitment to empowerment, self-help, and the development model of intervention. They prefer 'relief' to 'release' intervention and prefer to give material service or a gift to potential voters instead of encouraging target groups to be able to help themselves or create mutual help systems gradually. In the meantime the Thai people, particularly the disadvantaged, are pragmatic – they are not keen on long-term visions, goals, systematic planning, and continuous working processes (Heim, 1981, cited in Mongkolnchaiarunya, 2009).

The Origin of Social Work in Thailand

The origin of professional social work stemmed from the nationalistic ideology of Prime Minister Field Marshal Phibunsongkram in 1938. The policy, intentionally, was to create public support and strengthen the Thai state as an institution upon which the Thai people could depend. The establishment of the Department of Public Welfare (DPW) in 1944 is evidence of the government attempts to do this – the DPW was the government agency in which most social workers worked.

At present, there are approximately 2,600 social workers scattered around government social welfare agencies, including local administration. The rest include those who work in related practices such as community development workers, social development workers, and probation officers, as well as those who work in NGOs. Regarding the social work profession in NGOs, a large number of those who work as social workers do not have any degree in social work – there is no law or regulation which declares that social workers have to complete their degree from a school of social work. The NGOs in social welfare, therefore, can choose to employ anyone from any educational background to work in their agency. There are approximately 200 professional social workers in NGOs.

Laws Related to Strengthening Social Work Practices

In the last decade, social work practices in Thailand have gained great support from related social laws.

The Criminal Procedure Amendment Act (No. 20) (1999) mentions clearly the mandate of social workers in the interviewing of those who are under 18 years of age in criminal procedures. The Social Welfare Promotion Act (2003) and the Social Welfare Promotion Act (Amendment) (2007) encourage every sector to participate in social welfare services covered by, among others, the Child Protection Act 2003, the Elderly Person Act 2003, Domestic Violence Victim Protection Act 2007, Mental Health Act 2008, and the Anti-Trafficking in Persons Act 2008. There are more than 10 acts for facilitating social workers in working with various diversity groups. The Ministry of Social Development and Human Security has established at least five social resource funds to support practice and service delivery to a variety of social beneficiaries.

Regarding social work practice in NGOs, there are around 32,000 foundations, associations, and other organizations and the government has a duty to promote these organizations, businesses, volunteers, and so on to arrange social welfare services. They are all eligible to propose social welfare projects to be funded by the government. In fact, social welfare services are not provided only by government agencies but also by the local community, business sector, and civil society. The business sector can claim welfare services delivered to employees and society as corporate social responsibility (CSR) activities.

Social Work Licence and Professional Association

Although, the social work profession was established in 1942, a professional license is still not a reality. On 22 March 2010, the Cabinet of Abhisit Vejjajiva approved the Social Work Licence Bill – this is the most progress the profession's attempt has made. At present, the bill is under the scrutiny of the Office of Legislative and Judicial Board before being put to Parliament for approval. The licence process is still on the long and winding road.

Mongkolnchaiarunya (2009) contends that the main obstacle to issuing a Social Work Licence Law is the fundamental values deep in Thai society – the unique patron–client values which are culturally embedded in Buddhist practices. He points out that 95 per cent of Thai people are Buddhists. Giving food and providing help to the needy are believed to be good things that Buddhists should do. So, there is a kind of sharing among Thais in the local communities which indicates that the society/community naturally is able to provide a social safety net for its members and professional social work is not significant to the structure.

The Thai terms for 'social work' and 'social assistance' are confusing. At the top of the Thai social structure, social services, social assistance, or relief activities are rendered by the higher status politicians and the rich. As there is a channel for layman to receive royal medals by providing social services to the needy, many people enthusiastically demonstrate their good will by sharing their wealth. They also are called 'social workers' in Thai.

Meanwhile, a number of social activists and development workers who mostly work in advanced NGOs, and whose performance should be regarded as proactive social work activities, refuse to call themselves 'social workers'. They prefer to be community development workers and often express their intention to exclude and distance their work from the social work domain. Some of them even show negative attitudes towards 'social work' when speaking in public. This pattern exists alongside and parallels the mainstream charitable concept of social work.

The social work professional organization in Thailand, the Social Workers Association of Thailand (SWAT), was established in 1958. In 2009, SWAT had 1,170 members of which approximately 10 per cent are social work degree holders. The administration team is elected every two years and most of the presidents have been senior officials in the Ministry of Social Development and Human Security. The association hardly takes any significant role in social work and the development of social welfare and is now operating on a deficit as a result of lack of income from membership fees or other fundraising projects. The current president, Associate Professor Apinya Wechayachai, is working hard to activate the association by developing an internal communication system and submitting training proposals to the national social welfare fund. This proposed program is useful for social work professional development and will help generate some income for the association.

Although a social work licence is still not a reality, the social work profession has been acknowledged to some degree by the government. The Civil Service Commission (CSC), which has the mandate to identify and validate all professions that can be recruited to work as civil servants, has announced that 'social worker' is such a position, and qualification requirements and a job description are also clearly stated. Due to the scarcity of graduates from the social work field in the past, persons with sociology and psychology backgrounds will be accepted as social workers. A social development degree is included but high-ranking social workers are often promoted to lead social welfare units as administrators and thus stop working as social workers.

Strengths and Opportunities in Social Work Profession

The 10th National Economic and Social Development Plan for 2007–2011 declares continuity from the eighth and ninth plans focusing on the 'human as the center of development' and His Majesty the King's Philosophy of Sufficiency Economy. The interpretation and implications of these two significant concepts are much more in-depth and practical, which reflects how the tenth plan is likely to cover social development to a greater extent than former plans. This would be a great opportunity for social workers to revise, review, and rethink generating a more advanced movement towards professional development.

The 1st Five Years Strategic Plan of Thai Social Welfare for 2007–2011 parallels the 10th National Plan. The Strategic Plan was drafted by the National Commission on Social Welfare Promotion and, if properly set up, should also encourage the professional development of social work.

Social work scholars and practitioners also are enthusiastic about raising the standard of social work practice to the higher levels of profession. In addition, they are aware of the important role of volunteers in social welfare as they proactively strengthen community welfare, which has great potential in the areas of social and human capital.

Last but not least, the schools of social work in Thailand have adjusted their education programs frequently with the intention of developing social work education proactively. Collaboration between educators and practitioners is well-established and this will have a positive effect on the social work profession in Thailand.

Conclusion

Social work and social welfare development in Thailand share the same path. The movement from mainstream residualism towards welfare pluralism is the current trend. There are many ways to interpret social work values in Thailand as a result of Thai social structure, which is uniquely hierarchical in nature and has significantly influenced both the traditional and narrower meanings of 'social work' in the Thai language.

At the same time, the genuine and broader meanings of social work are addressed among scholars and professional social workers. There are many ways to interpret social work values in Thailand. The positive trend of the social work profession is evidenced by (1) increasing laws related to strengthening social work practices, (2) the government trend towards universal social welfare by 2017, and (3) attempts to promote the social work licence law among professional organizations and social work schools.

References

Giddens, A. (2001), Introduction, in *The Global Third Way Debate*, edited by A. Giddens. Cambridge: Polity.

Hort, S.E.O. and Kuhnle, S. (2000), The Coming of East and Southeast Asian Welfare States, *Journal of European Social Policy*, Vol. 10, No. 2, pp. 162–84.

Mongkolnchaiarunya, J. (2009), Social Work Education and Profession in Thailand: Sunrise or Sunset, paper presented at the Seoul International Social Work Conference—Dean Forum: Social Work Education and Practice Development in Asia Pacific Region, Seoul, Korea, April 15–18, jointly organized by the Asia Pacific Association for Social Work Education (APASWE), Korean Council on Social Welfare Education (KCSWE), and Korean Association of Social Workers (KASW).

Nontapattamadul, K. (2011), Changes in Landscape of Social Welfare Administration in Thailand. Paper for the training workshop on Social Network: Application in Social Welfare Administration arranged by the Faculty of Social Administration, Thammasat University, incorporated with Thailand International Development Cooperation, Ministry of Foreign Affairs and Department of Social Development and Welfare, Ministry of Social Development and Human Security, 18 April to 27 May, 2011, at Thammasat University, Bangkok, Thailand.

Nontapattamadul, K. and Cheecharoen, C. (2008), Country Paper: Thailand, presented at the Planning Workshop to Establish an ASEAN Consortium of Social Welfare Practitioners, Educators and Schools of Social Work, 12–14 August, Pasay City, The Philippines.

Phongvivat, C. (2009), Social Work Education in Thailand, *International Social Work*, Vol. 45, No. 3, pp. 293–303.

Ramesh, M. (2001), *Welfare Capitalism in Southeast Asia: Social Security, Health and Education Policies.* Basingstoke: Palgrave.

Schramm, B. (2003), Explaining Social Policy: The Development of Social Security in Thailand, www.gtz.de/de/dokumente/en-explaining-social-policy-th.pdf.

SEAS (2013), www.seas.at/aseas/3_1/ASEAS_3_1_A6.pdf.

Sungkawan, D. (1992), Development of Social Insurance Policy in Thailand, PhD thesis, University of Chicago, Illinois.

Sungkawan, D. (2002), The Community and Culture-Based Welfare Provisions: The Emergence of a Thai Welfare Society, *Thammasat Review*, Vol. 7, No. 1 (December).

TDRI (2013), www.tdri.or.th/news/tdri/nation2010_09_07.pdf.

TO (2013), www.timesonline.co.uk/tol/news/world/asia/article5345646.ece.

Tonguthai, P. (1986), Social Security for the Thai People, *ASEAN Economic Bulletin*, Vol. 3, No. 1, pp. 145–56

Chapter 7
Social Work in Malaysia

Zulkarnain A. Hatta and Zarina Mat Saad

The salient features of social welfare history and social work development in Malaysia are reviewed in this chapter. The chapter begins with the history of social welfare in Malaysia during pre- and post- independence. It will then highlight the major organizations involved in the delivery of social welfare. The second part of the chapter examines the evolution of social work education, and the chapter ends with a discussion on future directions of social work profession in Malaysia.

History of Social Welfare in Malaysia

There has been welfare work in Malaysia for as long as people have inhabited the country. The activities were done purely out of the altruistic nature of humans, they were not given any training, titles, or work designations and there were no competency standards as they exist now; but nonetheless, they served the people that were in need. As society grew and became more complicated, more social problems occurred. A few decades ago, the majority of the Malaysian public had never actually heard of the term 'social work'. The most familiar terms were for the welfare department, community, and voluntary work (*gotong royong*), which are closely knitted and often used interchangeably.

Like in many other countries, the field of social work started with the establishment of social welfare agencies to address social issues and problems. Malaysia historically has been occupied by several colonial powers – that is, the Portuguese beginning in 1511, the Dutch in 1641, the English 1824, and the Japanese 1941–1945. During those periods, no proper documentation was kept (especially after Japanese occupation) regarding any organizations that offered social welfare services to the local community except during British rule.

Pre-Independence

Community work has been part of the traditional Malay community's customs and practices since long before being colonized by foreign powers. During the Sultanate of the Malay States, the local Malay community received protection, land to farm, and other basic needs such as shelter in exchange for work, including road building, palace construction, and conscription during war (Shaffie, 2003); however, this situation changed during British rule.

The British, through the East India Company, established their first South-East Asia trading base in the Island of Penang in 1786 and began expanding their influence throughout the Malay States, starting with Perak in 1874. Their main objective was solely based on economics and trade gains. The states of the Malay Peninsula were divided into three groups: the Straits Settlements, the Federated Malay States (FMS), and the non-federated Malay States (Kedah, Kelantan, Terengganu and Johor; Kratoska, 1997; Rudner, 1976; Shaffie, 2003).

As the economy flourished in the Straits Settlement (SS), the number of immigrants, especially from China, increased, which brought social problems to the SS. The Colonial Office then appointed William A. Pickering in 1877 to head the Chinese Protectorate in Singapore, to see solely to the welfare of these Chinese immigrants. Chinese Protectorate offices were also opened in Penang and Malacca. Their main functions included administering newly arrived 'coolie' laborers (known as *sinkeh*), monitoring secret societies, rescuing female immigrants from prostitution, and the containment of venereal diseases (Lim, 2008).

Another form of administration was the FMS, which consisted of the Malay states of Perak, Selangor, Negeri Sembilan, and Pahang. These states enjoyed not only greater economic benefits but social benefits ensuring better community welfare. Health efforts by the government significantly reduced the mortality rate in these states and smallpox vaccination was made compulsory in 1891. The Pathology Institute was opened in Kuala Lumpur and named the Institute for Medical Research in 1902. Malaria cases were reduced tremendously from 522 in 1901 to 32 in 1903. Dr Malcom Watson further introduced mosquito-breeding prevention by putting pipes in streams and spraying those streams with oil in 1914 (Beck, 2008).

Education for the community was also expanded. In 1903 R.J. Wilkinson introduced the study of Malay literature using the Roman alphabet and R.O. Winsted, the education director between 1924 and 1931 revived Malay vernacular studies. The Sultan Idris Training College (SITC) was founded in 1922 at Tanjong Malim in Perak to train Malay teachers in advanced agricultural techniques. In 1923 Labor Code enactment required that estate management companies provide education for 10 or more children of their laborers (Beck, 2008).

However, most of the health, social welfare, and education programs that were implemented in Malaya before Japanese occupation were not the result of the colonial rulers understanding the needs of the colonized. Rather, the implementation of new ideas and practices in public health originated from the United Kingdom, implicitly for their own agenda. In the case of British Malaya, the infant welfare programs were initiated to ensure the constant supply of laborers to continue operating the colonial estates and mines, just as in Britain the same program was set up to ensure the reproduction of the working class to fulfil strategic and military needs and of course the manufacturing industries that were fed by the empire's raw material from the colonies (Manderson, 2002).

On 8 December 1941, the day after the attack on Pearl Harbor, Imperial Japan invaded British Malaya. Many locals believed that the Japanese, who ended

British rule in Peninsular Malay, would liberate and grant them independence since the Japanese proclaimed the motto 'Asian for Asian'. Unfortunately, the welfare of the locals was not taken seriously into account except those who were beneficial to Imperial Japanese military expansion in Asia. Life under Japanese military administration proved to be harsh and the basic needs of the population were hardly fulfilled (Kratoska, 1997).

After World War II, when the British returned to Malaya and resumed control under the British Military Administration (BMA), the country was in chaos: high unemployment, malnutrition, child hawkers, war victims, comfort women, and a smallpox epidemic were among the problems plaguing the Malayan population, particularly in urban areas. The BMA set up a relief department to take care of existing problems, but its offices rapidly became a dole office. Remedial work was also hindered by the lack of resources and thus, the BMA was unable to develop more efficient and innovative methods of training. Training programs were provided for the local women by ex–Red Cross members and missionaries exposing them to Western education and ways of doing things, which proved effective regarding the issues of local women, prostitution, and child welfare (Harper, 2001). On 10 June 1946, the Malayan Governor of Malaya appointed J.A. Harvey to head the first Welfare Department with the help of Captain Mohamed Salleh (the first local to be appointed). The department's roles were specifically to overcome famine and poverty and aid war victims. The majority of welfare staff were trained at the London School of Economics with basic skills in youth, industrial, and rural welfare (Shaffie, 2003).

When the BMA shifted to civil administration, many of the welfare organizations were headed by women. The Welfare Council of Malaya, an organization to foster voluntary activities, was under the patronage of Lady Mountbatten; the Malayan Women's Service League was under the patronage of Lady Gent – their members were mainly Malays who sponsored nutrition schemes and voluntary work. Women of other races also played significant roles in the associations that fostered the welfare of women in Malaya. For example, the Ipoh Women's Association and Penang's New Democratic Youth League persuaded Chinese housewives to stop buying goods from the black market and looked after the welfare of prostitutes (Harper, 2001).

Malay women were also active in their associations and demanded equal rights for Muslim Malay women in education. In Johor, the wife of Dato' Onn Jaafar and Datin Halimah Hussein insisted on the improvement of health care for Malays in the *kampongs* or villages. Women's self-help groups from the rural *kampongs* of Province Wellesley, Perak, and Selangor came together to form the Women's Department of the United Malays National Organization (UMNO) to demand welfare for Malay women (Harper, 2001).

The FMS and the non-federated Malay States, together with the Strait Settlements of Penang and Malacca, were united under the Federation of Malaya on 31 January 1948 (Rudner, 1976). During the early years of the Federation of Malaya, many charitable and voluntary work associations were formed to address the needs of the marginalized groups. Among the first was the Malaysian Association for the Blind (MAB), established in 1951 in order to look after the welfare of the blind in the country. The founder, Major D.R. Bridges managed to set up the Job Placement Service in Kuala Lumpur in 1956 and transferred the Braille Publishing Unit and Braille Equipment Sales from the Ministry of Education to the MAB in 1959 (MAB, 2010).

Based on historical facts, welfare work in Peninsular Malaya (now known as Malaysia) had already begun in the late nineteenth century. Even though most of the programs were implemented to drive the British industries and economy, they nevertheless benefited the Malayan locals. Those programs, albeit serving the colonizers' agenda, had laid the foundation of modern Malaysian welfare programs.

Post-Independence

Shortly after gaining independence from the British in 1957, the government of the then Federation of Malaya began to prepare development programs for its community. Among the prioritized policies was the national social policy, the evolution of which began in the late 1950s and continues to be developed well into the twenty-first century. The national social policies tend to address and tackle social problems such as education and training, unemployment, poverty, income disparity, housing, substance abuse, domestic violence, crime, ethnic and community relations, and health care (Abbas, 2003; Rani, 2007). The main objective of social policy was to improve the welfare of the community and particular groups such as women, youth, children, the elderly, the disabled, and ethnic groups or minorities. Thereafter, the government allocated large amounts of financial capital to execute the national social policy, particularly in health and education.

In 1971 the government introduced the New Economic Policy (NEP), which is a 20-year economic policy aimed to accelerate the process of eradicating poverty and restructuring society to correct social and economic imbalances. The NEP achieved its objectives to some extent when the percentage of poverty fell from 42.4 per cent in 1976 to 17.1 per cent in 1990, but failed to reach 30 per cent enterprise ownership by *bumiputeras* (in English, 'son of the earth/soil') (Funston, 2001). Consequently, the Outline Perspective Plan 2 was put into effect for a 10-year period (1991–2000) and was formed as a basis for Vision 2020. The newly revised plan focused on unity of socioeconomic development in order to enable citizens to enjoy better material, spiritual, and social welfare (Abbas, 2003; Mohd, 2009).

The central component of a development strategy is investment in health. The Malay government aims to provide a comprehensive, quality service by ensuring fairer distribution of services and improved access to health care. In the 1950s the priority of health-care programs was rural areas due to high infant and maternal mortality, and general mortality and morbidity rates, which were associated with poverty and underdevelopment. Therefore, health care services provided at that time were maternal and child health care, medical and dental care, immunization, family planning, communicable disease control, and environmental sanitation. These services continue according to need and in addition, the government continues to establish hospitals that provide a wide range of care in urban areas and medical social workers in every state hospital. The government allocated Ringgit Malaysia (RM) 5.5 billion or 14.7 per cent of the social sector budget and 5 per cent of the total development budget to health services, for the period 2001–2005 (Abbas, 2003).

The federal government focuses on education for all while the state governments add to this with Islamic education. The objectives of the education policy are to (1) provide an education for all Malaysians; (2) generate an adequate pool of national human resources; (3) produce sound, well-rounded individuals; and (4) produce a loyal and a united nation. As a result, the literacy rate in Malaysia increased to 93.8 per cent in 2000. Preschool, primary, secondary, and tertiary education programs are implemented with 11 years of free schooling by the Ministry of Education. Allocation of RM 17.5 billion or 56 per cent of the development expenditure of the social sector and 17.7 per cent of the total development expenditure were spent on developing education, tertiary education, and training for the period 1996–2000 (Abbas, 2003).

Even after 52 years of independence, the government is still very attentive to the well-being of Malaysians. Various social policies have been introduced to safeguard the welfare of susceptible and vulnerable groups and the core of every policy promotes national unity and poverty eradication, which in turn form the basis of a stable nation preparing Malaysia to be a fully-developed nation by 2020.

Agencies Related to the Social Work Profession

Social work in Malaysia is generally related to many welfare programs and activities conducted by the government, nongovernmental organizations, and private agencies. On the government side, there are a few ministries directly linked to the social work profession, such as the Ministry of Women, Family and Community Development; the Ministry of Health; the Ministry of Rural and Regional Development; and the Ministry of Higher Education.

The Ministry of Women, Family and Community Development, for instance, consists of four departments including the Department of Women's Development, National Population and Family Development Board, Social Welfare Department and the Social Institute of Malaysia. The Department of Social Welfare Malaysia (DSWM) is the largest agency employing social work professionals, however, only one third of more than 3,000 employees are trained and involved in social work cases whereas the rest are either technical, support, or professional staff (Mohd, 2009).

The Social Welfare Department was established in 1946 with the task of developing the nation after World War II. In the past it was placed under several ministries such as the Department of Community Welfare (1946–1951), Ministry of Industry and Social Relations (1952–1955), Ministry of Labor and

Social Welfare (1958–1959; 1963), and Ministry of Health and Social Welfare (1960–1962). It was then ceded to the Ministry of General Welfare (1964), which became successively the Ministry of Social Welfare (1982), and the Ministry of National Unity and Community Development (1990) (SWDM, 2009). On 27 March 2004, the department was placed under the Ministry of Women and Family Development, Malaysia; on 1 April 2005, it was integrated with the Ministry of Women and Family Development, assuming the new name of the Ministry of Women, Family and Community Development (Rani, 2007).

The department's main mission is to develop society towards social well-being through realizing its four main objectives:

1. to provide shelter and rehabilitation for the department's target groups;
2. to develop the community through the process of changing attitudes and increasing capability for self-reliance;
3. to create a society with a caring culture, and
4. to improve the well-being of society through professional social welfare and social development services and strategic sharing of responsibilities.

The department has at least seven target groups including children, people with disabilities, older persons, destitute persons, family (women and girls, single parents, victims of domestic violence, the poor, people with problems, and juvenile offenders), victims of natural disaster, and voluntary welfare organizations. Amongst others, DSWM provides services in terms of prevention, protection, rehabilitation, development, and integration. There are seven laws that have been promulgated and put under DSWM administration: the Directive General of Social Welfare Act 1948 (Act 529); the Destitute Person Act 1977 (Act 183); the Childcare Act 1984 (Act 308); the Homecare Act 1993 (Act 506); the Domestic Violence Act 1994 (Act 521); the Child Act 2001 (Act 611) and the Disabled Persons Act 2008 (Act 685). There are also several policies being developed for the benefit of older people, disabled persons, and children.

Besides government agencies there are at least 200 voluntary organizations involved in numerous welfare activities like providing shelters and care for orphans, people with a physical or mental disability, elderly people, the poor, problematic children, women, and disaster victims, but there are still only a few workers trained in social work (Mohd, 2009). However, public and private institutions of higher learning are intensifying their efforts to offer more education and training for welfare workers in order to fulfill current national needs and social work professional standards.

There is a specific association for social workers in Malaysia known as the Malaysian Association of Social Workers (MASW) that works closely with government agencies, especially with the DSWM. MASW was formed on 3 March 1973, and registered with the Registrar of Societies on 28 March 1974. It was established as a result of a general agreement among professional social workers from social welfare services, general hospitals, and the University

Hospital, University of Malaya, that MASW should be a body to unite social workers from diverse backgrounds, to meet professional standards, and also to promote and maintain the quality of social work practice and education in the country (MASW, 2008).

MASW has three main missions to accomplish including to be an active advocate for professional competency in social work practice, education, and research; to be a relevant forum for assessing, identifying, and managing social problems; and to be an effective resource of professional support to its members. It also aims to participate dynamically in networking with government and nongovernmental agencies locally and internationally in the pursuit of professional competency in all areas of social work. The association is currently working on the establishment of national competency standards for social work practice and education; enactment of a Social Workers' Act and regulatory certification and licencing; training welfare workers; organizing workshops/seminars on social work issues to enhance competency in practice; conducting talks and public forums to increase awareness; participating and presenting papers at conferences; and conducting social research (MASW, 2008). Even though social work professionals are not on a par with some other professions in this country, they are beginning to receive adequate recognition from the government agencies and NGOs. This is proved by their continuous collaboration in organizing social work activities and programs.

Social Work Education in Malaysia

For welfare work to be effective, it needed coordination and organization. Prior to 1952 social workers engaging in welfare work in Malaysia (then called Malaya) were sent primarily to the United Kingdom for training and education for the very purpose of better organizing the welfare system. In 1952 professional social work courses were introduced at the University of Malaya (UM) in Singapore (Singapore was part of Malaysia until 1965 when it seceded). Hence, between 1952 and 1975 about 150 students graduated from UM, and approximately 50 per cent of these graduates were employed by the welfare department (MSW, 2006).

In 1975, Universiti Sains Malaysia (USM) became the first university in Malaysia to introduce a social work program. The impetus for the establishment of the social work program at USM was initiated by several bodies: the MASW, the Malaysian Ministry of Social Welfare, and the Social Development Division of the United Nations Economic and Social Commission for Asia and the Pacific. Instead of making the program independent, it was placed under the School of Social Sciences, along with other fields such as sociology, anthropology, economics, development studies, and political science. During those years, it was considered that such a program placed in a school of social sciences would benefit from the expertise of other social scientists. The presumption then was that in this manner it would avoid some of the pitfalls of social work development and evolution, as had happened in some Western countries (Yasas, 1974). Initially, the social work program at USM was named Social Development and Administration (SDA).

Malaysia during those years was basically a developing country and still very rural. The SDA program was created to cater to the needs of the country at that time, and it was going to train social workers not simply as social work practitioners but also as administrators. SDA had a development perspective, quite different from the traditional concept of 'social work'. The social work program at USM at that time was heavily influenced by prevailing views of the 1970s Asian social workers and the personalities of the staff (Fattahipour, 1991). While the program benefited from input from other social scientists of the School of Social Sciences, as time went by it was realized that if the program was to be sustainable, more well-trained, qualified professional social workers were urgently needed. Throughout the 1980s a recruitment process was launched nationwide and the successful candidates were sent to either the United Kingdom or United States to pursue their doctorate in social work.

Today, Malaysia is rapidly industrializing and many areas are being urbanized; since the 1990s it has not been the same society as when the SDA was established in 1975. Rural life has been transformed, and the same kinds of economic and technological development that many industrialized countries experienced are also being experienced by Malaysia. With the transformation, which is also occurring in other social institutions, particularly the family, the demand for change was heard. Problems that once society faced no longer can be seen from the development perspective, a change in perspective needed to be adopted.

Up until a few years ago, USM's social work program was the only one in Malaysia responsible for educating social workers (cf. USM, 2006). However, not all graduates turn out to be social workers; some simply found better paying jobs in other settings, and left the social work field. A major concern was that some did not consider themselves social workers because the SDA program did not clearly and strongly gave them a sense of identity as professional social workers (Fattahipour and Hatta, 1992). Many simply saw themselves as 'personnel officers', 'administrators', 'social developers', or just 'jack of all trades' (Fattahipour, 1988).

One of the original intentions of the establishment of the social work program at USM was to produce graduates who were trained for the Ministry of Social Welfare at that time. A few others were employed by the Ministries of Health, Rural Development, Youth and Sport and Education. Over time, the program received students that came from high school with no work experience or any social work related background. In 1996, after years of debates and discussions, the program was finally named Social Work. The rationale for the change was simply that the contents of the program were generic social work in nature (Fattahipour and Hatta, 1992) and that the change in name would give a strong sense of identity to the program (including students) and with other social work programs internationally. Additionally, the change of name was consistent with the name of international social work bodies like the International Federation of Social Workers (IFSW), Asia-Pacific Associations for Social Work Education (APASWE), International Association of Social Workers (IASW), and local organizations such as the MASW.

Realizing the importance of social work in a country facing many social challenges, during the 1990s three more universities started offering similar programs, and three more introduced a social work program during the new millennium. The establishment of social work programs in other universities reflected the need for more social workers to meet the many challenges. Respectively, the universities are Universiti Putra Malaysia (UPM) in 1991, Universiti Malaysia Sarawak (UNIMAS) in 1993, Universiti Utara Malaysia (UUM) in 1997, Universiti Kebangsaan Malaysia (UKM) in 2000, Universiti Malaya (UM) in 2000, and Universiti Malaysia Sabah (UMS) in 2002 (MSW Report, 2006).

Status of Programs of Local Universities

A total of seven local universities offering social work as a major bodes well for the country. Apart from USM, most of the other universities are still in their formative years. Nonetheless, all of the programs offer a broad social work curriculum. Although there are variations among the courses offered, they all include basic core courses such as (1) Introduction to Social Work, (2) Values and Ethics in Social Work, (3) Social Work Practice with Individual and Family, (4) Introduction to Social Work Research, (5) Introduction to Group Work, (6) Theory and Practice of Community Work, (7) Field Work, (8) Social Psychology, and (9) Human Behaviour and Personality.

Apart from that, all the universities offer optional courses such as (1) Social Policy and Welfare System, (2) Health Psychology, (3) Abnormal Psychology, (4) Human Service Organization, (5) Law for Social Workers, (6) Medical Social Work, (7) Gerontology, (8) Juvenile Delinquency, (9) Criminology, (10) Substance Abuse, (11) Social Work in Industry, (12) Religion and Social Welfare, (13) School Social Work, (14) Counselling, (15) Family Dynamics, (16) Social Work with Youth and Children, and (17) Social Work Skills in Rehabilitation Institutions.

USM, UNIMAS, and UMS are more oriented towards producing a general social work graduate, while UPM tends to focus more on human development, and UM towards social administration and social justice. UKM on the other hand, is known for its emphasis on medical social work, and UUM primarily focuses on the management aspects of social services. To graduate, apart from other general requirements of a particular university, most programs require students to take a minimum of eight core courses and four option courses and another four elective courses.

Each course carries between three to four credit hours. At USM each course carries four credit hours (two hours lecture and two hours tutorial), while at UUM each course is three hours (two hours lecture and one hour tutorial). Apart from the courses offered, all of the universities offer field work or practicum for the students. Prior to the 1996/97 academic year, the social work programs were based on a four-year program. However, decisions made by political leaders changed most of the universities' programs to three years, social work not being spared.

Before the 1996/97 academic year, there were three field work components (stretched over three semesters – working with individuals, working with groups, and working with the community, respectively. As a result of the reduction to three years, all of the field work components were reduced to two semesters instead of three – one semester working with individuals and another semester working with groups/community.

Theoretically, the courses and curriculum offered by the Malaysian universities are generally in line with international standards. However, one of the main concerns is the qualification of teaching staff in each university – many of the universities still do not have adequately trained and qualified staff. Many still do not have doctorate degrees in social work, and those that do have doctorate degrees that are not in the area of social work. UUM, for instance, has several MSW holders, while at UKM, most do not even have a social work degree at any level.

Arguably many of the problems of social work education in Malaysia will be alleviated if there is a body to monitor social work programs towards achieving professional standards. The MASW recognize and register members who have a degree/diploma in social work or in social science with more than five years' working experience in a social work setting. In the last three years, MASW has initiated moves towards competency standards and professional accreditation for practitioners.

Since social work education is relatively young and most of the universities are still developing, there is obviously a need to establish standards. Standard-setting will enable social work to move towards a higher level of professionalism, this will also be in line with the national plan. The accreditation body is to set internationally recognized standards in governing the universities' curriculum, contents, length and hours of practicum, staff qualification, and the ratio of students to staff.

Social Work Educational Policy and Accreditation in Malaysia

Social work as a discipline has its own body of knowledge, values, and skills. As a discipline that prepares its students to work with people and societies, it is important for all the universities in Malaysia that offer social work programs to have standards consistent with global social work expectations, while at the same time taking into consideration the local context. The initiative to set up an accreditation body started around 2002/2003 when an ad hoc committee was established compromising all seven universities and the MASW. The committee was called the Malaysian Committee of Social Work Education and has since changed its status to a council, the Malaysian Council of Social Work Education. The discussion that follows will outline the objectives and plans of the intended accreditation body.

While taking the definition of social work adopted by IFSW and IASSW in Montreal, 2000, Malaysia's definition will be influenced by the country's national social policy. In the said policy, social work has an important role to play in promoting social harmony and stability, strengthening and enhancing the family unit and social cohesion, and fostering a caring society (cf., e.g., Hatta and Pandian, 2007).

Towards that end, social work in Malaysia commits itself to:

- Bring about optimal social functioning of individuals, families, and communities by utilizing all necessary intervention approaches;
- Enhance human well-being and alleviate poverty, marginalization, and other forms of social injustice;
- Formulate and implement social services, programs, and policies that will meet the basic needs of all and maximize the capability of all for betterment; and
- Emphasize research and development in social work to help solve existing and emerging social problems.

In clarifying the objectives of their social work program, the local universities should reflect on:

- The purpose and aim of Malaysian's definition of social work;
- The long-held value and ethical principles of social work;
- The incorporation of MCSWE's benchmark in developing curriculum; and
- Teaching–learning strategies.

The Proposed Curriculum Benchmark

Social work curriculums have to be developed with contents, teaching, and learning strategies that will prepare students for general competency and professionalism. With regards to practicum, it should be appropriately administered and supervised utilizing appropriate social work theories and practices. The curriculum must include the following four main components:

1. Core social work courses that encourage the development of professional competency in dealing with individuals, families, groups, and communities; using social work intervention inventories; working with the appropriate ethics and values; working professionally in organizations; and the ability to make a self-reflection on the work done. These core courses should focus on the following themes:
   - Social work values and principles – the ability to adopt them in different situations and cultural contexts;
   - Social work theories and practices that cover working with individuals and families, group work, community work, social policy, and social work research;
   - Interpersonal communication skills in helping;
   - Knowledge of human behaviour and social environment with an emphasis on person-in-environment perspective, lifelong development perspective, loss and attachment issues, and the ability to understand critically social structure and cultural factors that influence human behaviour;
   - Social policy and welfare system;

- Social work history and development at the international and local levels;
- Knowledge and skills working in a social service organization;
- Social work practices that are based on various cultural settings; and
- Social work practices that are based on an international, global context.

2. Foundational courses in the social sciences such as psychology, sociology, anthropology, economics, and political science. These courses are necessary in developing students to become wholesome in their generic competency. In order to achieve that end, the following themes must be incorporated in the courses: (a) Society and Culture, (b) Race and Ethnicity, (c) Gender Relations, (d) Multiculturalism, (e) Power Analysis, (f) Development Issues, (g) Social Ecology, (h) Social Dynamics, (i) Social Changes, (j) Displaced Population, (k) Indigenous People's Issues, (l) Globalization, (m) Cognition and Learning, (n) Deviance, (o) Social Psychology, (p) Human Development, (q) Philosophy and Ethics, and (r) Religion and Spirituality.

3. Courses which prepare students for selected fields of practice: (a) Family and Child Welfare, (b) Reformatory Service, (c) Health and Medical Social Work, (d) School Social Work, (e) Gerontology, (f) Women and Minorities, and (g) Disability.

4. Practicum/field work that provides students with clearly designed learning experiences in a practice setting:
   - A minimum of two field placements, which make up a total of 800–1,000 hours, is required;
   - A minimum of eight weeks per semester in an agency and community respectively to facilitate students' development of professional competencies;
   - Prerequisite courses must be taken before students start their practicum;
   - A minimum of one hour per week supervision where at least 50 percent are being conducted by a professional supervisor who should be a qualified social worker;
   - Planned coordination and liaison between the university and agencies to ensure the field work experience meets the program planned objectives and outcomes;
   - A minimum of two site visits by the academic supervisor per semester; and
   - The proportion of core social work and foundational courses in the curriculum has to be 85 per cent for core courses including practicum, and 15 per cent for foundation courses.

Resources and Structure

A good social work program will require the proper and adequate supply of resources. One of the most important variables in effective teaching is the classroom size. A ratio of 1:18 staff–students should be attempted by the universities. At a minimum, 80 per cent of the teaching staff must have a social work academic qualification that is recognized by the government, along with contemporary practice experience. Consequently, only these staff can teach the core courses.

In terms of the structure of the program, to be deemed as viable it should have at least five full-time staff of which three must have a degree in social work at the master's level. Following the IFSW guidelines, the head of the program, be s/he the dean, director, or chairperson, must have at least a master's degree in social work (an MSW). To further improve the program, evaluation of the program must be conducted by an external and internal assessor periodically. The MCSWE will act as the internal assessor and a reputable social work academician from outside the country will be the external assessor.

Students Professional Development

Student intake should be governed by the university's policy, and their admission criteria should be in line with the program's objectives. Students' aptitude and attitude must be taken into consideration; s/he for instance should be evaluated for any judgemental traits and ethical issues. On the other hand, students should never be discriminated against based on race, religion, culture, gender, physical impairment, or sexual orientation. Special intake should be allowed for those who might not have the necessary academic qualifications but do have more than sufficient work experience in related areas of social work. Special intake should also be allocated to minority ethnic groups and disabled persons. The social work program should facilitate students' cognitive and affective development of competency and a system of mentoring and supervision should be established to assist in the students' total learning process.

Staff Professional Development

Social work academicians need to retool themselves periodically with the latest knowledge. They should be given support and encouragement to attend workshops, seminars, and conferences both locally and internationally. These experiences are also an avenue for them to establish networking, which is vital for exchanges of ideas and collaboration. Incentives should be given to those who present papers rather than just attending as participants. Additionally, apart from undertaking individual research, staff should collaborate in the research arena both at the local and international stage.

Membership of the Accreditation Body

The main responsibility of the accreditation body is to accredit social work programs. As a responsible entity, a dependable membership must be ensured. The following people should make up the membership: two members from each university, two members from the National Association of Social Workers, and two members from relevant government agencies (Malaysian Welfare Department, Ministry of Education of Higher Learning, and from the Health Ministry). Their task is to ensure that all of the above-mentioned objectives vis-à-vis the curriculum, contents, and structure of each university are accomplished.

Current Challenges for Recognition

Social work as a profession is still relatively unknown to the public. Many still see it as welfare-related work (giving charity and dole-out by ministers' wives), or volunteer work (*gotong royong*). There is a paradox among the policymakers; while they are concerned with the affairs of social issues in the country and see the need for social work programs, there exists a certain vagueness of understanding of what social work education and practice really entails. If social work is truly understood by the authorities, the Social Workers' Act would have long since been tabled and approved in the Malaysian Parliament.

Despite the late start, in April 2010 the Malaysian government approved a proposal by the Ministry of Women, Family and Community Development to establish the Social Workers' Act. Among the significant components of the act are the following: establishing a social work council to regulate social work practitioners and educators; ensuring the Public Service Commission and Public Service Department recruit qualified social workers into the public sector; and upgrading the Social Institute of Malaysia and other accredited institutions to offer social work courses at certificate and diploma levels. With the establishment of the act, the job designation of 'social worker' hopefully will be assigned in schools, rehabilitation institutions, and prisons, just to name a few. As of now there is no official job designation for social workers in the public sector. Instead, those individuals who do the social work task are being given titles such as counsellors, welfare officers, and the like. One of the most unfortunate situations in Malaysia today is that most social work jobs are being given to those who do not have formal social work education. The problem occurs in part due to the recruitment process of the Public Service Department and the Public Service Commission (government agencies that set rules and criteria for employment in the public sector). The main criterion for recruitment is a candidate's university grade point average. Priority is given to graduates that have a high grade point average. For example, if a student majoring in history has a higher grade point average than a social work major, and both are competing for a social work job, the former will get the job.

The implication of this recruitment practice is dire: clients of that history 'social worker' will be victimized by the latter's lack of social work education. It actually renders him/her incompetent and inefficient in trying to serve the client. Despite being given in-house training, it is no substitute for three or four years of formal social work education. To remedy the problem, these agencies have spent huge amounts of money to train these non–social workers by university academicians. A crash course will be given with the hope that it will replace the missing three to four years of formal social work education. Another ill effect of this unsound recruitment practice is the increasing unemployment and underemployment of social work graduates.

Things are no better in the private sector. It is a well-known fact that social work is not a high-paying job. Hence, the private sector does not attract fresh graduates to seek employment with them simply because of the salary factor. Social workers need to take care of their basic needs as well, especially new graduates who are about to enter the job market.

Conclusion

Social work practitioners and academics have to be activists in promoting and educating both the public and government officials. They have to align and find allies with sympathetic ears, especially among members of Parliament, ministers, and policymakers. The task is to make social work officially recognized as a 'professional' profession (similar to architects, medical doctors, and lawyers). Along with that recognition, the salary scheme will have to be adjusted to make the lives of social workers comfortable, rather than the meager amount that entry levels are getting now for a job that is not labelled 'social worker'.

The irony of the situation is that most who call themselves 'social workers', both in the public and private sectors, are not trained formally. A medical doctor, a counsellor, a minister, a politician, an activist – all can lay claim to be a social worker, while the real social worker still struggles to be recognized. Some of them are of the opinion that one need not be trained formally to be a social worker. If one is to accept their line of reasoning, the effort of MASW to create competency standards for practitioners, and MCSWE's efforts to establish an accreditation body will be to no avail:

> However, with the soon to be approved Social Work by the government, the situation looks promising in mitigating these 'professionalism' issues. The term 'professional' in Malaysia in the context of social work is still a contentious issue. Hence, the effort to define professional social work must be carried out vigorously, lest many think anyone can be a social worker by just having good intentions. (Hatta, 2007)

Much advance has been made in the practice of professional social work since colonial days, and since 1952 when the first few social work courses were introduced in Singapore. However, much more needs to be done. With the lingering uncertainty in public perception about social work and the contradictions of the authorities, the task to improve the condition of social work practice and education is still very challenging. The importance of having the Social Workers' Act and establishing the accreditation body should never be understated. The existence of the act and the accreditation body is not an end, but a part of the process to ultimately bring complete recognition of social work without any lingering ambiguity in Malaysia.

References

Abbas, F.A. (2003), *Social Policies in Malaysia*. New York: Economic and Social Commission for Western Asia.

Beck, S. (2008), *South Asia, 1800–1950*. Goleta, CA: World Peace Communications.

Council of Social Work Education (CSWE) (2006), *Educational Policy and Standards for Social Work Education in Higher Learning Institutions*. CSWE, Kuala Lumpur.

Fattahipour, A. (1988), A Search for Identity and Development, report, School of Social Sciences, Universiti Sains Malaysia, Penang, Malaysia.

Fattahipour, A. (1991), The Curriculum Review of the Social Development and Administration Program, report, School of Social Sciences, Universiti Sains Malaysia, Penang, Malaysia.

Fattahipour, A. and Hatta, Z.A. (1992), *Opportunities and Market Demands for Social Workers in Malaysia: 1992–2002*. Universiti Sains Malaysia: Penang, Malaysia.

Funston, J. (2001), Malaysia: Development State Challenged, in *Government and Politics in Southeast Asia*, edited by J. Funston. Singapore: Institute of Southeast Asian Studies.

Harper, T.N. (2001), *The End of Empire and the Making of Malaya*. Singapore: COS Printers.

Hatta, Z.A. and Pandian, S. (2007), The Dynamics of Issues and Social Services with the Roles of Social Workers in Urban Areas, *Malaysian Journal of Social Work*, Vol. 6, No. 2, pp. 31–44.

Kratoska, P.H. (1997), *The Japanese Occupation of Malaya, 1941–1945*. London: C. Hurst.

Lim, I. (2008), The Chinese Protectorate, retrieved from http://infopedia.nl.sg/articles/SIP_1346_2008-12-10.html.

Malaysian Association for the Blind (MAB) (2010), History, retrieved from http://www.mab.org.my/about/history.html.

Manderson, L. (2002), *Sickness and the State: Health and Illness in Colonial Malaya, 1870–1940*. Cambridge: Cambridge University Press.

Malaysian Association of Social Workers (MASW) (2005), Competency Standards Application Workshop, *report*, Malaysian Association of Social Workers, Kuala Lumpur.

MASW, (2008), Our History, retrieved from http://www.myasw.net.

Mohd, D.S.A.R.S. (2009), Development of a Career in Social Work Profession: Opportunities and Challenges, retrieved from http://www.jkm.gov.my/jkm.

Rani, Z.A. (2007), *Social Welfare Policies and Services for the Elderly: A Country Report (Malaysia)*. Kuala Lumpur: Social Welfare Department of Malaysia.

Rudner, M. (1976), The Structure of Government in the Colonial Federation of Malaya, *South East Asian Studies*, Vol. 13, No. 4, pp. 495–512.

Shaffie, F. (2003), Satu tinjauan mengenai latar belakang kerja sosial di Malaysia (A Study of Social Work Background in Malaysia), in *Pengurusan perkhidmatan kerja sosial di Malaysia (Social Work Services Management in Malaysia)*, edited by Z. Jamaluddin Sintok: Penerbit UUM.

Social Welfare Department of Malaysia (SWDM) (2009), History, retrieved from http://www.jkm.gov.my/jkm/index.php?option=com_contentandview=article andid=5andItemid=89andlang=en.

USM (2006), Report on the Proposal of the Master of Social Work Program, report, School of Social Sciences, Universiti Sains Malaysia. Penang, Malaysia.

Yasas, F.M. (1974), The Establishment of a Professional Course in Social Work and Community Development Training at the Bachelor's Level at the School of Social Sciences, report, Universiti Sains Malaysia, Penang, Malaysia.

Chapter 8
Social Work in Singapore

Rosaleen Ow

> Each country, according to its own culture, resources, and the extent of its human needs, has developed a unique mix of social welfare programs. The structures of those programs affect what services can be provided and, for social workers, the roles they will perform.
>
> (Morales et al., 2010: 239)

As such, this chapter will begin with a brief review of the structure of welfare services in Singapore as a backdrop for discussing the nature of social work within the context of these service provisions.

Singapore consists of a main island and some 59 small islands with a land area of around 700 square kilometers surrounded by the countries of Malaysia, Indonesia, the Philippines, and Indo-China. In 2008, the total population is close to 5 million consisting of 74.7 per cent with an ethnic Chinese background, 13.6 per cent from the Malay archipelago, 8.9 per cent with origins in India, and 2.8 per cent of mixed ethnicity (SDS, 2009: 5). Singapore represents a multicultural society in Asia. Although population groups originated from different parts of Asia, many of the common traditional values placed on the family and community remain. In spite of the Chinese majority in the Singapore population, social services in the community are not specifically tailored with a Chinese perspective in mind. In fact, ethnic-based social service agencies such as Mendaki for the Malay-Muslims, SINDA (Singapore Indian Development Association) for the Indians, the Eurasian Association, as well as the Chinese Development and Assistance Council (CDAC) for the Chinese also play a significant role in social service provision (Ow, 1999).

Social work as an organized profession first started in 1949 with the arrival of almoners from Britain, and in 1953 a group of almoners began formalizing the move towards developing indigenous practice. The formal training of social workers at the then University of Singapore began in 1952 (Ow, 2010b), followed by the formation of the Singapore Association of Social Workers in 1971 where membership included professionals from both academia and practice. An excellent account of the beginnings of social welfare services is available in a chapter by Wee (2004) and the development of the social work profession in Singapore (Wee, 1986).

Structure of Welfare Services in Singapore

Singapore's Welfare Philosophy is based on the concept of 'Many Helping Hands' (Abdullah, 1995), which reflects the partnerships between many stakeholders including the government, voluntary welfare organizations (secular and faith-based), and ethnic-based organizations as well as business corporations as part of their corporate social responsibility.

The Singapore government plans, regulates, and facilitates the provision of social services. It is often the catalyst of new services providing support through development costs, and recurrent costs of the services as appropriate. The spirit of volunteerism is promoted very strongly as it helps to develop civic consciousness and a sense of ownership for the well-being of the whole society. The Ministry of Community Development, Youth and Sports acts as the main initiator and provider of resources for community services. It is partnered by quasi-government organizations such as the National Council of Social Services, which oversees services provided by a large number of voluntary social service organizations. With subvention from the state, these agencies function with input of personnel resources from volunteers in the community as well as paid professional staff.

Social Work in Children and Youth Services

In the late nineteenth century, the British colonial government in Singapore recognized the need to treat adolescent offenders differently from adult offenders and instituted the Reformatory and Industrial Schools Ordinance for the detention of boys under 16 years old. When the immigrant population in Singapore stabilized in the early twentieth century and there were more children in the population, a Children's Ordinance was enacted in 1927 to protect them from acts of cruelty. Another related problem during that time was the purchase of young girls, some as young as 4–6 years old, from China to be brought up as *mui ts'ai* or bond servant girls in Singapore. While it was argued that the *mui ts'ai* was not a slave but usually a poor relation who might have died in poverty in China, the colonial government felt it was within its duty to protect these young girls until a suitable marriage could be arranged for them. Early legislation to protect these female relatives was not very effective until the 1949 Children and Young Persons Ordinance. By then, the communist government in China was established and the movement of *mui ts'ai* to Singapore virtually stopped. In addition to statutory interventions, many missionary societies also provided welfare and educational services for needy children in the early twentieth century as a supplement to limited state provisions (Wee, 2004).

Important changes came after World War II. A Social Welfare Department was established in 1946 with a more coordinated set of welfare services including the protection of young girls and the protection and rehabilitation of children in need or care, or who were in trouble with the law. The pre-war focus was to try and abolish the *mui ts'ai* system but given a changed social context, the post-war regulations and legislation for the welfare of children were focused more on protection and caregiving practices for children born locally. Although the earliest provisions were mainly for the protection of children from China, the beginning of a multi-ethnic population after the war meant that the services focused on Chinese welfare were no longer appropriate. Although early post-war interventions were mainly devoted to meeting basic human needs such as feeding malnourished children and housing orphans and those without family support, the high crime rate after the Japanese surrender revealed the need to work with juvenile delinquents. In 1951, the Probation Offender's Ordinance was instituted and was the beginning of a series of changes that provided intervention options for juveniles and young persons found guilty in adult courts.

Traditionally, a child is considered to be the property of the father and is under his care and control until marriage. In the context of present Singapore, children are to be nurtured and protected not just as an asset to the family but also valued in their own right. According to Khoo (2004: 127), 'Child welfare has to do with the legislation, policies, programs, and services that promote children's holistic development, protect children who are at risk from harm, and rehabilitate children if, and when they become a threat to themselves and to others.'

As such, from the perspective of human development in an ecological approach (Bronfenbrenner, 1979), services for children cannot be focused on the child alone but equally important is the focus on the family and community within which the child lives and develops. Varying official definitions of a 'child' and 'youth' exist in Singapore in accordance with the purpose of the different pieces of legislation. For example, under the Children and Young Persons Act (CYPA), Cap 38 (2001), a child is a person below the age of 14. A 'young person' is aged 14 but below 16, while a juvenile is someone between seven and 16 years of age. The Adoption of Children Act, Cap 4 (1985), defines an infant as a person under the age of 21 years. Under the Women's Charter, Cap 353 (1997), which governs matters related to maintenance, custody, and marriage, a child is defined as any person under the age of 21. Singapore is signatory to the United Nations Convention on the Rights of the Child (UNCRC) and accepts its definition of a child as someone below the age of 18. The Inter-Ministry Committee on Youth Crime, Singapore National Youth Council, 1999 defines youth as persons between the ages of 15–30 years of age (Nair, 2004).

Children are valued as the transmitters of traditional values and customs, as links between the past and the present. In a cosmopolitan and open society, children are also increasingly being valued for who they are, independent of family roles and responsibilities. Today, a child in Singapore is not only perceived as a family asset but also a national asset. Child well-being is now not just the responsibility of the family but also that of the state and the community. Therefore, child welfare provisions in Singapore include a variety of measures to improve family and community functioning and well-being as means towards nurturing and protecting the best interests of the child. In keeping with the many-helping-hands approach to social welfare, both the state and the community are involved in preventive, remedial, and developmental services for children and youth. Social work is

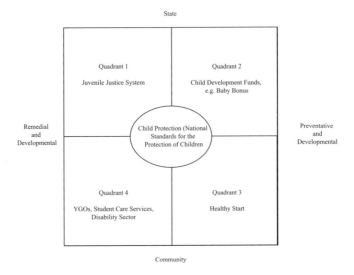

State

| Quadrant 1 | Quadrant 2 |
| Juvenile Justice System | Child Development Funds, e.g. Baby Bonus |

Remedial and Developmental

Child Protection (National Standards for the Protection of Children

Preventative and Developmental

| Quadrant 4 | Quadrant 3 |
| YGOs, Student Care Services, Disability Sector | Healthy Start |

Community

Fig. 8.1   Child and Youth Services in Singapore

engaged in the provision of such services using a systemic approach where the three traditional divisions of social work methods are integrated and the service holistic.

Singapore's provisions to enhance child and youth welfare and protection and the corresponding roles of social work in the current context can be conceptualized in the framework shown above.

In Quadrant 1 (Figure 8.1), the social workers' professional contribution can be demonstrated in the state's provision of remedial and developmental services for children and youth in the rehabilitation services provided under the jurisdiction of the Juvenile Court, the Family Court, and the Community Court system. One example is in the work of the probation service where social workers are called to oversee the custody and social care of the probationers under the Children and Young Persons Act. The act provides a wide range of options for managing juvenile offences and is the main tool for remedial and developmental services for the rehabilitation of youth offenders. The act recognizes the importance of the family in restoring the young offender into mainstream social life. Community-based rehabilitation such as the community service order (CSO), weekend detention order, and probation rather than institutionalization is therefore preferred.

The CSO, for example, opens the avenue for a value-added dimension to rehabilitation when youth offenders are provided with opportunities to carry out the CSO in projects such as wheelchair repairs, volunteering at eldercare services under the guidance of senior nurses, or painting community facilities. Such CSO activities may allow the youth offender to learn a skill or trade that may give them permanent employment after the CSO ends. Social workers providing professional services in such settings have many roles. They are accountable to the courts for social reports and recommendations that will help in sentencing or discharge, and works with the community in the course of rehabilitation and development of the juvenile offender, such as coordinating the input of volunteer probation officers and collaborating with parents and other family members in ensuring adequate social care and support after the probation period is over. While the judicial services may be perceived as remedial on one hand, the outcome is perceived as developmental as reflected by the involvement of professional social work in the process of rehabilitation and aftercare.

In Quadrant 2, at the preventive and developmental level, the state provides a range of child-friendly incentives and services such as the Baby Bonus Scheme and subsidized childcare. Within such services, the state not only concerns itself with the remedial and developmental perspective of child and youth welfare but also has a longer term perspective through preventive and developmental measures focusing on supporting families and marriage. Singapore has a very comprehensive national child development program. For example, beginning from birth, there is the Baby Bonus Scheme first introduced in April 2001 and subsequently enhanced in August 2008. Under the scheme parents are given a cash gift by the state depending on the number of children. In addition, there is the Child Development Account where the state contributes dollar-for-dollar to an account opened by the parents for the child. This not only addresses the concern about the low national fertility rates but also addresses the very Asian concern about savings and having the long-term means to bring up children. Savings in the Child Development Account can be used for a range of purposes, from paying fees for approved childcare services to education and health-care expenses for the child.

In 1993 the state also started the Edusave Scheme to ensure that all Singapore children have opportunities to maximize learning and to motivate them to excel. The state automatically opens an Edusave account for every child from age 6–16 years in a government, government-aided, or government-supported special schools. Yearly contributions from the state will be made to the account and children can make use of the money for enrichment programs or other additional courses that can benefit them. Various scholarships and awards are also available under the Edusave Scheme to motivate achievers. These preventive and developmental services by the state show that child and youth welfare in Singapore is a prominent feature of nation-building and begins as soon as a child is born, not when the child gets into trouble.

Social work supports the state's financial provisions in enabling children to develop in a nurturing environment through the provision of children services from a systemic perspective. Social workers' roles in this quadrant are preventive and developmental and include marriage and family casework and counselling, locating necessary resources, empowering clients towards self-reliance, initiating community support, evaluating existing services, and conducting research or data collation for input into policy discourses and service development.

In Quadrant 3, preventive and developmental services are also provided by community agencies. One example is the Healthy Start program, which is targeted at young, very low income and at-risk families with newborn babies or children aged six years and below. The program reflects the many-helping-hands approach to providing social services for children and youth that are primarily preventive and developmental in nature. The Healthy Start program was piloted by a voluntary welfare agency supported by state funding. As a result of the positive outcomes associated with the pilot program, the state expanded the Healthy Start program to include another five family service centres in the community. Social workers from these family service centres collaborate with hospitals and other community organizations to identify newborns from at-risk families and support them with parenting programs aimed at increasing parent-child bonding, marital relationships, and employment upgrading. In addition, Healthy Start also provides financial assistance, such as payment for kindergarten and childcare fees, to ensure that children of very low-income families can also benefit from these facilities. The ultimate goal is to give these children and the families the basic foundation for developing a low-risk trajectory for the future.

In Quadrant 4, at the remedial and developmental level, social workers in the community are involved in the provision of student care, youth guidance, and a range of services for individuals with disabilities. These include services for children and youths who are either in trouble with the law or are at-risk of trouble with the law. These community services are both remedial and developmental in nature and often work in conjunction with other state initiated remedial services. One such example is the wide range of resources available under the National Committee on Youth Guidance and Rehabilitation, whose primary aim is to identify and reach out to at-risk youths in the community. Among the developmental services provided under this national platform are those that help to strengthen families in their role of providing guidance and discipline to young members of the family, supporting other community agencies working with at-risk youths to reduce delinquency, and to intervene when delinquent behaviours are first detected.

An example of a community-supported program is the Youth Guidance Outreach Services (YGOS), a faith-based agency using local church communities to fund and support staff and services. Social work is focused mainly on reaching out to youths who have dropped out of school, and, youths with problems who are at risk of dropping out of school. In addition, this agency provides guidance services for first-time juvenile offenders who are caught for minor offences such as shoplifting. Such offenders are first given a police caution and put on a six-month voluntary guidance program with appointed community-based youth agencies. The program, through individual counselling and group activities, is aimed at helping such youths develop better self-control and to acquire life skills that will enable them to take responsibility for their own actions. The incentive for youths to stay on the program is that if they complete the program successfully, they will not be charged by the police for the offence. The Streetwise program has similar objectives but is targeted at youths with gang connections.

In Singapore, services for children and youth with disabilities are primarily provided by community-based agencies with some subvention of programs by the state. These services for persons with disabilities are initiated by and funded primarily through public donation with some state funding for educational programs. Social work in the field of disability is concerned with the long-term care of the person with disability from a life-course perspective, from birth to ageing. As such, apart from helping families with the day-to-day care and development of the child with the disability, social work is concerned with permanency planning issues for the time when the parents of the child with the disability can no longer take care of the child (Ow, 2004). In recent years, social workers are also increasingly aware of the need to address the double burden arising from disability and ageing (Chung, 2010).

Within this matrix of services provided by the state and the community is the strong national inter-agency collaboration by the state and the community in the management of child abuse. In addition to provisions under the Children and Young Persons Act, Women's Charter, and the Penal Code, Singapore is also a signatory to the United Nations Convention on the Rights of the Child in 1995. Every child therefore has the right to protection from abuse and neglect by parents and caregivers *and* appropriate treatment for recovery and social integration. Child abuse is defined as any act by a parent, guardian, or caregiver that endangers or impairs the child's physical and/or emotional well-being.

The Ministry of Community Development, Youth and Sports documented the National Standards for Protection of Children (MCDYS, 2002; NSPC, 2002), which sets out the framework for the management of child protection in Singapore to ensure good practice. Collaborative tasks of the legal system, the police, child protection agencies in the community, the schools, the private and voluntary sectors, the health-care agencies, and the public in child protection are emphasized. Although reporting of child abuse is not mandatory, the public is encouraged to report to the relevant authorities if they have knowledge that a child is being abused so that investigation by the police can proceed. The Child Protection and Welfare Officers at the Ministry who are trained in social work practice act as the case managers. They ensure the follow-up of all cases through regular case conferences with the child abuse and protection team consisting of a range of multidisciplinary professionals from government and community agencies to the hospitals.

Social workers involved in the work of child protection must work in a multidisciplinary context with professionals from the other care systems such as the hospitals, the courts, the police force, schools, community social service agencies, policy makers, the media, and the public. The process of child protection and prevention of child abuse is placed within the centre of the matrix related to social work with children and youth because this area of social work practice requires active and clear collaboration between the state, other professional systems, and the community involving all the elements of preventive, remedial, and developmental work in the child's ecological environment.

Social Work and Family Services

In Singapore, a Confucian emphasis (Khan, 2001) on the family as the fundamental unit of society is emphasized by the government in nation-building discourses. This emphasis on family well-being and society continues to be the theme for discourse on the development of social services in the next 10 years (Mohamad, 2009). Singapore has also been deemed to be a patriarchal society that upholds traditional and conservative values emphasizing the role of the family rather than dependence on the state (Ganapathy, 2006). The cultural context of Singaporeans is heavily influenced by communal values, and family ties are prized (Leong, 1999, cited in Kee, 2004). The value and importance of children and young people feature prominently within this context. Although there are some sociocultural differences among the different ethnic groups in Singapore, there are also many similarities. State, community, and ethnic-based social services reflect these common dominant themes, such as the following:

1. The importance of interconnectivity, the nesting of the individual, the family, the community, and the nation;
2. The importance of education for upward mobility;
3. The importance of individual and community involvement in personal and national well-being, the many-helping-hands approach;
4. The importance of self-reliance as the first line of defense against challenges and external help only as a backup; and
5. The importance of developing basic building blocks in society (e.g., family unity, social security, future-orientation) through citizen-oriented programs.

In a multicultural context, there are some core values and principles of social interaction and behaviour that are shared among Singaporeans regardless of ethnic background and are the foundations for many of the social policies and social service programs in Singapore. The government together with the various ethnic communities worked together to identify these core family values. Since 1994, the Singapore Family Values has been strongly promoted and officially endorsed as the backdrop for social policies and family support and intervention (MCDYS, 2002). These Singapore Family Values are love, care, and concern; commitment to one's family; filial responsibility; mutual respect; and, communication. Traditionally, respect and communication tend to be unidirectional from the elder to the younger but with exposure to increasingly egalitarian social values supported through the media and education for all, mutual respect among individuals, including children and parents, is increasingly seen as a positive step towards generating better family and social harmony. In spite of the current emphasis on the rights of the child and the growing acceptance of a more egalitarian approach to social relationships, some traditional principles of social behaviour still govern the interaction of the average Singaporeans.

State of the Family in Singapore

Family Service Centers (FSC) are community-based social service providers located in the neighborhood in order to render social services more accessible to the public. Currently, there are 36 FSCs located in various parts of Singapore with more expected to be opened in the next few years to cater to the growing population from 4 million in 2000 to 4.8 million in 2008 (DYS, 2009).

All FSCs provide the following core services:

1. Casework and counselling, for example, marital counselling, child management, family violence, financial problems, and other interpersonal difficulties;
2. Information and referral – as a first-stop community-based service provider, FSCs act as links to other community resources and specialist agencies; and
3. Volunteer development – FSCs provide volunteer opportunities for members of the community to participate and assist in the provision of social services such as in elderly befriending; tuition programs for school children; reading programs, especially for those from low-income, non-English speaking homes; and mentoring of children and youth at risks.

Social Work and the Community

During the British colonial era, community development was perceived more as a remedial response to preventing ethnic competition and social problems rather than an aspect of social development per se. Community development then was the establishment of a few community centres that provided a point for residents to meet for social and recreational activities. Community work in Singapore began in earnest in the 1970s with the rapid development of new towns after self-government. The social implications of having a large proportion of the population living in high-rise, high-density neighborhoods include the lack of neighborliness, scarcity of social support within the community, social isolation, and a lack of ownership regarding public space and the environment (Vasoo, 2002).

New directions on community development were initiated through the formation of the People's Association comprising of a network involving both professional paid leadership and socially active community volunteers as grass-root leaders in the management of residents' committees and community centres. Over the years, social workers had been engaged in community development through the People's Association as well as through provision of community-based social services.

The most recent initiative to encourage community participation in caring for the community is the formation of the Community Development Councils (CDCs). Singapore is divided into five CDCs with the objectives of providing rapid assistance to the needy, building capacity among the people, and connecting the community. The CDC initiates, plans, and manages community programs in its own locality to promote community bonding and well-being. The welfare philosophy of many helping hands is again reflected here. The CDC provides opportunities for the more able and successful in the community to make life better for themselves and their fellow residents. It enables the residents to get involved in their community and develop a sense of care and ownership of the needs of the community they live in.

In terms of social work, the portfolio of the CDC is an example of locality development in which, for example, a number of social assistance programs exist to facilitate the social worker in helping service users to mobilize and maximize local and societal resources for meeting social and family needs. Some examples include the COMCARE GROW package where very low-income families are helped in paying for kindergarten fees through the Kindergarten Financial Assistance Scheme (KIFAS). Low-income families who need before and after school care for children aged 7–14 years can be helped under the Student Care Fee Assistance (SCFA) scheme. As part of their preventive and developmental roles, social workers can also assist service users to develop individual and family capacity through the Comcare Self-Reliance package. One example would be the Work Support Scheme in which families with low household income or no working members that demonstrate a willingness to become self-reliant can be supported. Various forms of financial assistance for a limited period are also available to enable recipients find time amidst crisis to develop skills and obtain a suitable job. The Home Ownership Plus Education Scheme (HOPE) is another scheme that encourages young, low-income families to keep their families small so that they can concentrate their resources on bringing up the children and break out of the poverty cycle. The educational grants are in the form of bursaries for the schoolgoing children up to university, as education is perceived to be the main route for upward mobility for such families.

Professional social workers provide the psychosocial and practical support required for the implementation of these programs to ensure that the service users are able to maximize on the intended benefits by accessing and continuing to be motivated to stay in these growth-inducing programs. Social workers do not provide the community resources. Their role is primarily to provide the services needed to family support and encourage the families to fully benefit from the existing community resources to enhance employability and family functioning and to provide feedback to policymakers and resource holders through their work in needs assessment.

Health and Social Work

During the post-war colonial period in the late 1940s through the 1960s, social workers in Singapore were confronted with a large segment of the population whose standard of living was characterized by malnutrition, poverty, underemployment, illiteracy, and exploitation. It is therefore no wonder that the first professionally trained social workers were employed as 'almoners' in the hospital settings dealing mainly with financial assistance and other welfare provisions under the then Social Welfare Department (Vaithilingam, 1980).

Malnutrition of children and its consequential long-term physical and mental damage meant that the work of the medical social workers was mainly focused on working with the doctors to ensure that parents understood and followed through on recommendations regarding the nutritional requirements for the children.

In addition to knowing the theory and process of working with the families, medical social workers also needed an understanding of basic dietetics.

Even then the medical social workers were engaged in work that in present-day terms could be defined as 'systemic' and ecological. For example, if parents were not able to care adequately for their children (such as being in ill-health or unemployed and lacking in means), the medical social workers sought fostering arrangements for the children. Readmission of malnourished children to hospitals was frequent, and medical social workers engaged in service development tasks such as galvanizing a voluntary welfare organization to provide convalescent care and helping to establish convalescence facilities for such children.

In the course of organizing foster and convalescent care, the medical social workers unearthed other social needs. Many children with intellectual disabilities (then labelled 'mentally retarded') also needed social care after being abandoned by the parents, and the medical social workers again had to work with community sponsors to provide residential and training facilities for these children. Medical social workers recognized that much of their tasks could not be fulfilled without the support and cooperation of the wider community outside the hospital setting and without influencing policymakers. Special education was recognized as an essential aspect of long-term care of children with intellectual disabilities by the Department of Education after a number of projects conducted by the medical social workers demonstrated its value. The role of the social worker in advocacy then as well as now must be based on evidence from the field and not on rhetorical statements about social needs. Today there are special education programs for children with different types of disabilities, with options for integration into mainstream education programs for children who are able to benefit from them.

Medical social workers have moved on from addressing challenges arising primarily from poverty and poor living conditions such as tuberculosis, leprosy, and malnutrition in the early years to challenges faced by demographic changes and rapid urbanization. Medical social workers now form part of a multidisciplinary professional team in health-care facilities such as hospitals and hospices to address issues arising from a rapidly ageing population, family challenges arising from health issues, and work-life stressors. Collaborating with a host of social service agencies outside the hospitals, medical social workers also address needs related to post-hospital care such step-down rehabilitative care in the community, domestic violence and child abuse, issues of death and dying, palliative care and bereavement, mental health, and illness.

Medical social work is therefore an important aspect of the seamless transition from health care in the hospital setting to community care and vice versa providing psychosocial support as well as practical resources to patients and their families. There are ample opportunities for training in medical social work, firstly from the perspective of a generic social worker and eventually specialization in specific areas of medical social work practice. Currently, close to 40 per cent of medical social workers have postgraduate training in social work practice and the sector enjoys firm support from the government as well as the employing agencies.

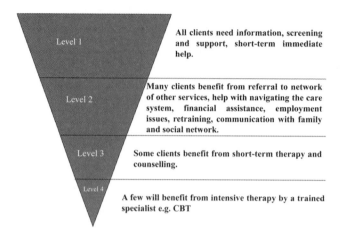

Fig. 8.2   Model for Reviewing Agency Intervention

Indigenous models of health and mental health are constantly being examined for differences in health and mental health constructs and preferred responses to health issues in the local context as a consequence of the multicultural mix among patient groups that are being documented.

Social Work in Singapore: Past and Present

The development of the social work profession has been influenced by many different beliefs, philosophies, and social theories. Historically, the underpinnings of social work had been said to include religion, charity/philanthropy, public relief through state provision, psychoanalysis, and psychotherapy (Specht, 1988). However, as has been illustrated above, the actual nature and practice of social work in any particular society is not always the intent of social work itself but a response to current major social, political, and economic forces. There is diversity in existing notions of the functions of social work that includes social reform/ advocacy, the provision of clinical/therapeutic services, and services to the poor and vulnerable. Most of social work practice in Singapore may currently be summarized briefly in the above manner:

As Figure 8.2 shows, the bulk of the service users meet social workers for the first time when they receive information and referral services at family service centres and community development councils in their neighborhood. The main intent of the information and referral service is to enable service users to access help for resolving immediate practical needs and assessment of longer term needs within their locality. Information and referral are challenging social work tasks as they function in detecting needs accurately that will lead to the provision of appropriate preventive or remedial and developmental intervention for the help seeker. As the clients are assessed and referred to appropriate social work services either within or external to the initial agency, the role and function of the social worker become better defined and the knowledge and skills more focused on helping to resolve specific identified needs. Only a small percentage of the service users however receive intensive therapy within the public social service sector. Most intensive therapies are provided by private practitioners who may not necessarily be trained in social work.

Social workers are not only engaged in the provision of direct services but also contribute to various initiatives of the government in social development and social policy (Tan and Ang, 2002; Osman, 2002):

> However, the success of social development and social policies may not always arise solely as a direct outcome of the social worker's contribution. Other factors such as the presence of political will, international collaboration and the participation of the beneficiaries of social development and social policies are also crucial. (Ow, 2010a)

Some of the challenges to the social work profession in Singapore in the future include

1. Attracting a sufficient number of university students to major in social work even though the profession obtains clear recognition and strong practical support from the government and the public through a formal comprehensive professionalization package and professional accreditation;
2. Attracting and retaining an adequate number of social work graduates for practice in areas related to ageing in comparison to more popular fields such as youth and child welfare;
3. Developing evidence-based texts on indigenous conceptualization of social needs and models of intervention as current texts and models are mainly imported from outside the Asian context;
4. Attracting an adequate number of university students from minority population groups to major in social work in spite of numerous scholarship and job opportunities; and
5. Finding evidence regarding the contexts under which a model of practice where ethnic-based agencies work collaboratively with other agencies to meet the needs of a variety of service users or ethnically integrated agencies with ample staffing from minority social workers is more useful. This issue is a challenging one for a multicultural society in which there are currently an inadequate number of minority social workers with formal social work training (Lai and Ow, 2004).

When Singapore was a British colony, social welfare was focused on mutual aid from clan associations; followed by the pre-war protection of migrant Chinese children (*mui ts'ai*), and post–World War II state provisions for the poor (Wee, 2004). The first social workers were 'almoners' meeting basic needs based on the British model of welfare and the mobilization of community voluntary organizations (charity/philanthropy) to augment state provisions. Post–independent Singapore after 1965 had to focus on economic growth and nation-building for survival. What of social welfare and social work in the new Singapore?

The philosophy of Singapore society is never about the individual but about the individual within the context of home and hearth. In order to achieve personal well-being, social workers and recipients of social services must realize that without the country, there will be no community; without the community, there will be no home; and without the home, there will be no self, in a circular, systemic chain of interdependence. The new paradigm for an emerging nation is collectivism and collaboration with an emphasis on a many-helping-hands approach to welfare (the interdependence of the self, family, community, and the state). Singapore has not emphasized social welfare and the provision of social work services as a right but as a response to inevitable calamities and personal needs. The ultimate goal is collective prosperity and harmony. Social work in Singapore exercises its mandate to exist and receives public support when the outcome of its contribution is in tune with human development and nation-building.

One of the most thoughtful conceptualizations of social work and its practice in Singapore is encapsulated in the following statements by Wee (1986: 65):

> Social work is concerned therefore with much more than just the enhancement of life for individuals and small groups in isolation: it is concerned also with enhancing their potential for contribution to the development and integration of the wider society to which they belong. ... To claim to be practicing professional social work, in a given society, is to make a statement of belief that the socio-political system is capable of change without armed struggle. Where political systems represent only sectional rights, where change is resisted by force of arms and where the rule of law is a fiction, there can be no social work profession. In such societies the worker may provide an ameliorative welfare service or join the guerrillas, but in neither case is this professional social work.

In concluding her historical account of early social work practice, another pioneer of professional social work practice in Singapore stated that

> these currently emphasized approaches to problem solving were in practice part of the Singapore social worker's repertoire long before they achieved their present status in the university's curriculum: we were generic before we knew the word. (Vaithilingam, 1980: 9)

Social work in Singapore is never just about the provision of remedial services, it is ultimately also about contributing to nation-building by participating in the development of human potential and building communities through the professional tasks of engaging and mobilizing human, economic, social, and political resources for the common good.

References

Abdullah, T. (1995), Statement by Singapore, World Summit for Social Development, United Nations Development Programme, United Nations Department of Economic and Social Affairs (DESA), http://www.un.org/ documents/ga/conf166/gov/950310074254.htm.

Bronfenbrenner, U. (1979), *The Ecology of Human Development: Experiments by Nature and Design.* Cambridge, MA: Harvard University Press.

Chung, A. (2010), Building Bridges: Integrated Care for Ageing Adults with Physical Disabilities and Senior Adults Who Acquired Disabilities in Later Life, presented at the Symposium on Critical Issues in Elderly Health, 5 March, National University of Singapore, Singapore.

Demography Yearbook of Statistics (DYS) (2009), Department of Statistics, Singapore, http://www.singstat.gov.sg.

Ganapathy, N. (2006), The Operational Policing of Domestic Violence in Singapore: An Exploratory Study, *International Criminal Justice Review*, Vol. 16, No. 3, pp. 179–98.

Kee, C.H.Y. (2004), Cultural Features as Advantageous to Therapy: A Singaporean Perspective, *Journal of Systemic Therapies*, Vol. 23, No. 4, pp. 67–79.

Khan, H. (2001), *Social Policy in Singapore: A Confucian Model?* Washington, DC: World Bank Institute.

Khoo, K.C. (2004), Child Welfare, in *Social Work in Context: A Reader*, edited by K. Mehta and A. Wee. Singapore: Marshall Cavendish.

Lai, A.E. and Ow, R. (2004), Cross-Cultural Issues in Social Service Delivery by Family Service Centres, in *Beyond Rituals and Riots: Ethnic Pluralism and Social Cohesion in Singapore*, edited by A.E. Lai. Institute of Policy Studies, Singapore: Eastern Universities Press.

Leong, J. (1999), Therapeutic Conversation through Confrontation: Reflections from a Singaporean Perspective, *Transactional Analysis Journal*, Vol. 29, No. 4, pp. 278–82.

Ministry of Community Development, Youth and Sports (MCDYS) (2002), *A Report of the Public Education Committee on Family*, Ministry of Community Development, Youth and Sports, Singapore.

Mohamad, M.O. (2002), Social Support Networks of Low Income Families in Singapore, in *Extending Frontiers: Social Issues and Social Work in Singapore,* edited by N.T. Tan and K. Mehta. Singapore: Eastern Universities Press.

Mohamad, M.O. (2009), Social Services: Perspectives in the Next 10 Years, presented at the Singapore National Council of Social Services Members Conference, Singapore.

Morales, A.T., Sheafor, B.W., and Scott, M.E. (2010), *Social Work: A Profession of Many Faces.* Boston: Allyn and Bacon.

Nair, S. (2004), Youth Issues, in *Social Work in Context: A Reader,* edited by K. Mehta and A. Wee. Singapore: Marshall Cavendish.

National Standards for Protection of Children (NSPC) (2002), *Child Protection and Welfare Services*, Ministry of Community Development, Youth and Sports, Singapore.

Singapore Department of Statistics (SDS) (2009), *Singapore in Figures 2009*, Singapore Department of Statistics, Singapore.

Ow, R. (1999), Social Work in a Multicultural Context. *International Social Work*, Vol. 42, No. 1, pp. 7–14.

Ow, R. (2004), Needs and Issues of Persons with Disability, in *Social Work in Context: A Reader*, edited by K. Mehta and A. Wee. Singapore: Marshall Cavendish.

Ow, R. (2010a), Negotiating Challenges: Social Development in Asia, *Asia Pacific Journal of Social Work and Development*, Vol. 20, No. 1, pp. 82–94.

Ow, R. (2010b), On the Move, Social Work Education: The Singapore Journey, in *Social Work Education in Countries of the East: Issues and Challenges*, edited by S. Stanley. New York: Nova Publishers.

Specht, H. (1988), *New Directions for Social Work Practice*. Englewood Cliffs, NJ: Prentice Hall.

Tan, N.T. and Ang, B.L. (2002), Social Development in Singapore Context, in *Extending Frontiers: Social Issues and Social Work in Singapore*, edited by N.T. Tan and K. Mehta. Singapore: Eastern Universities Press.

Vaithilingam, D.K. (1980), From 'Lady Almoner' to 'Medical Social Worker,' in *Towards the 1980s*, edited by: L.F.J. Cheng. Department of Social Work, National University of Singapore, Singapore.

Vasoo, S. (2002), New Directions of Community Development in Singapore, in *Extending Frontiers: Social Issues and Social Work in Singapore*, edited by N.T. Tan and K. Mehta. Singapore: Eastern Universities Press.

Wee, A. (1986), Early Social Work Resource Literature in Singapore, in *Singapore Sciences: Critical Surveys of the Humanities and Social Sciences*, edited by B.K. Kapur. Singapore: Singapore University Press.

Wee, A. (2004), Where We Are Coming From: The Evolution of Social Services and Social Work in Singapore, in *Social Work in Context: A Reader*, edited by K. Mehta and A. Wee. Singapore: Marshall Cavendish.

Chapter 9
Social Work in the Philippines

Jem Price

This chapter will attempt to 'map' the growth of social work in the Philippines, placing this account within a broader discussion of social work as an international activity (Harrison and Melville, 2010; Lyons, 2006). It will consider who 'counts' as a social worker and identify some of the key forms and features of social work in the Philippines. Consideration will be given also to the degree of professionalization of social work within the country, for example by looking at professional organization, regulation, and education. In doing this, I seek to offer a critical overview of the nature and preoccupations of social work in the Philippines and to celebrate the invaluable contributions it makes to the country and its people.

I will argue that the forms social work takes and the settings in which it happens reflect both contemporary societal and environmental factors (urban and rural poverty, concern with social and community development, the impact of conflict and 'natural' disasters) and the global development of social work as a response (noting in particular the historical influence of Spain and the United States). The impact of Roman Catholicism as the dominant national religion will be considered, as will the orientation of social work in relation to some enduring tensions and debates around social work purpose and potential (community and collective responses 'versus' individual approaches; the relative merits of radical/critical perspectives and those which seek social stability). The chapter also discusses the development of social work as a profession, examining for example its powers, recognition, and professional organization. Finally, the extent of the 'indigenous' social work knowledge base will be explored, alongside a commentary on social work education and training in the country.

Literature on the early historical development of social work makes links, explicit or otherwise, to what Hugman describes as, 'assistance for those people who were seen to be experiencing problems of daily life that were grounded in poverty' (2010: 1). This might seem a self-evident statement, and yet, of course, poverty existed long before social work. It is, therefore, suggested by many that social work evolved in individual countries as a 'modern' response to the impacts of 'modernization'. There is much truth in this. Social work did indeed evolve as a named occupation towards the end of the nineteenth century in North America, the United Kingdom, Germany, and the Netherlands (Midgley, 1981; Payne, 2005; Weiss and Welbourne, 2007). Social work, it seems, arose as a way of formalizing or bringing some coherence to a range of ad hoc responses, whether through religious organizations, institutional 'care', individual charitable works, or more politicized responses (Horner, 2009) and this is certainly true of the Philippines.

The social work profession continues to both reflect and wrestle with its own sense of purpose. Should it seek radical responses to poverty and marginalization (Brake and Bailey, 1980; Ferguson and Woodward, 2009; Lavalette and Ferguson, 2007) or the maintenance (Davies, 1994) of individuals and families in some socially acceptable place? Should social work seek collective or individualized responses to the issues which it seeks to address? How does, or might, social work engage with the complex and cross-cutting nature of social divisions (including poverty) in the societies in which it operates? To what extent should and does social work aim to influence the social policies which shape the lives of those whose needs it hopes to address? Does social work have or need boundaries or, indeed, need to be clear about its unique contributions and will this, in any event, be dependent on time and place?

All of these fundamental issues for social work are evident in the Philippines. In particular, I contend that social work in the country benefits from a certain flexibility of definition and boundaries, which means that many social workers are able to respond in less-restricted and more 'joined-up' ways than may be possible in some other countries within and beyond East Asia.

Development of Social Work in the Philippines in Global and Historical Context

Social work internationally is a relatively young profession and one which has arguably struggled to assert or even explain itself. Around the time that social work was developing in parts of the 'Global North', the Philippines was (in 1898) beginning a period of American rule which was to last for almost 50 years and which followed more than 300 years as a Spanish colony. Some parallels can be drawn with much of Northern Europe, at least in terms of the role which the Church played in encouraging private charitable acts and poor relief (Almanzor, 1966; Yu, 2006). The Roman Catholic Church remains a core participant, alongside state and voluntary sector agencies, in health and social care in the Philippines, whether through encouraging donors, providing care, or delivering social work education in Church-based universities across the country.

Prior to – and alongside – the development of professional social work around the world, family and community based informal caring and charitable acts were the primary ways in which human and social needs were addressed. However, as Dominelli puts it,

> Charitable giving was often rooted in a moralizing tendency that sought to affirm views of goodness and 'acceptable' behaviour. Such acts were normative, consistent with the dominant views held by society, and often punitive, in that they sought to limit claims on goodwill to avoid legitimating a desire to expect handouts rather than working for one's living. (2010: 18)

Social welfare in Southern (predominantly Catholic) Europe in the 1800s was significantly dependent upon faith-based charitable acts and individual donations, whilst the Protestant nations of Northern Europe, though also building upon and reflecting religious underpinnings, saw a growing State influence. The notion of charity itself was increasingly questioned, particularly in Northern Europe, on the grounds that it created dependence. Social welfare and social work grew more rapidly, typically as a state activity, in Northern Europe in the period from, say, 1945 to 1975, and less so in Southern Europe. 'Part of the reason for this was the reliance of the Iberian dictatorships until 1974 (Portugal) and 1978 (Spain) on the Catholic Church and charitable effort' (Payne, 2005: 72).

Whilst, as we shall see, the Philippines was, at this time, moving out of a long period of Spanish and then American rule, the combined influences upon social work of Church and charity remain. The interplay of 'traditions' of Catholic charitable giving when a Spanish colony and notions of targeted relief and limited state involvement in welfare introduced by the United States during their period of colonial rule have undoubtedly helped construct the Philippine approach to social work, though these influences now operate alongside (and at times in conflict with) community-focused initiatives aimed at promoting social and economic development. A specific influential dynamic in the early development of social work in the United Kingdom and United States was the growth of the settlement movement (Ferguson and Woodward, 2009; Horner, 2009; Payne, 2005), which emphasized living within poor communities, social education, community development, and (less so in America) social action. Projects such as these remain common in Philippine social work practice and also that social work in which students quite often move into deprived areas in order to undertake 'practica'.

Almanzor (1966: 27) notes that 'the humanitarian impulse' was present in the Philippines before colonial rule, but goes on to identify the influences of both Spain and the United States on the country and its social institutions. However, it fell to Yu 40 years later to offer a more critical account of the lasting impact which this had upon the profession (Yu, 2006). Both accounts present the period of Spanish rule as one in which social welfare developed, as missionaries converted most of the population to Christianity and developed schools, hospitals, and almshouses.

The period of American rule (1898–1946) saw the further development of charitable provision but also the gradual extension of public coordination and provision of welfare services. The position of the United States vis-à-vis the Philippines, however exploitative, was a different one to that with Spain. Howe (2002: 32) observes that

> the indirect or informal political control exercised by ... the United States over the Philippines, might (or might not, according to political preference) be described as imperialism. But it is not colonialism, since ... the Philippines retained formal political sovereignty. Nor is it colonization, since ... American migrants did not settle in ... the Philippines in significant numbers.

Social work is seen to have developed as a profession during the period following independence, initially by way of the influence of aid workers from the United States and elsewhere and then through a small number of Philippine social workers, trained in the United States, who established the Philippine Association of Social Workers (Almanzor, 1966; Yu, 2006).

Thus, writers on social work in the Philippines have broadly identified the adoption of Christian philanthropy/charity and aspects of American social work practice as the two major influences, with debate continuing around the interplay of those factors with indigenous culture.

Writing in 2006, Yu asserted that existing social work accounts within the Philippines of the development of its social welfare failed to engage critically with the repressive dimensions and lasting legacies of Spanish and American rule. He acknowledges that home-grown critical histories of the Philippines exist (Constantino and Constantino, 1978) but correctly sees these as absent from the work of many social work academics.

Thus, for Yu (2006: 561), 'The austerity of the Spanish colonial government and the omnipotence of the clergy created a model of social welfare that was dominated by the religious orders, with minimal government involvement.' Dominant accounts of social work in the Philippines continue to present Spanish rule as the time when hospitals and orphanages were established by a benevolent church and kindly individuals made private acts of giving as a route to salvation. Indeed, the ethos of charity and of donors is very much alive in Philippine social work and, for example, campaigning and community-based forms of social work exist alongside a deeply held faith which has the potential both to underpin committed and compassionate practice but also to limit expectations and individualize deservedness for support.

Again, for Yu (2006: 562), these beliefs 'hold perseverance in suffering as a virtue, fate as the will of God and misfortune and poverty as punishment for sin or a test of character'. Notions of individual failings and salvation, within welfare and broader society, would appear to have been a key legacy of Spain's colonization of the Philippines.

Developments under US rule included the establishment in 1915 of a Public Welfare Board to coordinate the efforts of charitable organizations and the setting-up of new charities, some initiated and sponsored by American citizens. A chapter of the American Red Cross was initially engaged in disaster relief but became increasingly concerned with health and social welfare. Institutional responses to need remained a core feature but with the gradual growth of health centres, social work offices in poor areas, some limited attempts to remove people from slum living, and so on (Landa Jocano, 1980).

The period also saw the registration of charitable providers, clearer eligibility criteria, and increased government and private funding of charitable services. However, the impact of economic depression in the 1930s, in a context of reliance upon the United States, was very significant, with a need for basic relief work (Lee-Mendoza, 2008). A small number of women gained scholarships to attend American universities for training from the 1920s onwards, and brought back social work theories and approaches to the Philippines.

In 1935, the Philippines entered a commonwealth period, with Manuel L. Quezon becoming the first president. The economy began to recover, a minimum wage was introduced and there was an expansion of public welfare legislation and programs, including some extension in rural areas. For Landa Jocano (1980: 63), the 1930s saw a transition in social welfare in the country (prompted by American influence), both in terms of a growing attention to 'professionalization' and an increasing emphasis on the need for coordination.

In 1940, the Department of Health and Public Welfare was established. However, the government was forced into exile from 1942–1945, during which time the Philippines was occupied by Japan and, again, emergency relief work became the focus of all agencies, governmental, religious, and charitable. After the war, the government faced 'the gigantic task of serving a war-beaten people, weakened by three painful years of enemy occupation' (Jocano 1980: 92). In 1946, the Philippines was proclaimed a republic. State engagement with welfare grew. The year 1947 saw a Social Welfare Commission being situated under the Office of the President which, for Lee-Mendoza (2008: 25) 'signified the formal recognition of social welfare as a responsibility by the state'.

The main areas of social welfare – and of social work activity – at this time were financial and other forms of relief, institutional care, work-training/income-generation projects, and rural welfare (not only concerned with relief but, very gradually, with the development of community kitchens, self-help programs and cooperatives, and the construction of basic road networks).

Building on the experiences of that small number of Filipinos receiving social work training in the United States, social work schools were established, initially in and around the capital, Manila. The Philippine Association of Social Workers was formed by that same handful of overseas-trained workers in 1947. Social workers in the 1950s and 1960s were, indeed, engaged in 'casework' rather than group or community work, mostly working in hospitals and mental health settings, assessing eligibility for free treatment and financial support (Lee-Mendoza, 2008: 56). UNICEF funding of training for children and families social workers provided a boost to the number of trained professionals at this time. A key development for the social work profession came in 1965, when Republic Act 4373 introduced regulation of social work and of the operation of social work agencies.

In 1965, Ferdinand Marcos became president of the country, a position he retained until 1986. The country saw a growing UN focus in the 1960s and 1970s on a development agenda. UNICEF, for example, became active in the Philippines. Funds were directed to national initiatives which aimed to tackle poverty and raise overall living standards. It has been suggested that Marcos's early years saw real attempts to achieve such aims, though he faced growing protest from students seeking educational reform, from the Filipino Communist Party, and from Muslim separatists in the south. In 1972, Marcos declared martial law, which was to stay in force until a visit of Pope John Paul II in 1981. Opposition leaders were silenced or forced into exile. Curfews were imposed and, seemingly, 'accepted' by much of the population. The armed forces grew in size very significantly. Yet the 1970s saw economic growth, relative prosperity, and a form of repressed stability. Much of this was sustained – if not created – by the billions of dollars of aid provided by the United States, coupled with the associated markets for Philippine products.

In 1976, existing government welfare agencies evolved into the Department of Social Services and Development, which for Lee-Mendoza (2008: 31) reflected the

> ... shifting emphasis from the traditional, often institution-based social welfare to community-oriented programs and services which underscored people's own capacities for problem-solving.

Social workers continued with activities such as emergency relief work and day care but became increasingly part of the drive for development, working with communities to develop businesses and skills for employment.

So, as martial law continued around it and the country became ever more reliant on a former imperial power, social workers and others (in government, voluntary, and private sector agencies) arguably engaged with a system which placed the onus on the poor to work their way out of poverty. Much of the social and economic development agenda was to be promoted through the existing political structure of *barangays*, a form of government at the very local level. The *barangays* remain very influential for social welfare and can have a key impact upon social work at the practice level. Long before Spanish rule, *barangays* were the main structure for settling disputes or seeking communal support at times of need (Zulueta and Nebres, 2003; Viloria and Martinez, 1987).

Spain introduced a centralized structure, with the country divided into *encomiendas*, or regions given limited fiscal powers and charged with promoting welfare and conversion of the population to Catholicism. Towards the end of the eighteenth century, a system of provincial government was introduced, in which the mayoral offices at the level of province and pueblo (town) were only open to Spaniards. Each *pueblo* was made up of a number of *barangays*, and it was only at this level that Filipinos were permitted to hold office. Zulueta and Nebres hold that corruption manifested itself at every level of the system and that, with the union of Church and State, a repressive state structure led to, 'much oppression and untold suffering' (2003: 60). Social workers in the Philippines today continue to grapple with a political system, and hence a welfare system, in which the personal power and influence of elected representatives and paid officials can hold huge sway. At the local level, social workers must typically inform and work through the barangay, which presents both potential barriers and an opportunity, a resource and a connection to local people.

Thus, for better and for worse, the community context is direct and real for much Philippine social work and those connections between *barangay* and welfare were first made explicit and formal as part of the development program under Marcos's 'New Society' policy ambition. Marcos undertook to breathe new life into the *barangays*, emphasizing their role as citizens' assemblies and as the focus for community decision making and planning to meet local needs. It is, however, difficult to see how this was to happen under a declaration which 'denied the people any meaningful participation [and] respected no constitutional rights, no civil liberties' (Zulueta and Nebres, 2003: 251).

Martial law was suspended in January 1981, though not fully in the predominantly Muslim regions of Mindanao. Marcos's final years as president saw economic stagnation and increasing levels of poverty and corruption. His position was, however, fatally damaged by the assassination of returning opposition leader Benigno Aquino, Jr., in August 1983. In 1986, Marcos sought to reassert his position by calling an election. Aquino's widow, Corazon 'Cory' Aquino, stood against him. When Marcos was declared winner of the election, tens of thousands took to the streets, demanding that Marcos stand down. Senior politicians and military leaders defected, throwing their support behind Aquino, and mass 'people power' demonstrations were held. Marcos went into exile and Aquino became president.

She, too, was keen to see a shift from welfare and relief to a development approach, creating the Department for Social Welfare and Development (DSWD) (2009, 2011a, b), which exists to this day. The Department was divided into five areas: family and community, children and youth, women, disabled and elderly people, and emergency assistance/disaster relief. By the early 1990s, the DSWD was the largest employer of licenced social workers in the Philippines and policy was focusing on 'Low Income Municipalities (LIMs) and other socially-depressed barangays' (Lee-Mendoza, 2008: 35–6).

The Local Government Code 1991 (Republic Act 7160) sought to increase accountability and autonomy by decentralizing a broad range of responsibilities and functions from national to local government, with associated funding. The majority of responsibilities (within government, at least) to provide social work and welfare services were devolved to the level of municipality, with some services, such as maintaining local health and day care centres, devolved to the *barangay*. The DSWD became a research and policy planning agency. This was a wholesale revision of the context in which most statutory social workers would operate and of the structures with which social workers in nongovernmental agencies would engage. Social workers employed within DSWD itself would, in future, be involved with support to – and regulation of – the services provided by local government, NGOs, and people's organizations. From the 1990s onwards, social work in the Philippines continued to operate within a pluralist structure of local government units, nongovernmental organizations, faith-based charitable providers, and some private sector agencies (such as private hospitals and industrial social work settings). All of this activity is, to varying degrees, subject to the oversight and 'vision' of the DSWD, which also employs some social workers in research and monitoring roles.

Legislation since 1990 has focused on empowerment/rights (for example, of Disabled People in 1992 and Indigenous Peoples in 1997) and on protection (of Children, in 1992, and through an anti-trafficking law in 2003).

The Philippine Council for NGO Certification suggests that there could be 60,000 NGOs in the Philippines and their work is seen very much as a part of social work and a place for social work. Thus, the Mission of the DSWD in 2011 was as follows:

> To provide social protection and promote the rights and welfare of the poor,
> vulnerable and the disadvantaged individuals, families and communities that
> will contribute to poverty alleviation and empowerment through social welfare
> development policies, programs, projects and services implemented with
> or through local government units (LGUs), non-government organizations
> (NGOs), people's organizations (POs), other government organizations (GOs)
> and other members of civil society. (DSWD, 2011a)

To conclude, one cannot understand social work in the Philippines without seeing
it in the context of its colonial and political history, much of which has been
shaped by foreign governments and international NGOs since independence.
Yu acknowledges that US rule saw the introduction of democracy and of public
provision and funding in welfare but holds that this happened in the interests of
retaining very significant powers over the Philippines and Filipinos. Furthermore,
Yu suggests that 'colonial rule' brought to the Philippines a form of social welfare
which was functional, residualized, and individualist (Yu, 2006). Though it is true
that casework models were adopted from US social work (and remain in some
areas of practice), it is also the case that the drive towards development (coupled
with very limited resources and reliance on overseas aid) has underpinned an
emphasis on community-based social work since the 1970s. Social development
remains a central focus of the DSWD.

In 2010, Benigno Aquino III was elected President of the Philippines, in part
on an anti-corruption manifesto. Whilst this may be seen as bearing some fruit,
corruption and graft remains a very significant dimension of Philippine society
and electoral politics. However, post-war experience has demonstrated to Filipinos
that protest can be a very powerful thing indeed. It is in this context that social
workers go about their day-to-day work and this chapter now turns to consider the
nature and features of contemporary social work in the Philippines.

Social Work in the Philippines Today

The history of the Philippines and of its social welfare system has had a profound
impact on what social work is and does in the country. There are broadly three
dimensions to professional practice, all of which remain core to the curriculum for
social work students and all of which are evident in practice and are considered
'professional social work'. These are Social Casework (conceptualized as
assistance towards individual adjustment), Social Group Work (group activities
organized for welfare purposes), and Community Organization (Landa-Jocano,
1980: 5–6). Whilst this suggests a breadth to social work in the country which is
less evident in many others, one could argue that social work in the Philippines,
whether at the individual, group, or community level, is often concerned with
maintenance, rather than opposition, and with notions of responsibility (whether
individual, family, or social).

Social workers in the Philippines commonly characterize their practice as
responding to poverty, and it is true that this very often underlies the issues which

they seek to address. However, as we have seen, the country imported an American model in which workers were expected to specialize in one of three forms of social work (casework, group work, or community organizing). Indeed, as we have seen, despite being a country which might be characterized as having a strong sense of community, social work did not take predominantly community (or generalist) forms until the UN push for development in the 1960s and 1970s. The preference for generalist skills and approaches, however, does also make pragmatic sense, in a context where just one social worker may cover a large area with extensive social need, particularly in rural parts of the country.

Lee-Mendoza tellingly comments that, even where social work in the Philippines does take the form of casework (for example, in responding to child abuse or to the needs adults with mental health needs), 'case managers have no choice but to also provide direct service which means ... resource provider, mediator, social broker, enabler, counsellor/therapist, and advocate' (2008: 529). Roles are perhaps defined 'softly', with social workers being able to conceptualize 'problems' broadly and to work across boundaries, in ways which do not occur in a good number of other countries.

This is, for many, a strength, and yet others in the profession argue for increasingly specialist training, practice, knowledge, and skills as the way forward.

Social workers in the Philippines work across a very wide range of organizational and practice contexts. They may, for example, be employed by international or national NGOs, central or local government, factories, charities, or faith-based organizations. The DSWD is the central government department responsible for the protection of social welfare rights and promoting and supporting social development. Whilst its direct social work functions and facilities are devolved to local government units (LGUs), the department employs social workers to devise and monitor national programs, undertake social research, and carry out training and capacity building across the country. According to its Annual Report 2011, the DSWD had a total staffing of 10,318 nationwide at the end of 2011, of whom 890 (less than 9 per cent) were based in the central office and the remainder were assigned to 16 field offices (DSWD, 2011b).

Areas of social work practice in the Philippines include child welfare and family support; work with older people, women, disabled people, and those with mental health problems; disaster management; community development and sustainability; community organizing; and advocacy and social action. Roles and tasks undertaken range from direct practice with individuals, families, groups, and communities to positions which focus upon social administration, project development, training, and the management of programs. Social work takes place in settings which include private companies, military contexts, private and public hospitals, courts, statutory and non-statutory welfare institutions, schools, and church-based services. Practice will sometimes focus upon particular 'groups' within the population, such as street children, farmers, the urban poor, or migrant workers.

However, it is equally likely to take the form of generic practice, tackling issues as they arise within a local area. A significant dimension of social work in the Philippines is that many qualified and registered social workers are in posts with titles which do not mention social work. Almanzor (1988) commented that this can be because they are working for NGOs or international organizations where the job title relates to funding requirements or specific agency aims (say, around youth work or campaigning for the rights of older people) or that they are in planning or research positions within, for example, the United Nations. Social work in the Philippines is, indeed a very 'broad church'.

This considerable range of sectors, settings, and roles has implications for the degree of autonomy afforded to social workers. Social workers do work in government positions but are also commonly employed by self-help/people's organizations (where the agenda should properly be set by clients or service users themselves) and by local and international nongovernmental organizations (which will, of course, have set aims and are likely to expect funds to be used for pre-agreed purposes). Workers and academics also recognize the impact of political influence and financial constraints on professional autonomy. As in all countries, therefore, one can identify significant differences in the extent to which social workers in the Philippines are able to act as autonomous professionals.

We now turn to look at the extent to which one might identify a body of Philippine social work literature, as one indicator of the maturity and establishment of social work within the country.

Indigenous Social Work Knowledge and Approaches

Midgley (1997: 176) describes a process in the 'Third World' whereby social workers and academics realized the limitations of imported individualized, remedial forms of practice, designed for Western urban settings, and instead set about designing methods which had more to offer for development in contexts where lack of food and mass illiteracy (often in rural areas) were more typical social problems. This section considers the extent to which social work in the Philippines has undertaken 'local' research and developed indigenous social work theory and methods for practice.

One form of indigenization of social work in the Philippines, though driven by an international agenda of development, was the aforementioned shift towards a generalist form of practice or what was known as the 'integrated method'. Practice which engaged at the individual level was not encouraged, as this did not easily support a development perspective. A response to poverty was seen as a community issue and social workers facilitated access to resources, fund-raised, motivated members of communities to participate, and trained local people to coordinate projects. Developmental social work uses a range of approaches to build capacity, self-sufficiency, and prevention in communities. Though areas of specialist practice exist (such as medical and forensic social work), many workers are in generic contexts and roles and adopt appropriate methods of intervention which draw on community social work theory and aspects of social pedagogy.

Weiss and Welbourne suggest that one indicator of the development of social work as a profession in a particular country is the development of 'country-specific knowledge', pointing out that most 'developing' countries come to identify the limited transferability of 'Western' casework models (2007: 227–28). As has been suggested, any account of social work in the Philippines must engage with the processes of colonization and globalization and of indigenization (Midgley, 1990; Lawrence et al., 2009; Harrison and Melville, 2010). At a pan-Asia conference held in the Philippines in 1976, for example, Delos Reyes noted that 64 per cent of the Philippine population lived in rural areas and urged that

> Noting the gross inequalities between urban and rural areas in income, facilities and opportunities, the thrust of rural development needs to be social justice and working towards a just society. The method best suited is that of social action-community organization. (1976: 89)

Though urbanized areas are expanding rapidly, approximately half of the Philippine population still live in rural areas and almost three-quarters of the poor live in those rural areas. Indigenous social work knowledge and forms of intervention are needed and, to varying degrees, evident.

Indigenous texts and journals which seek to explain social work in the national context certainly exist and have done so for many years (De Guzman, 1971; Glasser, 1970). However, they typically include theories and approaches which were mostly developed in the United States or United Kingdom. Whilst case studies and examples of agencies in the Philippines are employed throughout, to 'localize' the concepts presented, there is often little which might be described as 'Philippine social work theory'. There is evidence of a considered and well-developed knowledge base in terms of social conditions and issues in the Philippines (David, 2001, 2004; Landa Jocano, 2002).

Whilst there is also a literature engaging with structural factors such as poverty and gender, the social work literature does not appear consistently to be conceptualized in terms of social divisions or issues of power or anti-oppressive practice and a critical account of history is very often absent. Lee-Mendoza deserves much credit for writing a text for social work students and practitioners in the Philippines (2008). It was one of the very first to seek to account for social work in a Philippine context, to 'indigenize' Western practice models and to provide culturally recognizable case material and examples. The third edition was published in 2008, some time after Yu's previously discussed analysis had emerged (in which Lee-Mendoza is one of those authors whom he criticizes). Yet it retains an apparently 'neutral' (if not positively disposed) account of welfare development under Spain and the United States (and, for that matter, of the years of martial law in the 1970s and 1980s).

Lee-Mendoza is not alone in her take on Philippine history and the place of social work. Viloria and Martinez (1987) and Landa Jocano (1980) paint a similarly benign picture. Although Viloria and Martinez offer some critique of the long period of Spanish domination, highlighting the 'appalling rise in destitution' and the pain caused by 'The Sword and The Cross' (1987: 23), this is tempered with a somewhat grateful acknowledgment of the growth of education, of Christianity, and of charitable support for, 'the poor, the sick, the aged, the mentally ill and defective, the orphans, and youthful delinquents' (1987: 24). No critique of the motives or impact of the 'American phase' is offered or, indeed, of the Marcos regime, which had collapsed the year before this account was published. One can, therefore, identify social work literature written in and for students and workers in the Philippines but one might struggle to identify a critical indigenous social work literature.

In the Philippines, the cost of books is prohibitive for many students and university libraries to maintain stocks of current literature, and access to knowledge is certainly affected by limitations on resources. Having said that, a good number of local texts have been published and are reflected in the bibliography for this chapter. A number of social work and related journals are also published – albeit intermittently – within the Philippines (*Philippine Journal of Social Work; Social Welfare and Development Journal*). Finally, the various social work associations do hold conferences and other events at which research findings, theories, and practice issues are shared and debated.

It would seem fair to argue that social work in the Philippines has gone some considerable way towards developing unique areas of indigenous knowledge (Gray et al., 2008; Zhang and Huang, 2008; Veneracion, 2003) and methods for practice (Cordero et al., 2000a, b; Lee-Mendoza, 1999) but that the pervasive influence of global social work theory and limited resources for research and academic endeavor mean that there remains (as, of course, there always is) room for further development.

Social Work as a Profession in the Philippines

Accounts of the international development of social work typically point to professional development and recognition, the growth of social work education, the sharing of ideas through conferences and Internet-use, efforts to indigenize received methods and theories, and the increasing evidence of cross-national practice, student learning, and academic endeavor. Weiss and Welbourne name the 'drive for professional status' as a consistent – and consistently controversial – feature of the development of social work in all countries (2007: 1).

Indicators of 'degree of professionalization' (such as, the existence of codes of ethics and whether those codes are enforced, monopoly of specific roles, or protection of the title of 'social worker') suggest that social work is significantly more established and formalized in some countries than others. This section, drawing upon some of the main themes in Weiss and Welbourne's work, looks at core aspects of the social work profession in the Philippines.

One key aspect of professional development is that of public and governmental recognition, which can include restriction on use of the title 'social worker', licencing, and level of qualification. Here, social work in the Philippines 'scores well'. Republic Act 4373, passed in 1965, introduced the requirement that social workers complete a bachelor's degree, incorporating 1,000 hours of supervised field experience (typically in community, government, and private institutions) and pass a government board examination in order to be registered as a social worker (Lee-Mendoza, 2008; Viloria and Martinez, 1987). Such formal recognition and regulation took far longer to achieve in many other parts of the world, 'developing' or 'developed'.

Since the 1960s, the Philippines saw ongoing efforts to set and monitor standards in social work education (Lee-Mendoza, 2008: 61–4). For Midgley (1997: 167),

> American influences can be readily detected in Asian social work education, particularly in India and the Philippines, where the American preference for university-level training was adopted. ... While India, the Philippines and Korea have numerous schools of social work, countries such as Singapore, Thailand, and Papua New Guinea have more limited provision.

Social work qualifying programs in the Philippines are typically four years in duration. Admission requirements for social work training in the Philippines include the gathering of satisfactory references, health checks, evidence of appropriate qualifications, and the passing of a college entrance examination. A graduate of a social work qualifying course must pass the Board Examination for Social Workers in order to practice as a registered social worker in the Philippines. The Board of Examiners for Social Work was created in 1965, composed of a Chair and four members, appointed by the President of the Philippines. The examination is supervised by the Professional Regulation Commission (PRC).

In the 1960s, social workers demanded measures to raise the profile and status of the profession, resulting in Republic Act No. 5175 being passed in 1967. Among other provisions, this act permitted the qualification of master's degree holders in social work for board examinations and mandated the upgrading of the educational requirement of the members of the Board of Examiners from a bachelor's degree to a master's degree in social work.

A national curriculum has been in place for social work in the Philippines since the late 1960s, with the most recent version being developed by the National Association for Social Work Education (NASWEI) and the Philippine Association of Social Workers (PASWI) and approved by the Government's Commission on Higher Education in 2010 (CHED, 2010). These 'Policies and Standards for Bachelor of Science in Social Work Program' set out clear competency expectations (CHED, 2010: 3–4), which include skills in the helping process, critical understanding of discrimination and oppression, knowledge of social policy, applied psychology and sociology, and the ability to reflect critically and to make appropriate use of supervision. There is, therefore, considerable rigor in terms of expected standards of social work education across the country.

The long-standing existing of social work associations in the Philippines (especially the Philippine Association of Social Workers, Inc. [PASWI], established in 1947) is, in itself, another indicator of professional maturity. PASWI played a central role in the passage of the 'Act to Regulate the Practice of Social Work and the Operation of Social Work Agencies in the Philippines' in 1965 and subsequent legislation which created the Department of Social Welfare in 1968. It first adopted a Code of Ethics in 1964, with the most recent revision being in 1998 (Lee-Mendoza, 2008: 134). The association organizes regular seminars, workshops, and conferences. PASWI has been able to question government policies and actions on a number of occasions. For example, it, 'took a stand on such social issues like [*sic*] family planning, the integration of cultural minorities into Philippine society, the release of activist social workers who were detained for charges of rebellion during the Martial Law Period … [and it]… campaigned for opposition to the government initiated proposal to merge the DSWD and the Department of Health in the 1980s.' (Lee-Mendoza, 2008: 60–61). It is equally important to note that the National Association for Social Work Education, Inc. (Philippines), has been in existence and active, though with slightly changing names, since 1965. NASWEI operates as the national umbrella organization of schools of social work in the Philippines

One final indicator of professional organization and standing, again discussed by Weiss and Welbourne is that of prestige and remuneration. They comment that

> Generally, the status and prestige of social work … is not high. In half the countries … its status is particularly low relative to that of other helping professions. (2007: 240)

In the Philippines, again this in part depends upon the sector within which particular practitioners work but there remains a general concern that more could be done to improve the status and professional image of social work (vis-à-vis, say, medical professionals) and to broaden the public perception of social work among many Filipinos as primarily related to 'dole out' (Dineros-Pineda, 1992). Thus, Salvador-Tojos and Cabilao (2003) pose the following question:

> For all our efforts as social workers, why do some people still associate us mainly or solely with disaster management and the curative approach to providing assistance?

This section has sought to provide an overview of social work roles, education, and knowledge and of the place of the profession in the Philippines today. Social work in the Philippines is an established and comparatively well-developed profession but one which continues to tussle with the advantages and challenges of professional status and the inevitable tensions associated with practice in varied agency contexts.

Concluding Thoughts

Hugman (2010) makes the very significant point that 'social development' has constituted a core dimension of postcolonial social work. Whilst this may well be a response to poverty, Hugman also suggests that in Africa and Asia, social development forms a bridge between micro and macro approaches, and incorporates those notions of 'harmony and cohesion' which are central to those societies. Whereas Western social work tends to emphasize the interpersonal and individual social need, Hugman points out that social work in 'developing' countries typically engages with capacity building in communities and with economic development at the local level. It seeks to reconcile individual rights and wishes with those of family and community, in a way which might be considered contrary to Western ideas of anti-oppressive practice. However, for Hugman,

> Ironically, we have to recognize that the terms of this debate are couched in the value system derived from the European tradition, in which the post-Enlightenment notions of human rights and social justice are understood predominantly in a very individualistic way. ... For social work to operate only with an overly individualistic notion of how these values are to be achieved in such contexts may be both practically counter-productive and also constitute an implicit form of neo-colonialism. (2010: 85)

I hope to have shown that, though social work and social welfare in the Philippines has been influenced very considerably and directly by European and US social work, it has also developed its own policies and approaches in order to offer more culturally appropriate and economically realistic responses to human need and to contribute to a broader development agenda.

Social work is a well-established profession within the Philippines and one which is evident across a range of government and nongovernmental settings. Tensions within the profession include those around public perception and professional prestige, between specialist and generic practice, and between individualized and community-oriented approaches. Social workers uniformly describe their practice as being anti-poverty work (with many providing direct support to slum-dwellers, poor fishing communities, street children, and so on) and the profession is often conceptualized in terms of development objectives.

It is by no means uncommon to see social workers challenging social policy or protesting alongside marginalized people and communities, fighting for the extension of rights and welfare provisions, and supporting organized action. However, it is equally common to find social workers within private and public hospital settings, mental health or child protection contexts, working to something akin to a casework approach. Of course, social work in the Philippines also responds to the fallout of armed conflict and natural disasters. Social workers offer support, expertise, protection, and hope in a country whose people face many challenges.

Faith (predominantly Roman Catholic but with significant Muslim populations) brings much to social work in the Philippines: compassion, cultural understanding, a prime source of motivation and commitment, and a basis for ethical practice. The legacy of Spain (not least in terms of the Catholic faith) is very evident in the approach to welfare, the settings and services available, sources of funding and, perhaps, the ways in which clients or service users are perceived and approached. The impact of the much shorter period of American rule has also been discussed, with the early pioneers being trained in the United States.

Whilst many social workers are troubled by the common equating of their profession with 'dole-out', this does at least mean that the public perception of social work is largely positive and 'appreciative'. Social work in the country continues to provide tangible support at times of crisis and extreme need.

The relative fluidity of many social work roles, in terms of method or approach and of engagement with individuals within families and communities, is (for this author, at least) a real strength.

A further strength is the extent to which qualified social workers operate across government agencies, international and local NGOs, charitable organizations and campaigning groups (and that their roles and contributions in all of these contexts are considered social work).

If the Philippines is, indeed, moving into a period of economic growth, it is to be hoped that some of the increased wealth reaches those most in need and that social work continues to play a central role in protecting people and communities from the potentially detrimental effects of social and economic development.

References

Almanzor, A. (1966), The Profession of Social Work in the Philippines: Historical Background, *International Social Work*, Vol. 9, pp. 27–34.

Almanzor, A. (1988), The Fundamental Components of Social Work Practice: A New Look at Old Issues, in *Social Work in the Philippines: Tradition and Profession*, edited by C. Veneracion. Manila: PASWI.

Brake, M. and Bailey, R. (eds.) (1980), *Radical Social Work and Practice*. London: Edward Arnold.

CHED (2010), *Policies and Standards for Bachelor of Science in Social Work Program*, Quezon City: CHED.

Constantino, R. and Constantino, L. (1978), *The Philippines: A Continuing Past*. Quezon City: Foundation for Nationalist Studies.

Cordero, E., Pangalangan, E. and Fondevilla, R. (eds.) (2000a), *Philippine Encyclopedia of Social Work: Volume 1*. Quezon City: Megabooks Company/ National Association of Social Work Education Inc.

Cordero, E., Pangalangan, E. and Fondevilla, R. (eds.) (2000b), *Philippine Encyclopedia of Social Work: Volume 2*. Quezon City: Megabooks Company/ National Association of Social Work Education Inc.

David, R. (2001), *Reflections on Sociology and Philippine Society*. Quezon City: University of the Philippines Press.

David, R. (2004), *Nation, Self and Citizenship: An Invitation to Philippine Sociology*. Pasig City: Anvil.

Davies, M. (1994), *The Essential Social Worker*. Aldershot: Ashgate.

De Guzman, L. (ed.) (1971) *Philippine Encyclopedia of Social Work*. Manila: Philippine Association of Social Workers.

Delos Reyes, E. (1976), Country Paper: The Role of Social Work Education in Rural Development in the Philippines, in *Proceedings of the Group Training Course on the Role of Social Work Education in Rural Development*, edited by UNESCAP and University of the Philippines, and jointly sponsored by UN Economic and Social Commission for Asia and the Pacific and University of the Philippines Institute of Social Work and Community Development, Quezon City: University of the Philippines.

Dineros-Pineda, J. (1992), Beyond Nutrition: Empowerment in the Philippines, *International Social Work*, Vol. 35, pp. 203–15.

Dominelli, L. (2010), *Social Work in a Globalizing World*. Cambridge: Polity Press.

Department of Social Welfare and Development (2009), *Sama-Samang Pagtawid Tungo sa Kaunlaran: 2009 Annual Report*. Quezon City: Department of Social Welfare and Development.

DSWD (2011a), *About Us – Vision, Mission, Mandate*. Accessed 20 May 2011 at http://www.dswd.gov.ph/index.php/about-us.

DSWD (2011b), *Painting a Better Future: How DSWD's Programs Build the Filipino Family, DSWD Annual Report 2011*. Quezon City: Department of Social Welfare and Development.

Ferguson, I. and Woodward, R. (2009), *Radical Social Work in Practice*. Bristol: Policy Press.

Glasser, P. (1970), Present Status of Social Welfare Services in the Philippines, *International Social Work*, Vol. 13, p. 55.

Gray, M.; Coates, J., and Yellow-Bird, M. (2008), *Indigenous Social Work Around the World: Towards Culturally Relevant Education and Practice*. Aldershot: Asgate.

Harrison, G. and Melville, R. (2010), *Rethinking Social Work in a Global World*. Basingstoke: Palgrave Macmillan.

Horner, N. (2009), *What Is Social Work? Context and Perspectives*. Exeter: Learning Matters.

Howe, S. (2002), *Empire: A Very Short Introduction*. Oxford: Oxford University Press.

Hugman, R. (2010), *Understanding International Social Work: A Critical Analysis*. Basingstoke: Palgrave Macmillan.

Landa Jocano, F. (1980), *Social Work in the Philippines: A Historical Overview*. Quezon City: New Day Publishers.

Landa Jocano, F. (2002), *Slum as a Way of Life. A Study of Coping Behavior in an Urban Environment*. Quezon City: PUNLAD Research House.

Lavalette, M. and Ferguson, I. (eds.) (2007), *International Social Work and the Radical Tradition*. Birmingham: Venture Press.

Lawrence, S., Lyons, K., Simpson, G. and Huegler, N. (eds.) (2009), *Introducing International Social Work*. Exeter: Learning Matters.

Lee-Mendoza, T. (1999), *Social Work with Groups*. Quezon City: Megabooks Company.

Lee-Mendoza, T. (2008), *Social Welfare and Social Work*. Quezon City: Central Books.

LGC (1991), *Local Government Code 1991*. Manila: AVB Printing Press.

Lyons, K. (2006), Globalisation and Social Work: International and Local Implications, *British Journal of Social Work*, Vol. 36, No. 3, pp. 365–80.

Midgley, J. (1981), *Professional Imperialism: Social Work in the Third World*. London: Heinemann.

Midgley, J. (1990), International Social Work: Learning from the Third World, *Social Work*, Vol. 35, No. 4, pp. 295–301.

Midgley, J. (1997), *Social Welfare in Global Context*. Thousand Oaks, CA: Sage.

Payne, M. (2005), *The Origins of Social Work: Continuity and Change*. Basingstoke: Palgrave Macmillan.

Salvador-Tojos, L. and Cabilao, F. (2003), Foreword, in *Social Work in the Philippines: Tradition and Profession,* edited by C. Veneracion. Manila: PASWI.

Veneracion, C.J. (ed.) (2003), *Social Work in the Philippines: Tradition and Profession*. Manila: Philippine Association of Social Workers.

Viloria, E. and Martinez, J. (1987), Growth and Development of Humanitarian Services in the Philippines, in *Social Work in the Philippines, Tradition and Profession*, edited by C. Veneracion. Manila: PASWI.

Weiss, I. and Welbourne, P. (eds.) (2007), *Social Work as a Profession: A Comparative Cross-National Perspective*. London: BASW/Venture Press.

Yu, N. (2006), Ideological Roots of Philippine Social Welfare, *International Social Work*, Vol. 49, pp. 559–70.

Zhang, X. and Huang, Y. (2008), A Reflection on the Indigenization Discourse in Social Work, *International Social Work*, Vol. 51, pp. 611–22.

Zulueta, F. and Nebres, A. (2003), *Philippine History and Government through the Years*. Mandaluyong City: National Book Store.

Chapter 10
Social Work Services and Developmental Social Policy

Christian Aspalter

We are witnessing a great deal of development in the social work arena throughout all of East Asia, be it in the new, developing economies of Southeast Asia or in the generally already more developed countries of Northeast Asia. The above chapters have depicted past and ongoing developments with regard to the development of social work services and the institutionalization of social work as a profession in the region.

Each author has been given a relatively high degree of freedom to depict what is important to know about social work in his or her country or region. In this way, the findings of each case study have become richer, covering a wider spectrum of issues and developments. This book is in essence very explorative in nature, as it is the first book that collects data on social work developments all across a wide geographic area of Northeast and Southeast Asia.

This chapter will not repeat the findings, but rather it will add to 'the bigger picture' of social work development in this part of the world, in any part of the world (cf. Cox and Pawar, 2012; Healy and Link, 2011). The main part of this chapter concentrates on much-needed normative guidelines, as to *how to extend, improve, and adapt social work services to ongoing societal changes* – particularly the spread of post-industrial societies, fast aging of societies, and individualization of society, as well as continuous economic globalization.

All of these social problems acquire special solutions that require (1) monetary social policies (e.g., social security, or social assistance) and (2) non-monetary social policies that (a) develop social work services, (b) educate and guide the public in everyday life through 'advertisement in the public interest' (API), (c) city and rural planning and development, (d) develop physical and mental health care institutions, (e) develop community support and social capabilities, (f) develop cultural capabilities, (g) develop a natural and physical environment that is favorable for the prevention and cure of social problems (and less-favorable social outcomes), and so forth.

In a nutshell, this chapter seeks, with the help of normative theories in social policy and social work, to picture new needs, new methods, and overarching models for social policy and corresponding social work services.

What Are Normative Theories?

Scientists by and large follow three distinct objectives: (1) they observe developments, (2) they explain these developments, and then (3) they may add evaluative comments, distinguishing positive from negative practices and policies, as well as giving ideas of how things could be changed, what should be done, should be achieved, and what strategies and methods one should follow in doing so. The latter is the realm of normative theory (Table 10.1).

Table 10.1   Classification of Theories: With a Special Emphasis on Social Work Services

Descriptive Theories	Explanatory Theories	Normative Theories
• historical descriptions/ analysis • describing particular social work services • comparing social work services • comparing social policies for social work services • setting up classifications of social work services	• explaining determinants of the social work services and developments • explaining past and current developments • explaining comparative differences and similarities, deviations in social work services • projecting past trends and developments into the future	• evaluating/criticizing particular social work services, or overall social work systems • identifying particular failures and successes in social work services • proposing new methods, or new strategies/directions/ key solutions in social work services • proposing new social policies for social work services

Introducing the Paradigm of Societal Human Capabilities

Here, we define *societal human capabilities* ('capital') as the sum of 'individual human capabilities' or 'individual human capital' (i.e., physical and mental health, skills, knowledge, habits, personal traits, etc.), 'social capabilities' or 'social capital' (i.e., social skills, social support, political skills, and participation, etc.), and 'cultural capabilities' or 'cultural capital' (i.e., knowledge/skills/experience in sports, arts, and other cultural activities) (Table 10.2).

By and large, individual human capabilities comprise resources and capabilities that are associated with and generated by choices made and actions set by social individuals. Individual human capabilities include a person's physical and mental health, formal and informal education, general and professional knowledge, professional and technological skills and training, language skills, learning ability, creativity, adaptability, personal motivation, and other positive personal traits.

Social capabilities and cultural capabilities both represent societal factors that cannot influence or, in general, are not influenced by the immediate sphere of influence of each social individual alone – that is, by choices made and actions set by these social individuals:

Unlike human capabilities, social capabilities and cultural capabilities do not belong to or inhere in or reside in any one individual. Rather, they are part of a family, a clan, a network, a neighborhood, a community, a country. They are more public than private, more social than individual, at times more elusive than concrete for they exist and are sustained only in the relations among individuals. (Goldin and Katz, 1998: 28)

Social capabilities mainly refer to resources embedded in social networks accessed and used by actors for actions, plus the resources that are needed to access these resources (Lin, 2002: 25). It includes all sorts of political capabilities/capital, network capital, relationship capital, participation capital, trust relationships, social obligations, and social expectations (Landry et al., 2001; Gabbay, 1997).

Cultural capabilities are made up of a number of societal elements, such as traditions and customs; religious beliefs and moral codes; the culture to live a healthy life (cultural preferences regarding eating, drinking, exercise, and work); culture to study; a culture of seeking high work productivity or enduring long working hours; culture to take up entrepreneurial initiatives and risks; culture of social solidarity, cooperation, and mutual aid; culture that is rich in multicultural understanding; openness to new ideas and the outside world; and so forth.

Table 10.2　Three Elements of Societal Human Capabilities ('Societal Human Capital')

Individual Human Capabilities ('individual human capital')	Social Capabilities ('social capital')	Cultural Capabilities ('cultural capital')
• a person's physical health • a person's mental health • a person's spiritual health • education • general and professional knowledge • technological skills • professional skills and training • language skills • creativity • learning ability • adaptability, motivation • other positive personal traits etc.	• integration into family and community • family and community support • frequency and quality of interpersonal contact and communication • number of friends, strength of personal relationships • communication skills • social skills, etc.	• traditions • customs • habits • moral code • filial piety • religious believes • arts • culture to live a healthy life • culture to study • culture to save money • industriousness • entrepreneurial drive • culture of solidarity cooperation, and mutual aid • multi-cultural understanding • openness of society and community, etc.

Note: See Aspalter (2004, 2007a–c, 2010), Bourdieu and Passeron (1970), Bourdieu (1973, 1983, 1984, 1986, 1997, 2002), Bourdieu and Johnson (1993); for human capital/capabilities see England and Folbre (1997), OECD (1998a), Caputo (2002); for social capital/capabilities see Putnam (1993, 1995, 2000, 2001), Beverly and Sherraden (1997), OECD (1998b), Collier (1998), Montgomery (2000), Mondal (2000), Landry et al. (2001); Veenstra (2001), Woolcock (2001); Kumlin and Rothstein (2003), Chan et al. (2004), and for cultural capital/capabilities see Greene (2001) and Georg (2004).

Getting Away from a Sole Focus on *'Curative Social Work'*

The theory of societal human capabilities, since it belongs to the category of normative theories, suggests changes: that is, to add an additional focus in social work development, that of *all-encompassing preventative social work*. A number of steps have already been taken in the right direction, away from traditional, purely curative social work (e.g., DuBois and Krogsrud Miley, 2013; Van Wormer et al., 2012; Ife, 2012; Reichert, 2011; Ku and Yeun-Tsang, 2004; Adams, 2003; Morrow-Howell et al., 2001; Beverly and Sherraden, 1997; Gutierrez and Parsons, 1997, etc.).

In France, Pierre Bourdieu (1973, 1983, 1984, 1986, 1997, 2002) developed a theory that explains how we are, and why we are the way we are. The rich marry the rich, because they have a tendency to like each others' personal habits, social circles, each others' choices in music, sports, and the arts. The poor marry the poor, because they *may* prefer tattoos to fancy-colored polo shirts, drinking beer in a working-class bar instead of Riesling in a Five-Star Hotel, listing to rap music or techno music instead of Italian opera or classical music; and they may prefer soccer to polo, tennis, or golf.

If you combine Bourdieu's theory with the theory of communication of Niklas Luhmann (also known as Luhmann's social system theory) (e.g., Luhmann, 1984, 1995, 1997), then it becomes even more clear why past communication influences and even determines present and future communication, that is, social communication.

Each sentence limits the range of choices for the next, that is, subsequent, sentence; as much as each word limited the range of possible choices for the next word (in every sequence of communication, i.e., social system). In the same way, each year, or each part of our life, limits the possible range of choices we can or dare make in the following year or part of life.

What has this to do with social work? The answer is everything. If we know how we got our problems, we have a way to prevent them in the first place. Health is largely (but not entirely) a function of our past choices of place, time, education, work, social life, family, sports, and culture, and last but not least food.

Social work, hence, has to develop new perspectives that are capable of chaging people's lifetime and everyday choices, so that the personal and social problems may be prevented systematically and at a grand scale, nationwide, and for this one needs to invent and develop new policies and social work services on the ground.

Amazingly, many of the new model services – that are yet to be provided systematically and coordinated on a grand scale (with national policies, as well as textbook theories) – already exist, here or there, to a smaller or larger extent. What has calligraphy to do with social work? Visit, for example, a social work center for people with handicaps and migrant workers and their families in Chen Village in Shunde City (Guangdong, China) and you will know. Calligraphy is therapy and as a skill-development exercise, it is employed for preventative and curative purposes (HXJY, 2013).

Or, you may visit the Salvation Army in Hong Kong, where the elderly are planting tomatoes and other vegetables with children from the nearby primary school, passing on their knowledge and appreciation of nature – where both the children and the elderly are gaining, which is most important of all, a great deal of happiness and mutual support (HKSA, 2007). Happiness is a universal, most powerful cure. Happiness is a universal, most powerful preventative means to prevent social and personal problems.

Or, again, you may listen to a social worker from South Africa (François du Toit, 2006) who took his social work clients on foot into the Kruger National Park, to free them of their personal problems (having to focus on the environment, its beauty and possible dangers, instead of their personal problems, during the day when they were walking through the bush, or at night time when they listened to a myriad of strange noises outside their tents); and then to build them up again with social work techniques.

In the aftermath of the Asian tsunami in 2004, the very same social worker from South Africa (ibid.) applied a very different community social work method, one that builds on using the entire social capital of the community. In Sri Lanka, he went to the government officers, to the lawyers, the dentists, the rich, everyone that had political clout, economic power, and social esteem. He integrated them into the community social work effort in order to (a) get fully accepted and (b) build on their social and political strengths.

In 2007, I was giving a three-hour-long lecture to hundreds of government officers in Kuala Lumpur, at the headquarters of Institut Sosial Malaysia, from the Ministry of Women, Family and Community Development, Government of Malaysia. The then director of Institut Sosial Malaysia invited a group of 40 or so juvenile delinquents to attend the lecture. The lecture theatre was just big enough to hold them as well. The reason for doing so, I was told, was to let them feel they are part of society – to feel respected and in return to respect society. From their point of view, the lecture hall itself must have been very impressive, the kids also dressed up. I immediately understood that it was to build and strengthen their social and cultural capabilities (social and cultural capital).

Or, you may visit Kemerovo, an industrial city in Siberia, where, for example, the first row in the theatre is reserved for the socially weak, for social service recipients. In Kemerovo, there is free public transport for social workers, and social workers get a library card to be able to borrow books for their clients (Federova, 2006).

One of the biggest problems of Hong Kong is that people do not smile, they have forgotten how to smile, or they are too stressed out in their competitive grey asphalt jungle. A new social policy campaign emphasizing happiness could help to change this (Aspalter, 2004, 2007a–c, 2010), through (1) advertisements in the public interest (APIs); (2) massing planting of flowers throughout the city, particularly in the monotonous, neglected working-class areas; and (3) integrative social work services that not only focus on curing clients, but building the strengths and capabilities of all people in their particular neighborhood. A social work center that offers these kinds of extended services will then run, for example, a community gym, a community karaoke center, a community library, a community Internet center – like the ones I visited recently in Shunde. This would be in fact a living example of true social inclusion of the weak and the disadvantaged.

They do this to find and to get closer to the clients they focus on particularly. They will read the body language, facial expressions, and behaviour of potential clients to eventually be able provide further social work services. But also, they build the strengths of the whole community, all residents, be they problem cases or just ordinary members of the neighborhood. The social work center then has become a kind of 'living room' of the community – where social work services will have a deeper and longer impact, as well as a further reach.

The day that I visited a social service/social work center in Chen Village, I also visited an industrial social work center and a cultural services center (quite futuristic and very comprehensive, which the local government paid 120 million RMB to build; SBCC, 2013) in other parts of Shunde, both of which, in essence, follow a similar strategy: they try to get – if possible all – the families, the youth, the children, and the elderly to come to their services center, or even involve them in outdoor activities, to have as many interactions with them as possible, and – this is the key – *to also prevent rather than only to react to personal and/or social problems.*

All in all, these few examples show a small selection of the total possible variety of solutions. There is a truly infinite number of possible applications of social work services aiming to build and foster (defend) societal human capabilities: these are, individual human capabilities and social (including political) capabilities, and yet-much-neglected cultural capabilities.

The former Czech President Vaclav Havel once said,

> I consider it immensely important that we concern ourselves with culture not just as one among many human activities, but in the broadest sense—the "culture of everything", the general level of public manners. By that I mean chiefly the kind of relations that exist among people, between the powerful and the weak, the healthy and the sick, the young and the elderly, adults and children, business people and customers, men and women, teachers and students, officers and soldiers, policemen and citizens, and so on … however important it may be to get our economy back on its feet, it is far from being the only task facing us. It is no less important to do everything possible to improve the general cultural level of everyday life … I would go even farther, and say that, in many respects, improving the civility of everyday life can accelerate economic development. (Vaclav Havel, cited in Lavoie and Chamlee-Wright, 2002: 78)

The same holds true for the personal and social problems that social work tries to cure – and prevent. We have to improve the 'culture of everything', to focus on (a) poor and the rich, (b) the weak and the powerful, (c) the sick and the healthy, (d) the ones that have a particular handicap and the ones that have not, (e) the abused and the abuser, (f) the neglected and the ones that neglect, (g) the ones that are socially excluded and the ones that are at the center of society's attention and social activity, (h) the ones that are not allowed, or cannot afford, or have not yet learned to participate in all facets of cultural activities of everyday life or special once-in-a-lifetime cultural activities and the ones that are at the center of the cultural life of our society, and so on. This is what we can call *a truly comprehensive, and thus preventative, strategy in social intervention.*

It is also vital to begin with social work services before personal and social problems begin to manifest, before they grow in quantity, and before they worsen in quality.

A 'very early intervention strategy' is another key aspect when it comes to prevent problems and to address them as early on as possible. Esping-Andersen (2002, 2007) and countless other social policy experts around the world (e.g., Krieger, 1969; Newman-Williams and Sabatini, 2000; Zollinger Giele and Holst, 2004; Georg, 2004; Gitterman and Schulman, 2005; OECD, 2007) have emphasized the fact that early intervention needs to focus on people's childhoods, as much as possible.

Anger, anxiety, depression, lack of enthusiasm, lack of confidence, social exclusion, cultural exclusion, lack of social skills, lack of cultural competence, abuse and neglect of any kind, and so on, have their roots often in one's family or other social environment, or one's early life experiences. Poverty and lack of education are other examples, of how the history of personal conditions and choices earlier on in life (not necessarily in childhood) affect our later phases of life.

Certainly negative effects of vital or repeated conditions or experiences will multiply over one's lifetime, and cause a 'negative domino effect' throughout a person's lifetime. But also, conversely, we can say that positive effects of vital or repeated conditions or experiences will cause – and this is the good news – a 'positive domino effect' throughout a person's lifetime.

Developmental Social Policy (DSP) for Social Work Services

The theory of developmental social policy (Midgley, 1993, 1994, 1995, 1996 1999, 2001, 2003, 2008) has developed independently from the theory of societal human capabilities (Aspalter, 2004, 2007a–c, 2010). Yet, the normative strategies of both have been very synergetic if not overlapping. Social capabilities have been proposed as a cornerstone of social policies and social services alike by both theories. Midgley and Aspalter (forthcoming) have simply extended the realm of developmental social policy to include cultural capabilities, and a new focus on the importance of the physical and natural environment in achieving the goals of social policy and social services at hand, while also focusing on marketing techniques to deliver social development and other social policy goals (e.g., for DSP's application in the area of active aging, cf. Aspalter, 2014).

Developmental social policy was championed by the United Nations in the 1950s, especially under the umbrella of development aid, for so-called third world countries. Throughout the 1960s and 1970s, this idea was heavily promoted with policies focusing on people's basic needs for water, food, shelter, and education (Midgley, 2008: 16).

The Need for Progressive Social Change

In the developmental social policy approach, the need for progressive social change is pivotal to achieving the goals of social development. Representatives of the developmental social policy approach stress the negative effects of 'merely transferring resources to the poor [by way of asset- and means-testing!]' (Midgley: 2008: 21).

The reason for this are the twin evils of the 'poverty trap' and the 'savings trap' that are inherent to any attempt to condition social benefits and social services to a certain income, or wealth/savings criteria – that is, the unfortunately widespread practice of asset-and means-testing of social transfer payments and social services in general (Midgley and Aspalter, forthcoming).

Asset and mean-tests (AMTs) simply cause the poverty trap and the savings trap. Once people cross a certain income or savings threshold, they get penalized for doing the right thing.

Benefit recipients and service recipients, here, simply act as rational people that are responsible for their families and who try to make ends meet, to feed their family, and to pay their bills – and it is not them who are 'lazy', it is the policymakers and experts who look the other way or who simply have not realized that the rising number of poor people, ever since the War on Poverty, is caused by the War on Poverty itself *as it chiefly uses the AMT method, that is, asset- and means-testing.*

Proponents of developmental social policy try to ensure better outcomes, and to learn from empirical evidence. Some people may call it pragmatism, others may simply call it science. Empirical evidence guides and strengthens theory. No theory can stand alone for long, sooner or later it has to integrate empirical evidence. The developmental social policy approach, from its very beginning, is firmly rooted in empirical evidence – that is, pragmatic programs – and yielded tangible outcomes (Midgley, 2008: 16).

The theory of developmental social policy, therefore, strongly rejects the long-term tradition of AMT (asset- and means-testing) in the provision of social transfer payments and social services of all kinds due to the very harmful, and over time strengthening, effects of AMT benefits and services, that cause poverty to increase in the long run.

AMT need, therefore, to be replaced with (1) universal and/or (2) non-economically targeted (NET) cash transfer and social service programs. NET, such as geographically targeted social welfare benefits and services, fulfil the promise of poverty reduction, without the twin effects of the poverty trap and savings trap.

Social Planning and Social Intervention

Another keystone of developmental social policy is the insight that *social planning is key in achieving and fostering social development.* The empirical reality of the world is supporting the idea that governance is most important in guaranteeing a take-off in economic, social, and cultural development (e.g., Hobhouse, 1924; Hardiman and Midgley, 1982; Falk, 1984; MacPherson and Midgley, 1987; Estes, 1988, 1990, 1993, 2003; Jones, 1990; Chen and Desai, 1997; Mehrotra and Jolly, 1997; Ghai, 2000; Tang, 2000; Gough et al., 2004; Singh and Aspalter, 2008).

No 'invisible hand' can ever fix social problems, nor prevent them. The very principles and logic behind social work intervention of all kinds is the need of intervention and guided social development:

> ... developmental social policy stresses the need for purposeful interventions that direct the process of change and bring about significant improvements in standards of living. Human agency is, therefore, a key feature of this approach. Developmental social policy scholars believe that social problems must be solved through deliberate, planned human effort. Acting collectively, human being can find effective solutions to the urgent social problem that plague human societies. Therefore, developmental social policy stresses the need for interventions by collective institutions. Collective action at the community and regional level is vital but many believe that developmental social policy is most effective when implemented through the agency of government. This requires that governments be responsive to the needs of people, be committed to raising standards of living for all and when it funds, supports and coordinates development effort at all levels. (Midgley, 2008: 22)

Social work, just like social policy in general, needs the planning of the 'guiding hand' of (a) government agencies at all levels, (b) social work associations, as well as (c) social work movements, (d) major social work agencies, and (e) social work and social policy experts.

Social workers therefore should work with (as agency managers, as professionals) and for the government (as government employees) to achieve the goal of improving people's standard of living through comprehensive preventative and curative social work services for all layers and all corners of society.

The Guiding Principles of Universalism, Equality and Inclusivity

Other leading principles of developmental social policy are 'universalism, equality and inclusivity' (Midgley, 2008: 23–25). Midgley (1995, 1996, 1999, 2001, 2003, 2008) proposes to focus on *universal* social policies and universal social services. In line with the previous examples I have given above: *we may understand 'universalism, equality and inclusivity' as a paradigm that exceeds the realm of universal education and universal health care services, to also include 'truly universal social work services' – not only in terms of coverage of people but also in terms of coverage of services, and in terms of coverage of people's strengths and weaknesses, and this also very early on in their lives.*

The aims of social policy are basically threefold:

1. To reduce dis-welfare (suffering, hunger, thirst, death, disease, crime, discrimination, exclusion, homelessness, poverty, etc.);

2. To increase welfare, that is, people's well-being (increase quality of life, confidence, happiness, skills, knowledge, physical and mental strength, social support networks, cultural and social participation, etc.); and
3. To achieve, strengthen, and maintain overall social development, including social, political, and legal institutions, as well as a large number of economic, social, and cultural development standards.

For social policy, this means to focus on the reduction of dis-welfare, especially in the context of the developing world, particularly for example here in East Asia. Also, we need to prevent problems rather than wait for accidents to happen and diseases to manifest and spread. Social work services are a fundamental aspect of social policy in general, and particularly developmental social policy, which can look back on a long history of program-level focus on policy planning and policy development.

For this reason it is necessary to create a new space for 'preventative social work services' for the entire community, with the support of the entirety of social services available, throughout the entirety of people's lifetime.

In the following, I will show new areas and new ideas of how to expand the umbrella of social work services, from a mostly responsive force for social change to a comprehensive, all-encompassing engine that drives, rather than passively responds to, social development, in today's increasingly complex world of everyday life in a post-industrial, soon super-aged, and already heavily globalized societal setting.

Developing and Defending People's Human, Social, and Cultural Capabilities

Social policy has expanded (was forced to expand) its scope of social policies to address an ever-increasing number of social problems. Economic problems, such as unemployment, were thrown out of the standard economic policy repertoire. Work creation policies, public works programs, public infrastructural projects, however, cannot be replaced with monetary policy that regulates the supply of money, to either stimulate or reduce economic activity. Low inflation now coexists with high rates of unemployment and together these seem to form the parameters of a new evil kind of economic equilibrium, that is supported by 'not empirically founded' neoliberal, neoclassical economic thought, based on the theories of Carl Menger (1871, 1994), Eugen von Böhm-Bawerk (1890, 1891), Friedrich von Wieser (1893), Ludwig von Mises (1912, 1927, 1929, 1940, 1952, 1977), Friedrich A. von Hayek (1941, 1944, 1960, 1972, 1978, 1990), and Milton Friedman (1962, 1973, 1976, 1989).

New social problems caused by aging of societies and the onset of new modern mass diseases, such as cancer, Alzheimer's disease, diabetes, asthma, and cardiovascular disease, have changed the landscape of personal human needs, and changed the conditions current health-care and long-term-care systems and policies are built on. Health-care and long-term-care costs, now more than ever before, threaten existing health-care systems and economic systems as a whole (with US health-care costs quickly approaching 20 per cent of GDP (Aspalter, 2012)!

Therefore, social policy experts and governments alike need to focus on new social policies, especially those that do not rely on additional funding in times of prolonged fiscal austerity of national states, federal states, and local governments alike.

Non-monetary social policies are not to replace monetary social policies (such as, social assistance or social security systems), but instead to complement them, increasing the reach and output of overall social policy in the short as well as in the long run.

Social policies that invest in people's human capabilities, social capabilities, and cultural capabilities are among the most efficient policies there are, since they are very much preventative in nature. If applied very early, there is a very positive multiplying effect, since a life 'saved' very early is a life that will avoid a great deal of personal problems.

Societal human capabilities policies prevent individual problems before they evolve and social problems before they spread and spiral out of control.

For social work services, investing in people's individual human capital would mean focusing, for example, on (a) character-building; (b) helping people with character weaknesses; (c) improving their skills; (d) knowledge and self-awareness; (e) education on how to prevent mental and physical health problems; (f) educating people on healthy and unhealthy lifestyle choices, including food choices and hygiene matters and how to keep up with sports and/or physical and mental exercises; (g) educating and counselling people on economic as well as employment and career choices; (h) educating and counselling people on how to avoid and deal with loneliness; (i) educating and counselling people on family matters, including family planning; (j) educating and counselling people on how to open their own small-scale businesses or on how to become a self-employed professional, and so on; and (k) educating people on financial and legal affairs for everyday life, and so forth. This is only a short (not exhaustive) list of goals for extending existing and introducing new social work services with regard to creating and strengthening people's individual human capabilities.

With regard to social capabilities, social work agencies and professionals may in the future focus more on (a) training people in how to make, keep, and look after friends; (b) teaching people how to create family habits such as Friday night dinners, Sunday picnics in the park, and so on; (c) teaching and enabling people in how to join social events such as chess circles, poetry/literature circles, dance groups (which is very popular, especially among middle-aged and elderly women in China, to be found in almost every larger community and central parks/squares), and so on, or irregular community events, such as, balls, theatre, and musical performances, and so forth; (d) integrate the wealthy, the powerful, and people with high social standing to participate and support social work programs and/or community activities for the weak and the disadvantaged; (e) facilitating and/or organizing hospital visits to terminally or severely ill people and to people who are alone; (f) facilitating and/or organizing self-help groups for people who face old or new kinds of problems or risks; (g) facilitating singing, dancing, acting classes, and so on for children, their parents, and grandparents, that is, for everyone in the community; (h) facilitating dating groups for the younger and older people alike; (i) facilitating or organizing group excursions and hiking events, or other sports events and physical exercise (e.g., like water gymnastics groups); (j) facilitating or organizing tourist trips (one of my own grandma's favorite activities, where she met with people from her local community and travelled the country, Austria, and Europe – she was a mountain farmer with a very small pension), and so on.

This way, social workers get to know the community at large better, and find more potential clients for further consultations, and/or therapy, and so on. This will help to loosen people's shyness, and increase their acceptance and willingness to seek help in everyday and exceptional lifetime situations, as well as referrals from relatives and friends of persons in need.

In the realm of creating and strengthening people's cultural capabilities, social work agencies and government agencies alike may in the future concentrate their efforts in the direction of (a) increasing people's participation in cultural activity at the community level (e.g., Beijing Opera, theatre and circus performances, group meditations, Taiji courses and groups, etc.); (b) increasing people's cultural activities at the personal level (e.g., calligraphy, painting, etc.); (c) increasing people's cultural sports activities/participation, such as, golf, mini-golf, cricket, Japanese arrow shooting, playing Korean drums, joining or watching cultural dance performances (indigenous or traditional dances, etc.), joining a ball or dance event/competition; (d) organizing a talent show for younger and older people; (e) organizing cooking courses and cooking competitions for children, people with handicaps, senior citizens, whole families, or organize cooking courses that teach people how to cook healthily and/or with very little money at hand – especially for the poor, and so on; (f) bringing the traditional local and national cultures closer to people by, for example, organizing or facilitating cultural classes and cultural activities for everyone to join; (g) teaching family values (including filial piety, etc.); (h) educating people to save money and to make their own investments, be they on a very small scale or not; (i) educating children to create a culture to study and work, and to help their parents, wherever they can; (j) educating people to eat healthily, to exercise, to rest and play – in short, to develop a healthy lifestyle.

Investing in 'Environmental Social Policies'

'*Environmental social policy*' is a new concept in social policymaking (Aspalter, 2007; 2010; Aspalter and Midgley, forthcoming). 'Environmental social policies' are social policies that focus on the physical environment in order to help people succeed in their lives, to do away with their problems, to enhance their capabilities and long-term development prospects. Planting trees and flowers in a rundown neighborhood may have more deep and long-lasting effects in avoiding lack of investment, unemployment, desperation, depression, addiction, crime, and so on than short-term monetary programs that do not alter behaviours and attitudes, that do not do away with vicious cycles of desolation, neglect, abuse, crime, and underdevelopment.

Environmental social policies can be found in an array of contexts and in most countries around the world, for the most part, on a case-by-case basis. The physical arrangements of housing complexes, public transportation access, public safety, and, for example, a healthy integration of shopping and housing units to provide jobs in the vicinity of working-class housing complexes, all matter to the positive social, economic, and cultural development of a community or city.

Environmental social policies are, in their very essence, urban social policies and rural social policies that follow (i) the principle of positive domino effects and (ii) the principle of the physical environment changing individual behaviour and development, all to be integrated and orchestrated under a common umbrella of developmental social policy.

For social work services, we have to get more and more out of the counselling room, into the community and, very important, into the natural environment. It would be great if social work clients could meet with their professional counsellors in a nearby park or in a coffee shop, lifting ever-more existing barriers to communication and decreasing opportunity costs of the clients, who then may even bring their kids along who then play in the park or read their magazines, and so on, in the coffee shop.

The colleague from South Africa I mentioned above took this concept much further. But, one must imagine a counsellor or a couple of counsellors hiking with a group of clients, be it for a couple of hours, or a couple of days. One can do so much more out there in the open, among the trees with the birds singing, while one is enjoying the wonderful scenery that nature provides us with. This will be so much more rewarding than sitting in a relatively sterile, even though nicely decorated, small counselling room of any social work agency.

It would be nice if, for example, my social work colleagues in Hong Kong could take their clients to enjoy the view at Victoria Harbor, or to walk around Kowloon Park with its beautiful rose garden and its pink flamingos – then sit down with their clients, spend some quality time with them, while providing professional social work services.

Investing in 'Communicational Social Policy'

Aspalter (2007a–c, 2010) developed the idea that 'social policy marketing' should play a pivotal role in the application of developmental social policies that span the entire playing field of social policies, that is, the 'old heartlands of social policy' (poverty reduction and prevention, health-care systems, pensions, child welfare policy, drug addiction, etc.) as well as 'entirely *new heartlands of social policy*' (social integration policies, long-term care systems, population policy, tsunami warning and evacuation systems, etc.).

Social services may be made public, awareness of the very same created, but also the social standing and acceptance of social work services may be boosted with the help of 'social policy marketing' tools, such as 'advertisements in the public interest' (or APIs).

The government of Hong Kong, for example, utilizes 'advertisement in the public interest' which is a cost-effective means to achieve social policy objectives, especially the preventative aspects, but also to support curative efforts such as finding and motivating the target clientele to seek and accept help from particular social work services.

Particularly interesting is the near neutral effect of APIs on public social welfare budgets, since they can be made mandatory and free-of-charge (for example, by mandating TV and radio channels to provide five minutes of API time for every two or three hours of broadcasting). Marketing and communication professionals may work hand-in-hand with social policy and social work experts in developing, supervising, and evaluating APIs or other means of communicational social policies, to support conventional social work services, as well as new innovative, integrative social work services of all kinds that target the entire population.

Investment in Cost-Effective and Outcome-Oriented Social Service Programs

Like any social service programs, social work programs need to follow the principles of cost-effectiveness and outcome-based goal orientation. Too often, social programs are proposed, sustained, and extended in scope simply because that is the way things have been done in the past. Social work services, to gain continued financial and political support – especially in times of continued fiscal austerity – need to apply thoroughly and universally (for all programs, at all times) the principles of social service management, such as cost-effectiveness (i.e., achieving the highest levels of 'output to input ratios') and the principles of science, in such a way that belief is replaced with thorough, careful testing of any outcomes. Outcomes are not to be assumed, but tested scientifically, that is, empirically (not just logically).

The term 'poverty reduction' carries the word *reduction* for a purpose. When one does not succeed in reducing poverty, but just continues to administrate or manage people in poverty, one clearly misses the goal. Outcome-based goal orientation mandates strict goal setting and outcome testing, on a recurrent basis.

For this very reason, developmental social policy scholars reject the application of the method of asset- and means-testing (AMT) for social transfer benefits and social services. AMT benefits and services need, in their entirety, to be replaced by (a) NET ('non-economically targeted' benefits and services) and/or (b) universal benefits and services, to the very same extent, and put to the very same purpose.

Cash transfers and services that are designed with the method of non-economically targeting (NET) – for example, through targeting on citizenship, residence, age, gender, ethnic groups, religious groups, work performance, school attendance, study performance, and so on, and endless combinations thereof – completely avoid the evil twin problems of the 'poverty trap' and the 'savings trap'. The same is true with universal benefits and services.

People who want to receive NET benefits and services will not (need to) crowd out their work efforts, labor force participation, total working hours, their efforts to save and invest money, and so forth, as these will have no effect on getting or not getting any in-cash or in-kind benefits or social services. They will not be put into the awkward position of worrying about crossing the poverty threshold when their employer gives them a higher salary, or a promotion, or increases their overall working hours. People, then, will not worry about losing out on a vast number of in-cash transfer benefits and social services that are based on the condition of them not surpassing a certain income and savings threshold.

People, by the millions, will simply not change their age, gender, residence, or the ethnic group they belong to – and in most cases, they cannot do it anyway, and this is the point – *just to get additional social welfare benefits or services.*

The ongoing, and mostly blind and automatic, support of AMT benefits and services is ideologically driven. Many times, social workers control the levers of power, in government or in important social organizations. Therefore, they could exert a great influence to change, once and for all, the fatal conundrum of delivering benefits and services with the wrong method – that is, AMT – instead of delivering them along the methods of universalism and/or non-economic targeting (NET).

Concluding Thought

Developmental social policy (DSP) may serve as yet another fountain of inspiration and a guiding star on the horizon of developing social work services in the years and decades ahead. In a changed societal and industrial setting, where problems are mounting and resources are more and more permanently drained, social work services need to increasingly accommodate themselves to the requirements of society, its human, social, and cultural resources.

To adequately address the mounting number of personal and social problems in today's society, we have to (1) find new ways to deliver new social work services, and at the same time, (2) support the operation of traditional, existing social work services. The latter can be achieved through

a. change of awareness, acceptance, and appreciation;
b. increasing reach, that now includes a wider range of clients over a wider range of their lifetime;
c. better screening of needs and potential clients within the whole community through a much wider range of cultural and social activities;
d. 'very early' intervention;
e. better funding through multiple channels, not only the government but also more private donations, and more contributions from private businesses, which will be attracted by the extended range and reach of old and new activities;
f. better public relations, media coverage, and social networking; as well as
g. more opportunities for social enterprises that help to finance traditional and new innovative social work services across the board.

References

Adams, R. (2003), *Social Work and Empowerment*. Palgrave Macmillan: London.

Aspalter, C. (2004), Human Capital and Filial Piety, keynote speech delivered at the conference on Filial Piety in Chinese Societies, Social Service Development Institute, Hong Kong, 30 November.

Aspalter, C. (2007a), Towards a Human Capital Welfare State? In Search of Win-Win Solutions, paper presented at the conference Partnership for People-Centred Development: Challenges and Responses in a Globalising World, International Association for Community Development, City University of Hong Kong, 27–29 June.

Aspalter, C. (2007b), Towards Human-Centred Social Development: An Asian Perspective, paper presented at Harmony and Social Development, Bi-Annual Conference of the International Consortium for Social Development, The Polytechnic University of Hong Kong, 16–20 July.

Aspalter, C. (2007c), New Paradigms in Social Service Provision: A Global Perspective, keynote lecture given at Institut Sosial Malaysia, Ministry of Women, Family and Community Development, Government of Malaysia, 17 December.

Aspalter, C. (2010), Towards 'Human Capital Solidarity': Emphasizing Justice in the Distribution of Physical, Mental, Social and Cultural Capabilities: A Normative Study in Social Policy, ISSA International Social Security Association, Geneva, Global Research Conference, Luxembourg, 30 September.

Aspalter, C. (2012), European and Asian Health Care Systems in Comparative Perspective, in*Health Care Systems in Europe and Asia*, edited by C. Aspalter, Y. Uchida and R. Gauld. London: Routledge.

Aspalter, C. (2014), New Perspectives for Active Aging: The Normative Perspective of Developmental Social Policy, in *Active Aging in East Asia*, edited by A. Walker and C. Aspalter. London: Routledge.

Beverly, S. and Sherraden, M. (1997), Human Capital and Social Work, Center for Social Development, Washington University St. Louis, CSD working paper, No. 2.

Böhm-Bawerk, E.v. (1890), *Capital and Interest*. London: Macmillan.

Böhm-Bawerk, E.v. (1891), *The Positive Theory of Capital*. London: Macmillan.

Bourdieu, P. (1973), Cultural Reproduction and Social Reproduction, in *Knowledge, Education, and Social Change*, edited by R. Brown. London: Tavistock.

Bourdieu, P. (1983), Ökonomisches Kapital, kulturelles Kapital, soziales Kapital, in *Soziale Ungleichheiten*, edited by R. Kreckel. Göttingen, Germany: Otto Schwartz.

Bourdieu, P. (1984), *Distinction: A Social Critique of the Judgment of Taste*. London: Routledge.

Bourdieu, P. (1986), The Forms of Capital, in *Handbook of Theory and Research for the Sociology of Education*, edited by J.G. Richardson. Westport, CT: Greenwood.

Bourdieu, P. (1997), The Forms of Capital, in *Education: Culture, Economy, and Society*, edited by A.H. Halsey et al. Oxford: Oxford University Press.

Bourdieu, P. (2002), Cultural Power, in *Cultural Sociology*, edited by L. Spillman. Oxford: Blackwell.

Bourdieu, P. and Johnson, R. (1993), *The Field of Cultural Production*. New York: Columbia University Press.

Bourdieu, P. and Passeron, J.-C. (1970), *La reproduction: Éléments pour une théorie du système d'enseignement*. Paris: Minuit.

DuBois, B.L. and Krogsrud Miley, K. (2013), *Social Work: An Empowering Profession*. Boston: Pearson.

Caputo, R.K. (2002), Discrimination and Human Capital: A Challenge to Economic Theory and Social Justice, *Journal of Sociology and Social Welfare*, Vol. 29, No. 2, pp. 105–24.

Chan, R.K.H; Cheung, C.K., and Peng, I. (2004), Social Capital and Its Relevance to the Japanese-Model Welfare Society, *International Journal of Social Welfare*, Vol. 13, pp. 315–24.

Chen, L. and Desai, M. (1997), Paths to Social Development: Lessons from Case Studies, in *Development with a Human Face: Experiences in Social Achievement and Economic Growth*, edited by S. Mehrotra and R. Jolly. Oxford: Oxford University Press.

Collier, P. (1998), Social Capital and Poverty, Social Capital Initiative Working Paper, No. 4. Washington, DC: World Bank.

Cox, D.R. and Pawar, M. (2012), *International Social Work: Issues, Strategies, and Programs*. London: Sage.

Du Toit, F. (2006), lecture given at the Annual Conference, organized by the Russian Federation of Social Workers, Kyzyl, Tuva Republic, Russian Union.

England, P. and Folbre, N. (1997), Reconceptualizing Human Capital, working paper, Network on the Family and the Economy, August.

Esping-Andersen, G. (2002), *Why We Need a New Welfare State*. Oxford: Oxford University Press.

Esping-Andersen, G. (2007), Investing in Children and Their Life Chances, paper presented at the workshop Welfare State and Competivity, Madrid, 26–27 April.

Estes, R.J. (1988), *Trends in World Social Development: The Social Progress of Nations*. New York: Praeger.

Estes, R.J. (1990), Development under Different Political and Economic Systems, *Social Development Issues*, Vol. 13, No. 1, pp. 5–19.

Estes, R.J. (1993), Towards Sustainable Development: From Theory to Praxis, *Social Development Issues*, Vol. 15, No. 3, pp. 1–29.

Estes, R.J. (2003), *Social Development in Hong Kong: The Unfinished Agenda*. New York: Oxford University Press.

Falk, D. (1984), The Social Development Paradigm, *Social Development Issues*, Vol. 8, No. 4, pp. 4–14.

Fedorova, I. (2006), lecture given at the annual conference, organized by the Russian Federation of Social Workers, Kyzyl, Tuva Republic, Russian Union.

Friedman, M. (1962), *Capitalism and Freedom*. Chicago: University of Chicago Press.

Friedman, M. (1973), *Money and Economic Development*. New York: Praeger.

Friedman, M. (1976), *Price Theory*. Chicago: Aldine.

Friedman, M. (1989), Using the Market for Social Development, *Cato Journal*, Vol. 8, No. 3, pp. 567–79.

Gabbay, S.M. (1997), *Social Capital in the Creation of Financial Capital* Champaign, IL: Stipes.

Georg, W. (2004), Cultural Capital and Social Inequality in the Life Course, *European Sociological Review*, Vol. 20, No. 4, pp. 333–44.

Ghai, D. (ed.) (2000), *Social Development and Public Policy: A Study of Some Successful Experiences*. London: Macmillan.

Gitterman, A. and Schulman, L. (eds.) (2005), *Mutual Aid Groups, Vulnerable and Resilient Populations, and the Life Cycle*. New York: Columbia University Press.

Goldin, C. and Katz, L.F. (1998), Human Capital and Social Capital, National Bureau of Economic Research, working paper, No. 6439, March.

Gough, I. et al. (eds.) (2004), *Insecurity and Welfare Regimes in Asia, Africa, and Latin America: Social Policy in Development Contexts*. Cambridge: Cambridge University Press.

Greene, J.P. (2001), Social and Cultural Capital in Colonial British America: A Case Study, in *Patterns of Social Capital: Stability and Change in Historical Perspective*, edited by R. Rotberg. Cambridge: Cambridge University Press.

Gutierrez, L.M. and Parsons, R.J. (1997), *Empowerment in Social Work Practice*. Pacific Grove, CA: Brooks/Cole.

Hardiman, M. and Midgley, J. (1982), *The Social Dimensions of Development: Social Policy and Planning in the Third World*. Chichester: John Wiley and Sons.

Hayek, F.A.v. (1941), *The Pure Theory of Capital*. Chicago: University of Chicago Press.

Hayek, F.A.v. (1944), *The Road to Serfdom*. London: Routledge and Kegan Paul.

Hayek, F.A.v. (1960), *The Constitution of Liberty*. London: Routledge and Kegan Paul.

Hayek, F.A.v. (1972), *The Road to Serfdom*. Chicago: University of Chicago Press.

Hayek, F.A.v. (1978), *Law, Legislation and Liberty: The Mirage of Social Justice*. Chicago: University of Chicago Press.

Hayek, F.A.v. (1990), *The Constitution of Liberty*. London: Routledge and Kegan Paul.

Healy, L.M. and Link, R.J. (2011), *Handbook of International Social Work: Human Rights, Development, and the Global Profession*. New York: Oxford University Press.

Hobhouse, Leonard T. (1924), *Social Development: Its Nature and Conditions*. London: Allen and Unwin.

Hong Kong Salvation Army (HKSA) (2007), organized visit, 29 June, Hong Kong.

Hua Xiang Jia Yuan (HXJY) (2013), organized visit, 22August, Chen Village, Shunde, Guangdong, China.

Ife, J. (2012), *Human Rights and Social Work: Towards Rights-Based Practice*. Cambridge: Cambridge University Press.

Jones, H. (1990), *Social Welfare in Third World Development*. London: Palgrave Macmillan.

Krieger, M. (1969), *The Life-Cycle as a Basis for Social Policy and Social Indicators, Center for Planning and Development Research,* University of California at Berkeley.

Ku, B.H.B. and Yeun-Tsang, W.K (2004), Capacity Building and Rural Social Development in China, in *Social Work Around the World: Globalization, Social Welfare and Social Work*, edited by N.T. Tan and A. Rowlands. Geneva: International Federation of Social Work.

Ku, Y.-W. (2000), Social Development in Taiwan: Upheavals in the 1990s, in *Social Development in Asia*, edited by K.L. Tang. London: Kluwer Academic Publishers.

Kumlin, S. and Rothstein, B. (2003), Investing in Social Capital: The Impact of Welfare State Institutions, paper delivered at the Annual Meeting of the American Political Science Association, Philadelphia, 28–31August.

Landry, R.; Amara, N., and Lamari, M. (2001), Social Capital, Innovation, and Public Policy, *Isuma – Canadian Journal of Policy Research*, Vol. 2, No. 1, pp. 63–71.

Lavoie, D. and Chamlee-Wright, E. (2002), *Culture and Enterprise: The Development, Representation and Morality of Business*. London: Routledge.

Leung, J.C.B. (1995), From Subsistance to *Xiaokang*: Social Development in the PRC, *Social Development Issues*, Vol. 17, No. 3, pp. 104–14.

Lin, N. (2002), *Social Capital: A Theory of Social Structure and Action*. Cambridge: Cambridge University Press.

Luhmann N (1984). *Soziale Systeme* [Social systems]. Frankfurt a.M.: Suhrkamp.

Luhmann, N. (1995), *Social Systems*. Stanford, CA: Stanford University Press.

Luhmann, N. (1998), *Die Gesellschaft der Gesellschaft* [The Society of Society]. Frankfurt a.M.: Suhrkamp.

MacPherson, S. and Midgley, J. (1987), *Social Welfare in Third World Development: Comparative Social Policy and the Third World*. London: Palgrave Macmillan.

Mehrotra, S. and Jolly, R. (eds.) (1997b), *Social Development in High Achieving Countries: Common Elements and Diversities*. Oxford: Clarendon Press.

Menger, C. (1871), *Grundsätze der Volkswirthschaftslehre*. Vienna: Wilhelm Braumueller.

Menger, C. (1994), *Lectures to Crown Prince Rudolf of Austria*. Aldershot: Edward Elgar.

Midgley, J. (1993), Ideological Roots of Social Development Strategies, *Social Development Issues*, Vol. 15, No. 1, pp. 1–13.

Midgley, J. (1994), Defining Social Development: Historical Trends and Conceptual Formulations, *Social Development Issues*, Vol. 16, No. 3, pp. 3–19.

Midgley, J. (1995), *Social Development: The Developmental Perspective in Social Welfare*. London: Sage.

Midgley, J. (1996), Toward a Developmental Model of Social Policy: Relevance of the Third World Experience, *Journal of Sociology and Social Welfare*, Vol. 23, No. 1, pp. 59–74.

Midgley, J. (1999), Growth, Redistribution and Welfare: Towards Social Investment, *Social Service Review*, Vol. 77, No. 1, pp. 3–21.

Midgley, J. (2001), Growth, Redistribution, and Welfare: Toward Social Investment, in *The Global Third Way Debate*, edited by A. Giddens. Cambridge: Polity Press.

Midgley, J. (2003), Poverty and the Social Development Approach, in *Poverty Monitoring and Alleviation in East Asia*, edited by K.L. Tang and C.K. Wong. New York: Nova Science.

Midgley, J. (2008), Developmental Social Policy: Theory and Practice, in *Debating Social Development*, edited by S. Singh and C. Aspalter. Hong Kong: Casa Verde.

Midgley, J. and Aspalter, C. (forthcoming), Theory of Developmental Social Policy, in *Development and Social Policy*, edited by C. Aspalter and K. Teguh-Pripadi.

Mises, L.v. (1912), *Theorie des Geldes und der Umlaufmittel*. Berlin: Buncker & Humblot.

Mises, L.v. (1927), *Liberalismus*. Jena, Germany: Gustav Fischer.

Mises, L.v. (1929), *Kritik des Interventialismus: Untersuchungen zur Wirtschaftspolitik und Wirtschaftsideologie der Gegenwart*. Stuttgart: Gustav Fischer.

Mises, L.v. (1940), *Nationalökonomie: Theorie des Handelns und Wirtschaftens*, Geneva: Editions Union.

Mises, L.v. (1952), Middle-of-the-Road Policy Leads to Socialism, in *Planning for Freedom and Other Essays and Addresses*, edited by L.v. Mises. South Holland, IL: Libertarian Press.

Mises, L.v. (1977), *A Critique of Interventionalism*. New York: Arlington House.

Mondal, A.H. (2000), Social Capital Formation: The Role of NGO Rural Development Programs in Bangladesh, *Policy Sciences*, Vol. 33, pp. 459–75.

Montgomery, J.D. (2000), Social Capital as a Policy Resource, *Policy Sciences*, Vol. 33, pp. 227–43.

Morrow-Howell, N.; Hinterlong, J., and Sherraden, M. (eds.) (2001), *Productive Aging: Concepts and Challenges*, Baltimore: Johns Hopkins University Press.

Newman-Williams, M. and Sabatini, F. (2000), Child-Centred Development and Social Progress in the Caribbean, in N. Girvan (ed.), *Poverty, Empowerment and Social Development in the Caribean*. Kingston, Jamaica: University Press of the West Indies.

Organization of Economic Cooperation and Development (OECD) (1998a), *Human Capital Investment: An International Comparison*. Paris: OECD.

OECD (1998b), *Social Capital: An International Comparison*. Paris: OECD.

OECD (2007), *Modernising Social Policy for the New Life Course.* Paris: OECD.

Putnam, R.D. (1993), The Prosperous Community: Social Capital and Public Life, *American Prospect*, No. 13, Spring, pp. 35–42.

Putnam, R.D. (1995), Bowling Alone: Americas Declining Social Capital, *Journal of Democracy*, Vol. 6, No. 1, pp. 65–78.

Putnam, R.D. (2000), *Bowling Alone: The Collapse and Revival of American Community.* New York: Simon and Schuster.

Putnam, R.D. (2001), Social Capital Measurement and Consequences, *Isuma – Canadian Journal of Policy Research*, Vol. 2, No. 1, pp. 41–51.

Reichert, E. (2011), *Social Work and Human Rights: A Foundation for Policy and Practice.* New York: Columbia University Press.

Shunde Beijiao Culture Center (SBCC) (2013), organized visit, 22 August, Beijiao, Shunde, Guangdong, China.

Singh, S. and Aspalter, C. (eds.) (2008), *Debating Social Development.* Hong Kong: Casa Verde.

Tang, K.-L. (2000), *Social Development in East Asia.* Basingstoke: Palgrave.

Van Wormer, K.; Kaplan, L., and Juby, C. (2012), *Confronting Oppression, Restoring Justice: From Policy Analysis to Social Action.* Alexandria, VA: Council of Social Work Education.

Veenstra, G. (2001), Social Capital and Health, *Isuma – Canadian Journal of Policy Research*, Vol. 2, No. 1, pp. 72–81.

Wieser, F.v. (1893), *Natural Value.* New York: Macmillan.

Woolcock, M. (2001), The Place of Social Capital in Understanding Social and Economic Outcomes, *Isuma – Canadian Journal of Policy Research*, Vol. 2, No. 1, pp. 11–18.

Zollinger Giele, J. and Holst, E. (eds.) (2004), *Changing Life Patterns in Western Industrial Societies.* Amsterdam: Elsevier Science Press.

Index

180   *Social Work in East Asia*